The Political Economy of Modern Britain

The Political Economy of Modern Britain

Andrew Cox
Professor of Strategic Procurement Management, University of Birmingham, UK

Simon Lee
Lecturer in Politics, University of Hull, UK

Joe Sanderson
Research Fellow at the Centre for Strategy and Procurement Management, University of Birmingham, UK

Edward Elgar
Cheltenham, UK • Lyme, US

Published by
Edward Elgar Publishing Limited
8 Lansdown Place
Cheltenham
Glos GL50 2HU
UK

Edward Elgar Publishing, Inc.
1 Pinnacle Hill Road
Lyme
NH 03768
US

A11414 324493

A catalogue record for this book is available from the British Library

Library of Congress Cataloguing-in-Publication Data

Cox, Andrew, 1951–
    The Political economy of modern Britain / Andrew Cox, Simon Lee,
Joe Sanderson.
        Includes index.
        1. Great Britain—Economic conditions—20th century.
    2. Industrial policy—Great Britain. I. Lee, Simon, 1963–
    II. Sanderson, Joe, 1969– . III. Title
    HC256.C65 1997   96-48952
    338.941—dc21   CIP

Printed and bound in Great Britain by
Hartnolls Limited, Bodmin, Cornwall

ISBN 1 85278 411 3 (cased)

Contents

Figures and tables

Preface

The Description and Explanation of Britain's Relative Economic Performance

It is a difficult task to explain Britain's relatively poor economic performance since 1939. The reasons for this are complex. The first problem is that there is no unambiguous data about economic performance. This is because governments have a vested interest in manipulating data to suit their own purposes. Secondly, there is disagreement amongst analysts about the relative causal importance of specific data and phenomena in explaining specific political and economic events. Finally, there is a lack of consensus about which key events are or were pivotal in determining economic performance.

This volume does not address these contested issues directly. Rather, it seeks to provide the reader with a basic understanding of the key issues which are contested amongst analysts. The hope is that in doing so the volume will provide a basis for students to understand the basic facts of Britain's relative economic performance and how they have been explained and interpreted.

In providing a description of policy and an analysis of different schools of thought, we do not seek to provide an alternative framework for analysis. Our aim is more limited. We seek merely to provide readers with a range of tools which they can use to understand the performance of the British economy since 1939 and why it has been relatively less successful than other advanced industrial economies. In so doing, the basis for a more informed and knowledgeable citizenry may have been established.

Many debts of gratitude have been incurred in the writing of this book, and limitations on space make it impossible to thank everyone individually. We would, however, like to offer our special thanks to Jackie Potter, who undertook the task of preparing the manuscript for publication. The responsibility for all sins of error and omission, of course, remains wholly our own.

Andrew Cox, Simon Lee and Joe Sanderson

PART A:

Describing Britain's Relative Economic Performance

1. The Political Economy of Britain since 1939

Andrew Cox and Joe Sanderson

INTRODUCTION

This chapter performs two basic tasks. First, it develops a continuum of six ideal type relationships between the state and the market. Having outlined the basic distinctions between these idealised state–market relationships, it provides a history of the key economic policies pursued by British governments since the beginning of the Second World War in order to discover to what extent Britain's politico-economic experience between September 1939 and the present day fits into each category. The value of using a continuum of theoretical state–market relationships is that it helps us to think more logically and coherently about the policies which were actually being pursued after 1939. It allows us to be critical and to ask whether it is correct, for example, to characterise both the Conservative government of 1959–64 and the Labour governments of 1964–70 as 'corporatist', simply because they established a number of tripartite planning bodies. If we begin with a clear conception of what these theoretical types imply, then such assertions will have a more intelligent basis.

Before moving on to the first of these tasks, however, it is necessary to make some general comments about state–market relations as a theme in British party political debate. The first is that since the creation of the Labour Party there has been a rhetorical lack of consensus between the major parties in Britain about the proper role for the state in the economy. The Conservatives have spoken the language of the free market, while Labour has been much more in favour of using the state as an agent of social and economic advancement. This remains equally true today, because although the Labour Party has abandoned its historic commitment to public ownership of the means of production, it still seeks to differentiate itself from the Conservatives by talking about the importance of 'community' and 'social responsibility' in framing economic policy. This lack of consensus has led a number of commentators to attribute Britain's relatively poor economic performance, particularly since 1945, to adversary politics (Finer, 1975). The thrust of the adversary politics thesis is that British economic policy has been ineffective, because it has lacked continuity and a sense of national purpose. Every change of governing party, it is argued, has produced a damaging period of instability as the course of policy has been reversed.

The weakness of this argument, however, is that it overemphasises what parties say they will do if they are re-elected, rather than what they actually achieve once in office. This leads us to our second point. Concentrating on what British governments have done since 1939, this chapter argues that changes of governing party at general elections are not a satisfactory guide to Britain's position on the continuum of ideal state–market relationships developed below. Indeed, as the following discussion will reveal, there was a surprising degree of consensus between 1939 and 1979 as to the proper relationship between the state and the market. Only after the election of Margaret Thatcher in 1979 could the adversarial nature of British politics be said to be anything more than rhetorical. As Dutton comments, however, even this conclusion should be regarded as provisional, because the radical overhaul of Labour Party policy initiated after their third successive election defeat in 1987 may presage the emergence of a new centre-right consensus (Dutton, 1991, p. 92). Dutton's argument has been given added weight by the deepening of this reappraisal following Labour's fourth successive election defeat in 1992 and the election of Tony Blair as Party Leader in 1994.

If the adversary politics thesis can thus be regarded as largely redundant as an explanation of Britain's relative economic decline, the alternative question is why consensus politics have failed to address the economy's weaknesses. While this question is explicitly examined in later chapters, a few general comments can usefully be made at this stage. It is well documented that the consensus between 1939 and 1979 was built around an active and, on occasion, interventionist role for the state in economic affairs, but the use of the word 'consensus' does not imply that there was an absence of disagreement over this state activism. Each of the major political parties is in reality a coalition of often conflicting interests, many of which are explicitly opposed to state intervention. The Labour Party is a coalition of social democrats, trade unionists and socialists (Coates, 1975, pp. 177–230). The Conservative Party is a coalition of industrialists, financiers, property owners and commercial interests (Harris, 1972, pp. 23–76). The Liberal Party was historically a coalition of landowners and industrialists, but today, in combination with what was the SDP, it is primarily a middle-class party based on intellectuals and party activists committed to the devolution of political power and electoral reform. Given that none of the parties speaks with a single voice, there is always likely to be a significant minority of the government who disagree with the prevailing relationship between the state and the market. While this significant minority may desire either a more or a less extensive role for the state, the important point is that once any of the parties enters office its actions are constrained by the need to maintain unity. Applying this insight to the failure of the postwar consensus to stem the tide of relative economic decline, it can be argued that the role chosen for the state was ultimately always compromised and made ineffective by the demands of governance.

A number of other factors can be added to this party political influence on the relative failure of state activism in the postwar period. The first of these is the defensive strength of a trade union movement committed to wage militancy and the protection of free collective bargaining in industrial relations – free, that is, from state interference (Cox, 1981, pp. 61–99). Resistance to an expanded role for the state can also be traced to the crucial contribution to Britain's balance of payments made by the invisible earnings of the financial services sector. The success of financial capital, or the City of London as it is more usually called, has historically depended on a commitment by the British state to free trade and minimal regulation of business (McRae and Cairncross, 1977, pp. 1–20). Next, it has been noted that the British civil service, the group of people ultimately responsible for implementing a policy of state activism, lacks a well-developed culture of interventionism (Hayward, 1977, pp. 120–90). Finally, this cultural thesis has also been applied at the wider level of society, where it is argued that the commitment of the British public to liberal values and parliamentary forms of representation means that state intervention and a growing public sector are generally regarded as illegitimate (Dyson, 1980, pp. 186–204). This means that both main political parties have been constrained in their attempts to use the state to deal with economic problems by their need to maintain a solid base of electoral support. Thus, if there is any single explanation of why consensus politics have failed to address the weaknesses of the British economy it lies in the inability of the state to impose its desired policies on key social and economic actors. This failure lies not in a lack of purpose, but mainly in the ability of electoral opinion and trade union, financial, and bureaucratic interests to veto an expanded role for the state in economic affairs.

STATE–MARKET RELATIONSHIPS: A CONTINUUM OF IDEAL TYPES

As was suggested above, the value of a continuum of ideal types is that it helps us to think more logically and critically about the terms which are regularly used to describe the approach to economic management adopted by each of Britain's postwar governments. The continuum employed in this chapter encompasses six ideal type relationships between the state and the market, ranging from socialism at one extreme to laissez-fairism at the other. The full range of relationships is shown in Figure 1.1. Each of these will be discussed in detail below, but first it is necessary to make a number of more general comments about the continuum.

As can be seen from Figure 1.1, the continuum is organised on the basis of an increasing degree of state involvement in the economy as we move from right to left. This somewhat broad notion of 'involvement' has been used, because it allows us to think about the role of the state both in terms of its *ownership* of industrial and financial concerns and in terms of its *control* over the activities of these concerns. Clearly, it is logical to argue that where the state owns all or a substantial majority of a particular industry then it is likely to wield a significant measure of control over its activities, but this does not deny the possibility of state control without state ownership. It is for this reason that the continuum separates the issue of ownership from that of control for each of the six ideal types.

The continuum is further divided into the relationship between the state and the market at the *macroeconomic* level and that between them at the level of the *microeconomy*. Simply expressed, the term macroeconomy refers to the operation of the economy as a whole. At this level, the relationship between the state and the market is concerned with aggregate economic phenomena such as the level of unemployment, the rate of inflation, the rate of growth of the money supply, and the general levels of saving and investment. Thus, when we talk about ownership and control in the macroeconomy we are referring to those institutions and organisations which have a direct influence on these and other economic aggregates. In effect, this means the whole range of financial institutions including the clearing banks, the investment banks, the insurance companies, the building societies, and the stock and currency markets. The term microeconomy, on the other hand, refers to the behaviour of individual economic units such as firms and consumers, although in the context of this chapter the use of the term only extends to the former. At the level of the microeconomy, therefore, the state–market relationship is concerned with firm or industry-specific phenomena such as the level and duration of

	Socialism	Dirigisme	Corporatism	Macmillanism	Keynesianism	Laissez-fairism
The macroeconomy: ownership	Wholly state.	Mixed: mainly market, but state owns the largest financial institutions.	Wholly market.	Wholly market.	Wholly market.	Wholly market.
The macroeconomy: control	Wholly state.	Mixed: principally state.	Mixed: mainly state. State works with key financial interests to agree detailed compulsory investment plans.	Mixed: mainly market. State relies on the voluntary participation of private companies to ensure effective implementation of broad investment plans.	Mixed: principally market, but state intervenes indirectly through fiscal levers to manage aggregate effective demand.	Fundamentally market, but state provides a system of legal guarantees for private property, creates a system of exchange, controls inflation and maintains internal and external order.
The microeconomy: ownership	Wholly state.	Mixed: mainly market, but state owns the largest companies in strategically important sectors.	Mixed: principally market, but with selective state ownership of strategically and socially important industries, ie. the utilities.	Mixed: principally market, but with selective state ownership of strategically and socially important industries, ie. the utilities.	Fundamentally market, but with limited, ad-hoc state ownership to support ailing and strategically important industries in the national interest.	Wholly market.
The microeconomy: control	Wholly state.	Mixed: principally state. State ownership of leading companies is used to control the priorities of the market.	Mixed: mainly state. State formulates compulsory plans for industry working with key representatives of business and labour in institutions which it licenses and controls.	Mixed: mainly market. Key representatives of business and labour work together in state-sponsored institutions but state relies on voluntary participation.	Fundamentally market, but with limited, ad-hoc state intervention to correct "market failures".	Wholly market.

100% ← ——— Degree of state involvement: in the economy ——— → 0%

Figure 1.1: A continuum of ideal type relationships between the state and the market

investment, the number and size of firms in a particular industry, wage, price and profit levels, and the terms and conditions of employment. By extension, ownership and control should be understood in terms of individual firms or industries.

One final point should be made before we move on to a detailed consideration of each of the ideal types covered in the continuum. As with many of the concepts and theoretical categories employed in the social sciences, the meaning of several of these categories is open to debate. Socialism, for instance, is a notoriously complex and multi-faceted concept, which operates both on the level of values and on the level of the concrete social and political institutions which are supposed to embody those values. In terms of values, socialism is equated with freedom, equality, community, brotherhood, social justice, the classless society, co-operation — to name just a few of the most commonly used ones. In terms of social and political institutions, socialism is seen as the replacement of private property by the 'common' or 'public ownership' of the means of production. The problem of definition is not simply a function of the plurality of words and phrases used to capture the essence of socialism, but derives from the fact that each of these words can itself be defined in several, often conflicting, ways. By 'equality', for example, some socialists mean 'equality of opportunity' while others mean 'equality of remuneration', definitions which are clearly very different. The institutional term 'public ownership' is similarly problematic. It can refer to central planning with complete state ownership of the means of production; to the nationalisation of large and strategically important industrial and financial concerns only; to partial state equity in private companies; to public corporations; to producers' co–operatives; and so on (Berki, 1975, pp. 9–10).

These observations should not, however, lead us to despair, but should rather act as an incentive for us to develop a clear, simple and unambiguous *working* definition of each of the ideal types in the continuum. Such a definition is explicitly limited in its application, being specifically designed for the purposes of a particular piece of work. The organising theme of the continuum developed here is the extent to which the state replaces the market as the mechanism of ownership and control in economic affairs. Our working definitions will, therefore, avoid the question of 'values' and will be couched in purely 'institutional' terms.

Socialism

For the purposes of this analysis socialism refers to a situation in which the means of production − land, and industrial and financial capital − are completely owned and controlled by the state. In this ideal type, therefore, the market has effectively been abolished and replaced by state direction. The allocative decisions (where to direct investment and resource flows) and the productive decisions (what and how much to produce) which form the basis of all economic activity are taken in accordance with a centrally-defined plan, rather than in response to market-based prices and profit levels. This does not, however, mean that prices and wage rates do not exist, but rather that they are set by the state in order to achieve the objectives of the plan.

Dirigisme

Dirigisme is a term derived from the French verb 'diriger', which means to manage, conduct or steer. It refers to a situation in which the state proactively manages the economy in accordance with a comprehensive plan which it has formulated. Although at this level dirigisme sounds very much like socialism, there are several fundamental differences. The most important is that the state has not completely replaced the market. Ownership of the means of production is mixed, with the state owning only the largest companies in strategically important sectors such as banking, insurance, steel, computers, chemicals, and the utilities (water, energy, transport and telecommunications). The rationale of this pattern of ownership is that it allows the state to steer the economy along the lines set out in the plan, without the need for detailed intervention in all sectors. It is assumed that where state ownership, and therefore control, leads these companies, the market will follow. For this reason, dirigisme is often also referred to as 'indicative planning'. State ownership and control of the leading banks and financial institutions is seen as particularly significant in this connection, because these have an enormous influence on the strategic direction of the economy through their control over credit and investment flows.

Corporatism

The essential characteristic of corporatism is the creation by the state of a privileged policy-making role for those organisations that are based on the division of labour in society. Thus, the state works with key representatives of business and labour in institutional frameworks which it licenses and controls to formulate detailed plans for the management of the economy at both the macro and micro levels. The state does not, however, implement these plans directly, but instead works through the incorporated interest groups. In other words, corporatism represents *indirect* state intervention. Nevertheless, this is a strong and comprehensive form of state intervention. Strong, because the policy bargains reached in discussions between the state, capital and labour impose compulsory responsibilities on the partners to implement the agreed objectives. Comprehensive, because these three-way discussions operate at both the macro and micro levels, and they are consciously linked as part of a national economic strategy (Grant, 1985, pp. 8–9).

It might seem strange, therefore, that corporatism is characterised by the continuum as exhibiting a lesser degree of state involvement in the economy than dirigisme. This observation serves to highlight the difficulty of representing these complex concepts along a simple dimension of more or less state involvement. The problem is that while corporatism describes a situation in which the vast majority of the means of production are privately owned, the state still actively controls the operation of the economy. Corporatism might, thus, legitimately be placed immediately next to socialism. It needs to be emphasised, therefore, that the decision to put corporatism to the right of dirigisme was based on two main criteria: first the relatively insignificant degree of state ownership linked to this ideal type; and second, and perhaps more important, the central role played by non-state actors in the formulation of economic policy.

Macmillanism

This ideal type takes its name from the former British Prime Minister, Harold Macmillan, and is a distillation of the ideas contained in his 1938 book, *The Middle Way*. On a superficial level, Macmillanism seems indistinguishable from corporatism. The essence of this ideal type is the progressive development of the mixed economy, with a clear distinction being drawn between the proper sphere of state activity and those functions best carried out by private enterprise. As with corporatism, therefore, the importance of maintaining both state and market in the management of economic affairs is explicitly recognised. Furthermore, the core objective of Macmillan's approach is the adoption of rational and comprehensive planning of the national economy rather than the piecemeal planning of individual sectors. It is on the level of institutions, however, that the similarity between Macmillanism and corporatism appears most marked. Macmillan calls for the establishment of tripartite bodies, made up of representatives of the state, business and labour, which would formulate policy in accordance with a national plan agreed by a tripartite co-ordinating body, the National Economic Council (NEC). He envisages three distinct, yet interrelated, strands of policy covering industry, finance, and foreign trade, each being managed by a tripartite body immediately subordinate to the NEC. The policies agreed by these three bodies would then be implemented by business and labour in the relevant sectors of the economy. Macmillanism is, therefore, an explicitly indirect form of state intervention (Macmillan, 1938, pp. 194–300). As Wyn Grant comments, however, a properly corporatist approach to economic management requires more than the setting up of tripartite institutions to agree general policy guidelines. Corporatism proper imposes *compulsory* responsibilities on business and labour to implement the agreed policy objectives in detail (Grant, 1985, p. 9). Furthermore, the essence of corporatism is that it extends across all sectors of the economy. It is on these points that Macmillanism emerges as a theoretical category in its own right.

Macmillan's approach to industrial planning, for instance, is based on two key ideas. First, he argues that there are three main categories of industry to which different approaches should be taken. For simplicity we will call these three types of industry new, mature, and strategic. New industries are those which are rapidly expanding and in which over-capacity is not yet a problem; mature industries are those in which competitive expansion has slowed down and the productive capacity is beginning to outstrip market demand; and strategic industries are those, like the utilities, which are important to other productive enterprises and to general economic welfare and stability. Macmillan makes it clear that his model for industrial planning would not apply to either new or strategic industries. In the case of the former, he comments that 'new industries, in the early stages of their development and during the period of their rapid expansion, are best left to the vigorous initiative of private enterprise and uncontrolled competition' (Macmillan, 1938, p. 237). In the case of the latter, he states that 'certain industries and services which are of key importance to the vigorous economic life of the community ... should be brought under either some suitable form of public ownership and management or, in certain cases, a form of statutory control or supervision which may not involve public ownership' (Macmillan, 1938, pp. 237–8). It is only in the case of mature industries, therefore, that the indirect planning elements of Macmillanism are to apply.

This brings us to the second of Macmillan's key ideas, which is that where industrial planning is used, it should be on the basis of *voluntary* participation and co-operation by the key economic interest groups. The whole thrust of Macmillanism is that planning should not be forced on industry by the state, but should instead be based on the initiative of a substantial majority of the employers and employees in an industry. He comments that the enabling powers for industrial reorganisation 'would be available when a sufficient majority in an industry had agreed upon a scheme and had convinced an Industrial Reorganisation Advisory Council, appointed by Parliament, that the scheme would not be injurious to the public interest' (Macmillan, 1938, pp. 202–3). Furthermore, Macmillan argues that 'the role of the state would merely be one of vigilant neutrality ... That is to say, it would be vigilant in the devising of safeguards to defend the interests of the workers employed and of the consumers of the industry's products. It would be neutral as to whether the industry made use of the powers, or as to the extent to which it made use of them' (Macmillan, 1938, p. 219).

Macmillan develops similar ideas with regard to the management of investment finance. He calls for the setting up of a National Investment Board (NIB), which would be a meeting ground for representatives of the state, the Central Bank, and those members of the NEC with expertise in financial affairs. The key function of the NIB would be to provide facilities for the exchange of securities so that investment decisions could be taken under circumstances free of short-term speculative pressure. Again, however, Macmillan draws a distinction between new industries, in which he regards speculative investment as essential and socially useful, and mature industries, which he argues should be under the jurisdiction of the NIB. Macmillan stresses, though, that privately-owned, mature industries would not be forced to come within the NIB scheme; participation, again, is voluntary. Only in those industries which fall into the strategic category would the NIB be able to exert compulsory control over investment flows (Macmillan, 1938, pp. 260–2).

To sum up, Macmillanism appears superficially synonymous with corporatism, but a closer consideration reveals at least two important differences. First, Macmillanism does not apply indirect planning across the whole economy; it leaves room both for unfettered private enterprise and for direct state ownership and control. Second, where indirect planning is employed, it relies on the voluntary participation and co-operation of business and labour.

Keynesianism

This ideal type is based on the ideas of the economist John Maynard Keynes as set forth in his seminal work, *The General Theory of Employment, Interest and Money*. It posits an important yet fundamentally limited role for the state in the management of the economy. In essence, the state is limited to indirect intervention at the macroeconomic level. Its role is to manage aggregate 'effective demand' with the aim of keeping the economy operating at, or as close as possible to, 'full employment'. Effective demand simply means demand backed by money (Stewart, 1986, p. 68).

Keynes argues that the level of employment in an economy of a given population with a particular degree of technological development is determined by the level of aggregate effective demand, which in turn depends on the levels of consumption and investment in the economy. In simple terms, consumption refers to spending by individuals on goods and services to satisfy their own wants, while investment refers to spending by firms on buildings and machinery in order to produce goods and services in the future. Keynes assumes that aggregate consumption is a relatively fixed proportion of aggregate effective demand and that consumption will, therefore, automatically adjust to a new level of demand in the economy. This means that the level of employment is largely determined by the level of investment. The key question for the state, therefore, is what determines the level of investment and how can it be effectively managed? This brings us to the most important element of Keynesianism, which is the observation that there is no simple causal relationship between the rate of interest and the general level of investment. Keynes notes that even when the interest rate falls, people have a tendency to retain their savings as a hedge against an uncertain future. This 'liquidity preference' theory of interest rates leads to the conclusion that lowering the interest rate will not produce a commensurate increase in the level of investment. The practical implications of this theory are that monetary policy in general, and interest rates in particular, cannot be used to manage aggregate effective demand in pursuit of full employment (Stewart, 1986, pp. 68–80).

The Keynesian solution to managing effective demand is, therefore, based on the manipulation by the state of fiscal policy instruments, which in essence means taxation and public spending. In other words, Keynes argues that when the level of private sector investment in the economy is below that needed to produce full employment then the state should make up the shortfall by increasing public spending and reducing taxation. An important addition to this line of argument is the notion of 'the multiplier effect', which means that a relatively small reduction in taxation or injection of state investment into the economy will produce a larger increase in aggregate effective demand. This insight is based on the idea that there will also be an increase in private sector investment as the confidence of business in the future state of the economy is boosted by public sector action. The actual size of this multiplier effect depends on the marginal propensity to consume and the marginal efficiency of capital. On the other side of the equation, Keynes argues that when there is an excess of private sector investment, and the economy is in danger of overheating, then the state should dampen down economic activity by increasing the burden of taxation and cutting public spending. The impact of tax increases and cuts in public spending is, again, subject to the multiplier effect (Stewart, 1986, pp. 86–97).

Keynesianism is, thus, presented as means of using the state to avoid the excesses of boom and slump, while maintaining a fundamentally market-based pattern of ownership and control. It should be noted that we refer to Keynesianism as a *fundamentally* market-based ideal type, because, beyond the state's indirect macroeconomic role, there are a small number of circumstances in which Keynes sanctions limited and ad-hoc state intervention at the microeconomic level. As the continuum suggests, this intervention can either take the form of public ownership to support ailing and strategically important industries in the national interest, or the form of targeted fiscal measures – tax incentives and subsidies – to correct market failures. Amongst such market failures we might include under investment in areas of high unemployment, and a lack of properly trained workers for high-technology industries. The essence of Keynesianism, however, is that the state engages in indirect macroeconomic management in order to create a level of aggregate effective demand at which privately-owned and controlled industrial and financial capital can flourish.

Laissez–fairism

The final ideal type, laissez-fairism, presents an almost entirely market-based pattern of ownership and control. In this category the state is described as 'minimalist' or as 'a night-watchman'. Amongst its limited number of functions the most important are the provision of a system of legal guarantees for private property, the creation of a system of exchange (money), and the maintenance of a stable business environment by controlling inflation and defending the nation against internal and external threats. All of these functions are directed towards ensuring the success of private enterprise. Unlike the Keynesian ideal type, the state has no legitimate role in managing the level of employment (or unemployment) in the economy. Allocative and productive decisions are taken entirely on the basis of market signals – prices and profits. The only legitimate concern of the state is the general price level, which it influences by means of monetary policy instruments such as interest rates and credit controls.

Having outlined the basic distinctions between these idealized state—market relationships we are now in a position to consider how closely Britain's politico-economic experience since the beginning of the Second World War fits into each category.

CORPORATISM AND THE BRITISH WAR ECONOMY (1939–45)

During the early days of the Second World War it became clear that the British state had learnt a number of valuable lessons from the economic experiences of 1914–18. The machinery of government was much better prepared for the conduct of a total war, because since the early 1930s a number of departments had been engaged in the preparation of elaborate war plans. In the first two weeks of the conflict alone some forty Acts of Parliament were passed. This legislation created a vast array of new government machinery, including the Ministries of Supply, Economic Warfare, and Food and Shipping. Recruitment was added to the responsibilities of the Ministry of Labour, making it a linchpin in the combined economic and military strategy of total war. Perhaps the most important realisation to come out of the First World War was that, in order to fight a truly 'total' war, the state would have to extend its apparatus of control far beyond those sectors of industry which were explicitly engaged in military production. Britain, therefore, came the closest it has ever done to the creation of a corporate state, based upon public control of a principally privately-owned economy.

The key developments in this regard came after the formation of Churchill's Coalition Government in May 1940. The immediacy of the German threat, following the defeat of the British Expeditionary Force at Dunkirk, required the Coalition to pursue policies which signalled a radical shift in the prevailing relationship between the state and the market. Policy-makers realized that they would have to plan and control profits, rents, consumer prices, wage rates, and the supply and use of raw materials and commodities in production if the war was to be fought effectively. While the state did own the Royal Ordnance factories, the dockyards, and 170 'agency' factories, and exerted direct control over the railways and the ports, the mechanisms of control were primarily indirect and used on privately-owned industries. As outlined above, an extensive system of bureaucratic planning and control was established at the national level. The activities of these ministries were co-ordinated by the Production Executive, a committee of the War Cabinet staffed by the Minister of Labour, the

Minister of Aircraft Production, the Minister of Food and Shipping, the President of the Board of Trade, the First Lord of the Admiralty, and members of various economic departments serving in an advisory capacity. The Executive's main objectives were the ending of all unnecessary industrial activities, achieving smooth co-operation between all sectors of industry, and ensuring the most efficient and effective use of the available workforce.

Below the Executive level, key representatives of business and labour were compulsorily incorporated into state policy-making and they took part in the formulation of detailed plans with regard to production, wages and profits. The most important state agencies in this process were the Ministry of Labour and the Ministry of Supply (the latter became the Ministry of Production in 1942). The plans drawn up by these ministries in partnership with business and labour were implemented by a network of tripartite and bipartite institutions at national, regional, district and factory level. The agreements reached nationally on production, wage and profit levels imposed explicitly compulsory responsibilities on employers and workers. Given the exigencies of the war, however, the state rarely had to use its statutory powers to enforce such agreements. The high degree of consensus over the role of the state engendered by the national emergency enabled the Coalition Government to control price, wage and profit levels, to redirect industrial output to military ends and, thus, to fight the war to a successful conclusion (Middlemas, 1980, pp. 266–306).

KEYNESIANISM AND THE POSTWAR SETTLEMENT (1945–59)

Despite ample evidence of a wartime consensus supporting the development of a corporatist relationship between the state and the market, it would be wrong to argue that this consensus was sustained after the end of hostilities. There was scant support amongst trade unionists, employers, financial interests and the general public for the maintenance of the extensive role which the state had adopted. Similarly, there was significant disagreement within and between the two main political parties as to the proper role to be played by the state in the management of the postwar economy. There was, however, one fundamental point of consensus based on a political commitment to the creation of a welfare state as a means of compensating the British people for the privations of the war effort. This commitment had been institutionalised in the Cabinet Committee on Reconstruction set up in 1943. Debating a series of reports and white papers, the Committee had reached broad agreement on the need for universal systems of education, health care and social services. Perhaps most important from the perspective of the present analysis, however, was an agreement reached on the need to adopt Keynesian demand management techniques as a means of maintaining 'a high and stable level of employment' after the war. This became a firm commitment in the form of a White Paper on employment policy published in May 1944 (Dutton, 1991, p. 17).

When the Labour Party returned to office in July 1945 it was without a clear and unified conception of the proper role to be played by the state in the management of economic affairs. The left wing of the Party wanted the new government to create the Socialist Commonwealth by progressively taking the means of production into state ownership. According to their plan of action, the strategically important utilities and staple manufacturing industries would be nationalised first, followed by land and property, then the financial sector, and finally the remaining small and medium-sized enterprises. This view was opposed by the social democrats in the Party, who were in favour of nationalising only the inefficient utilities and staple industries such as coal, steel and railways. The social democratic wing was also in favour of a massive extension of social welfarism which might mean the maintenance of a corporatist approach to the economy, but fell far short of a fully socialist system (Coates, 1975, pp. 44–74). The trade unions were also divided. Some trade unionists were in accord with the left wing of the Party in demanding complete state ownership and control of the means of production, but this group was in a minority. The mainstream trade union leaders were in favour of a limited programme of nationalising inefficient staple industries to protect jobs and a return to free collective bargaining over wages and conditions of employment. In their view, the state should work with the unions at a national level, but this did not amount to a commitment to corporatism. The agreements reached would be in the form of guidelines and would not impose compulsory responsibilities on workers. Equally, the state would have no powers to engage in detailed manpower planning. The unions, therefore, wanted to exercise an influence over state and employer policies without losing their traditional rights to bargain unilaterally with employers over wages and conditions on the factory floor (Panitch, 1976, pp. 7–40; Beer, 1969, pp. 160–2, 206–8).

The future relationship between the state and the market was also being hotly debated at this time by the Liberal and Conservative parties. The Liberal Party, while retaining some vestiges of its historic commitment to laissez–fairism and free trade, had been heavily influenced by the work of Keynes and Beveridge. Beveridge, who was essentially a non-party figure, had produced the report in 1942 which stood as the blueprint for the post-war welfare state. The report proposed the consolidation of existing schemes of welfare support into a universal national scheme, the creation of a national health service, and the maintenance of a high level of employment (Dutton, 1991, pp. 14–15). The ideas of Keynes had come to prominence in both political and bureaucratic circles during his wartime attachment to the Treasury, and the majority of Liberals were happy to argue for the use of Keynesian demand management techniques to ensure full employment. Keynesianism recommended itself to the Liberal Party, because it asserted that, while the state might need to take on a limited ownership role in inefficient and strategically important industries (coal, steel, railways, and so on), the state need not involve itself in widespread ownership and control of industry, nor was it necessary for the state to directly control investment flows and the supply of goods and raw materials in the economy. Keynes argued that by using fiscal policy tools (taxation and public spending) growth and full employment could be maintained without the risk of inflation. According to this approach, in a depression the state would increase public spending and reduce taxation to stimulate demand, while in an inflationary period the state would cut public expenditure and increase taxation to take demand out of the economy. In this way, a high and stable level of employment would be sustained, growth would exponential, and the business cycle of booms and slumps would be eradicated without the need for direct ownership and control by the state. It would then be possible, given sustained economic growth, to underwrite the extensive welfare state envisaged by Beveridge (Stewart, 1986, pp. 141–56). Keynesianism also commanded some support from a broad range of industrial and financial interests. This support was, however, essentially negative, being built on the view that if state intervention was to be maintained after the war, then this was the least painful form available. The best case scenario for the majority of these interests would have been the dismantling of wartime corporatism and a speedy return to a laissez-faire relationship between the state and the market (Blank, 1973).

Finally, the Conservative Party was also debating alternative prescriptions for the role of the state in the postwar economy. Ever since the publication of *The Middle Way* in 1938, Harold Macmillan and a number of fellow MPs and industrialists (Boothby, Stanley and Mond) had been arguing for a rationally planned economy based on what we referred to earlier as 'Macmillanism'. This approach have would involved a range of voluntary planning agreements between business and labour with the state assuming a co-ordinating role of 'vigilant neutrality'. Like Keynes, Macmillan's ideas had been influenced by his experience of mass unemployment and economic inefficiency in the 1930s. In common with Beveridge, he was committed to developing an extensive welfare state and he regarded a planned economy as the only way to produce the growth necessary to make that possible. While 'Macmillanism', and a broad acceptance of the ideas of Keynes, were to have a marked impact on the postwar policies of the Conservatives, these were not the only state–market relationships debated within the Party in the immediate aftermath of the war. Churchill, a former Liberal free-trader, was the other main source of ideas. While he and his supporters recognised the need for a more extensive system of welfare, they were principally concerned to ensure that the state had a minimal role in economic affairs. As already mentioned, this view commanded significant support amongst the Conservative Party's traditional socio-economic base – property owners, financiers and industrialists – as well as amongst the general public, who wanted a swift end to wartime regulations, controls and rationing. It is not surprising, therefore, that a commitment to the restoration of a laissez-faire relationship between the state and the market was a continuing theme of Conservative rhetoric in the postwar era (Harris, 1972, pp. 77–148).

As a result of these contradictory pressures, the relationship which developed between the state and the market in the years immediately after the war was somewhat confused. The Labour Party was returned to office with a commitment to a massive shift of ownership and control to the state, but these plans were undermined by a number of serious short-term problems. A large proportion of the workforce was still in the armed forces, and a number of the staple industries were in need of fundamental modernisation and rationalisation. The industries producing consumer goods were similarly run down. More important still was the fact that Britain had technically been bankrupted by the immense financial burden of fighting the war. Without US aid any semblance of economic and social normalcy would have many years away. Labour, therefore, faced the twin tasks of reconstructing a shattered economy and transferring ownership and control of the means of production to the state, while having to depend on imported raw materials and consumer goods. Within these constraints, it is hardly surprising that the Attlee Government was unable to create the Socialist Commonwealth. Indeed, it is remarkable that Labour was able to fulfil as many of its manifesto commitments as it did. The major staple industries were nationalised, the national health service was established, social services were expanded, the Bank of England was brought into public ownership, and the extensive wartime systems of rationing and corporatist controls over production and manpower were maintained.

   Although this approach allowed the state to successfully direct resources
into export industries between 1945 and 1947, it was ultimately
undermined by an extensive range of socio-economic counter pressures.
Industry called for the nationalisation programme to be limited. The City of
London was active in preventing state intervention in the financial sector
from going beyond public ownership of the Bank of England. The trade
unions demanded, and achieved, a return to free collective bargaining and
continually campaigned against detailed manpower planning by the state.
Labour also faced mounting public demands for an end to rationing and
austerity. The major factor, however, which constrained the Labour
Government's desire to extend state ownership and control was an acute
shortage of foreign currency – in particular US dollars – to pay for
imported raw materials and commodities. Although progress was being
made by Britain's export industries, their earnings were still not large
enough to cover imports and foreign debt repayments. By 1947, therefore,
Britain was experiencing an enormous balance of payments deficit, which
necessitated a loan from the International Monetary Fund (IMF) and
further financial assistance from the Americans. This sounded the death
knell of Labour's plans to create a socialist pattern of ownership and
control, and marked the adoption of a broadly Keynesian approach to state
intervention. This meant that the state was committed to the maintenance
of high and stable level of employment through indirect budgetary
mechanisms (taxation and public spending), and the provision of extensive
social welfare benefits on the basis of sustained economic growth. The
nationalisation programme was limited to inefficient utilities and staple
industries, and rationing and the remaining corporatist controls on
production and manpower were progressively abolished. The only
exception to this shift towards Keynesianism was the nationalisation of the
steel and road haulage industries. These nationalisations were forced
through against the prevailing political and economic mood, because they
were supported by key trade union groups in the Labour coalition.
Nevertheless, the orientation of state intervention after 1947 was
overwhelmingly Keynesian (Howells, 1976, pp. 9–46).

   This broadly Keynesian approach was maintained by the Conservatives
when they returned to office in 1951, and it remained in place until the end
of the decade. Although the Conservatives denationalised the road haulage
and steel industries, and downgraded state aid for regions in decline, this
did not mark a fundamental dissensus with the policies of the Labour Party.
As the continuum developed earlier demonstrates, these policy shifts were,
in fact, fully within the bounds of the Keynesian approach which had been
adopted by the Labour Government after 1947. In reality, therefore, such

changes merely serve to mask the central continuity of Keynesianism. Amongst a number of reasons for the success of Keynesianism across the party political spectrum, perhaps the most important is that in the 1950s the world witnessed an unprecedented rate of growth which made it unnecessary for the state to intervene directly in the economy. Against this background, the desire of trade unionists and business interests to be free of state interference held sway easily. In a prolonged period of economic growth, and commensurate increases in material wealth, workers were quite content to use free collective bargaining to achieve wage agreements. Equally, the major industrial and financial interests were happy to underwrite an extensive system of welfare as long as rapid economic growth was the norm and the state did not attempt to adopt a more interventionist approach to economic management (Harris, 1972, pp. 149–248).

The durability of this Keynesian consensus should not, however, be taken to mean that there was an absence of alternative points of view. First, a significant minority of trade unionists and Labour Party activists were deeply disappointed by the record of the Attlee governments between 1945 and 1951 and by the Party's apparent shift, under the leadership of Hugh Gaitskell, away from a commitment to state ownership and control towards Keynesianism. There was also a significant minority of backbench Conservative MPs, supported by a range of business interests, who wanted to move towards a more laissez-faire relationship between the state and the market. Until the 1970s, however, when widespread evidence of Britain's relative economic decline began to undermine popular support for Keynesianism, neither of these groups was sufficiently powerful to seriously threaten the consensus. The long boom, which began in the early 1950s and lasted until the end of the 1960s, initially masked the fact that Britain's share of world trade and her growth performance were in relative decline. By the end of the 1950s, however, there was a growing awareness of this problem among informed academic and political elites. Although this awareness led to a questioning of the Keynesian consensus and a search for new policy ideas, the result was not adversarial politics at the level of the state. Instead, the focus of the consensus shifted towards Macmillanism and corporatism, as both main parties used the state more extensively to reconstruct British industry (Pahl and Winkler, 1974, pp. 72–6). The question to be addressed in the next section is which of these two theoretical categories best describes the state–market relationship developed in the 1960s.

MACMILLANISM OR A RETURN TO CORPORATISM? (1959–70)

The Conservative governments of the 1950s practised Keynesianism with a laissez-faire orientation. In essence this means that, while the welfare state was maintained and most of the industries brought into public ownership by the previous Labour governments were retained, the Conservatives consciously attempted to introduce a more commercial and market-based approach to the management of nationalised industries. In other words, the nationalised industries were not only to be used to achieve socio-economic objectives such as the maintenance of employment in depressed regions. Throughout the 1950s, therefore, state intervention at the microeconomic level was classically Keynesian in that it was designed to correct 'market failures', but not to replace the operation of the market. At the level of the macroeconomy, however, the state used fiscal policy instruments to defend the value of sterling and to support the role of the City of London as a major international currency market rather than to maintain a high and stable level of employment. The core objective of Keynesianism was being denied, because the significant invisible earnings of the financial sector were seen as an essential bulwark against the recurrent balance of payments problems stemming from visible trade deficits. The result was a 'stop–go' cycle of demand management, as the underlying weakness of the economy in manufacturing trade led to the use of Keynesian techniques to restrict consumer demands for imported goods (Brittan, 1971, pp. 179–226). Towards the end of the 1950s, however, a number of industrialists and politicians began to question the priorities of government policy and to call for increased state assistance to industry at the expense of the defence of sterling. The time was ripe for Harold Macmillan, who had achieved the Conservatives' third election victory in a row in 1959, to put the ideas contained in *The Middle Way* into action.

Although a number of commentators have argued that the strategy adopted by the Conservative Government after 1960 was corporatist (Pahl and Winkler, 1974, pp. 72–6), this chapter takes the view that the policies used were closer to the ideal type which we have called Macmillanism. This conclusion becomes clear when we consider that the Government relied on *voluntary* participation and co-operation by employers and trade unionists in the processes of policy-making and implementation. Furthermore, the approach to planning could hardly be described as comprehensive; there was no attempt to include the financial sector of the economy. The Government created a system of tripartite and bipartite institutions – the National Economic Development Council (NEDC), the National Incomes Commission, and the subsidiary Economic Development Councils (EDCs) – in order to bring business and labour together to discuss bottlenecks in industrial output, productivity and wage rates, but the approach was not compulsory. The Government merely encouraged union and employer participation, and the agreements reached imposed no compulsory responsibilities. Similarly, companies were never forced to accept the broad planning frameworks formulated by the NEDC. The only significant exception to this voluntary approach was the wage freeze introduced in 1961, but this fell apart after only six months. Ultimately, the Conservatives began to shift back towards a more Keynesian approach to the microeconomy. They increased state assistance to regions in decline and encouraged manpower retraining through the use of tax incentives and subsidies (Shanks, 1981, Ch. 1).

Despite the ritualised ideological battle which accompanied the 1964 general election, the new Labour Government led by Harold Wilson set out to implement a programme broadly similar to that attempted by the previous Conservative administration. The renationalisation of the steel and road-haulage industries did not, therefore, indicate a fundamental shift towards dirigisme or socialism, but was rather a sop to key trade unionists in the Labour coalition. It might be argued that Labour's policies were closer to the corporatist ideal type than those adopted by Macmillan. The Department of Economic Affairs (DEA) was established to co-ordinate the planning activities of the state and to act as a counterweight to the dominance of financial interests in policy-making, represented by the Treasury, the Bank of England and the City of London. A regional layer of tripartite institutions was added to the Conservatives' national and sectoral planning approach based on the NEDC and the EDCs. The centrepiece of Labour's approach was the National Plan, which was formulated by the NEDC on the basis of discussions held in the regional and sectoral EDCs. The Plan set out sectoral growth and reorganisation objectives, as well as guidelines for wage increases. The argument of this chapter, however, is that these policies did not amount to full corporatism because the National Plan did not impose compulsory responsibilities on business and labour to ensure effective policy implementation. Furthermore, and arguably the most important omission, the Labour approach left the financial sector free to decide the direction of investment flows. The state provided grants and subsidies to enable industry to relocate in line with the Plan, but companies were left free to decide whether they wanted to take advantage of these inducements. The Plan contained detailed guidelines for wage settlements, but, initially at least, union co-operation with these guidelines was entirely voluntary. Labour's approach is, therefore, best described as Macmillanism; the Government tried to use the state to indirectly control a principally privately-owned economy, but this was based on *voluntary* participation and co-operation by employers and unions (Young and Lowe, 1974, pp, 15–38).

This Macmillanist approach could not, however, be sustained in practice. This was revealed most emphatically in 1965–66, when a serious deterioration in Britain's balance of payments position induced a rapid depreciation in the value of sterling. Instead of adhering to the National Plan's strategy of ignoring the balance of payments constraint on economic growth, the Labour Government was forced to cut public spending and rein in consumer demand in order to defend the value of sterling and support the interests of the City of London. The National Plan was dealt a fatal blow by short-term financial problems, because the Treasury, the Bank of England and the City of London retained their historic stranglehold over policy-making. It thus became clear that the Plan would never be successfully implemented without effective state control over the priorities of the financial sector. The Plan was further undermined by its in-built assumption of wage restraint to combat rising inflation, and yet it did not impose compulsory responsibilities on the unions to ensure that they implemented this objective. Voluntary wage restraint ultimately crumbled in the face of vociferous rank-and-file opposition to bargains struck between union leaders and the state. Only then did the Labour Government begin to shift towards a more corporatist approach to wages policy. The National Board for Prices and Incomes was created in 1966 and its first action was to impose a statutory wage freeze lasting six months. This was followed by a further two years of severe wage restraint backed by a statutory policy (Crouch, 1979, pp. 45–65). The voluntary nature of the Plan also blunted its impact on industry. It was built on the premise that if the growth points in the economy were highlighted, and the state acted to sustain effective demand, then industrialists would invest and stimulate production and employment in the planned sectors. That this did not happen should not be surprising, because, left to make their own decisions, business leaders usually wait until effective demand rises before committing themselves to new investment. Unfortunately, Labour's macroeconomic strategy was being dictated by the interests of the financial sector. The defence of sterling required a reduction of effective demand, which meant that the majority of industrialists were unwilling to increase investment. Without effective state control over investment flows, therefore, the Plan was doomed to fail. As the weaknesses of the National Plan became increasingly obvious, the Labour Government tried to take a more proactive approach to industrial planning. At the heart of this policy shift were the Industrial Reorganisation Corporation set up in 1966 and the Industrial Expansion Act passed in 1968. This did not, however, come close to corporatism (Young and Lowe, 1974, pp. 31–7, 166–210).

As the preceding discussion makes clear, then, both the Conservative and the Labour governments of the 1960s set out to create a far greater degree of state involvement in the economy than had been thought necessary between 1947 and 1959. This shift was not, however, driven by adversary politics, but was rather a logical extension of the Keynesian consensus which had been institutionalised after 1947. Neither party tried to create a fully corporatist relationship between the state and the market. Instead, they were content to adopt a 'half-way house' between Keynesianism and corporatism, an approach which closely resembled what we have dubbed Macmillanism. The decision to take this voluntaristic approach is perhaps best explained by the dominance of liberal values in British society. This dominance has expressed itself in the trade unions' historic commitment to free collective bargaining and in the defence of free trade and laissez-fairism by the broad sweep of industrial and financial interests. Thus, both Labour and Conservative politicians would have been fully aware that any attempt to create an extensive interventionist role for the state would have been regarded as illegitimate by the mass of the electorate and by key socio-economic groups. A strategy based on voluntary co-operation with state-sponsored policies was, however, bound to fail, because it overlooked the lack of control which union leaders had over their members on the shop floor, the difficulty of achieving co-ordination in industry given its non-hierarchical and highly competitive nature, and the place of the City of London at the heart of an international financial system based on free trade principles.

As mentioned earlier, the Labour Government's response to the weaknesses of Macmillanism was to take a more proactive stance based on statutory powers designed to reorganise industry, direct industrial investment and manage labour relations. Unfortunately, this policy shift could only be achieved by reducing public expenditure on social welfare and by raising taxation to force resources out of consumption and into investment. The spending cuts undermined Labour's traditional electoral support amongst the working class, while the tax increases alienated all classes of voters. Added to this electoral dilemma, the Government's more assertive approach caused an intra-party conflict. Not surprisingly, the trade unions were violently opposed to any attempt to limit their traditional freedoms in order to achieve more disciplined labour relations, either through a compulsory incomes policy or by means of the legal restraints contained in Barbara Castle's 1969 White Paper, *In Place of Strife*

(Crouch, 1979, pp. 66–72). The left wing of the Party were alienated by the demise of the National Plan and by cutbacks in spending on social welfare. An important result of these factors was that the 1970 general election saw traditional Labour supporters abstain from voting in much larger numbers than ever before. This contributed to the victory of the Conservative Party under Edward Heath (Crewe et al., 1977, pp. 120–90). Significantly, Heath had been the first party leader in the post-war era to campaign on the basis of a manifesto which appealed to the base liberal values of the British people and the anti-statism of industrial and financial interests. Did this mark the demise of the post-war consensus?

A CHALLENGE TO THE POST-WAR CONSENSUS (1970–72)

While it would be somewhat excessive to argue that the policies adopted by Heath in the first two years of his administration marked the demise of the postwar consensus, they certainly constituted a serious challenge. The broad strategy of the Conservatives was to rebalance the state–market relationship in favour of the market. Pointing to the increasingly obvious signs of Britain's relative economic decline, Heath argued that the state activism employed by both Conservative and Labour governments since the war had not only failed to reverse this decline, but had actually made it worse. Despite the rhetoric, however, this did not herald laissez-fairism and a complete rejection of state involvement in the management of the economy. Instead, the policies adopted were Keynesian with a laissez-faire orientation. The state was, thus, to focus on the indirect management of demand at the macroeconomic level while returning to a fundamentally market-based pattern of ownership and control in industry and finance. Heath argued that unfettered private enterprise would be the source of Britain's economic renewal.

The laissez-faire orientation of Heath's approach was represented by his belief that new 'managerial' techniques and structures could be borrowed by government from the private sector to improve the efficiency of policy implementation. As a result of this belief, a number of central government's policy functions were 'hived-off' to autonomous agencies outside Whitehall, and the structure of both central and local government was rationalised. In line with a return to indirect Keynesian management, the degree of state intervention at the microeconomic level was drastically reduced. The National Board for Prices and Incomes (NBPI), the Monopolies Commission and the Land Commission were all abolished, as were a number of the regional and sectoral EDCs set up as part of the previous Labour government's Macmillanist strategy. In addition, state aid to industries and regions in decline was cut back to allow industrialists to make investment and location decisions on the basis of market signals. This policy was complemented by the removal of credit controls to give the financial sector more room for manoeuvre. Heath replaced Labour's statutory incomes policy under the NBPI with a policy of free collective bargaining between employers and workers in privately-owned industries, while an incomes policy was covertly maintained in the public sector. In order to provide private sector employers with a degree of protection as they bargained over wages with the unions, the Heath Government passed the 1971 Industrial Relations Act. The main effect of the Act was to outlaw unofficial, wildcat strike action, a measure which the Government claimed would help the labour market to operate more effectively. As we shall see, however, this claim proved somewhat ironic. In terms of state ownership Heath's approach was broadly Keynesian, in that he kept inefficient staple industries and the utilities in the public sector while profitable industries were sold off. Significantly, though, those industries remaining in public ownership were expected to operate in line with more commercial criteria. Similarly, the fundamental elements of the welfare state were retained, but the level of public spending on social services was to be held in check in real terms, and if possible reduced, in order to lighten the tax burden on the private sector. The final element in Heath's more market-orientated strategy was his decision to apply for membership of the EEC (British entry was achieved in 1973). To sum up, the policies adopted by the Conservative Government between 1970 and 1972 were seen by many commentators, particularly those on the Left, as a new departure for British capitalism (Blackburn, 1971, pp. 276–82). Although this position is understandable in comparison with what had happened in the 1960s, with the benefit of hindsight it would perhaps be more accurate to say that Heath had made a return to the Keynesianism of the 1947–59 period, albeit with a laissez-faire orientation.

Heath's return to Keynesianism was, however, to prove spectacularly unsuccessful as a means of dealing with the difficulties faced by the British economy in the early 1970s. The core assumption of this strategy was that, left to its own devices, the market would be able to regenerate industry and create the rapid economic growth necessary for an extensive welfare state to be maintained. Unfortunately, this line of reasoning ignored the fundamentally weak and uncompetitive position of much of British industry. This meant that, even if the state were to maintain a full employment level of effective demand, the market would be unlikely to choose to invest in manufacturing industry given that profits were at an historic low. Heath's macroeconomic strategy, which stimulated the flow of investment funds through tax cuts and the deregulation of the financial sector, therefore led to speculation in the property market rather than increased investment in industry and job creation. The result was a boom in property prices which fed through into rapidly rising inflation. This domestic inflation was fuelled by the effects of an appreciation in the value of sterling after the collapse of the Bretton Woods system of fixed exchange rates in 1970, and by an international shortage of, and therefore speculation in, raw materials and commodities (Young and Lowe, 1974, pp. 131–64).

The political costs of these economic difficulties were enormous. Inflation in the prices of property and consumer goods, with implications for the general cost-of-living, led to increasing unrest and demands for higher wages among workers. This worker militancy was further exacerbated by the legal restrictions on strike action which the Government attempted to introduce under the 1971 Industrial Relations Act. Rather than helping the labour market to operate more effectively, therefore, the Act led to a massive increase in strike activity with obvious implications for output and productivity levels in an already weak industrial base. The final nail in Heath's strategy, however, was the end of the postwar boom which had allowed policy-makers since the beginning of the 1950s to ignore the signs of Britain's relative economic decline. In the recessionary world market of the early 1970s, the structurally weak and inflation-prone British economy faced a rapidly falling demand for its products, low investment in industry and rising unemployment. By mid-1972, therefore, the Heath Government came under increasing pressure to change its approach as a number of strategically important companies employing very large numbers of people went bankrupt (Young and Lowe, 1974, pp. 131–64). These included Upper Clyde Shipbuilders, Rolls-Royce, Alfred Herbert Engineering, Ferranti and British Leyland. Heath's response, despite vociferous opposition from the right wing of the Conservative Party, was to move back towards a Macmillanist approach to economic management.

PRAGMATIC MACMILLANISM (1972–79)

As the title to this section indicates, the Conservative Government's return to Macmilllanism in 1972 was pragmatic rather than principled. This is true both in the sense that the policy 'U-turn' came about through force of circumstances, and in the sense that Heath did not attempt to apply a fully Macmillanist planning strategy. In addition, we should not assume that

Heath's challenge to the postwar consensus had left the landscape of British politics unchanged, and that this was simply a return to share that same centre ground with the Labour Party. As will be discussed later in this section, Labour used its time in opposition to move its broad policy stance back to the kind of dirigiste/socialist position that it had held in 1945. The postwar consensus was, therefore, being challenged by both main parties at a level beyond mere rhetoric. Both parties felt that the consensus had not been effective in addressing Britain's long-term economic difficulties, and that the time was ripe for new and more radical answers.

As we have seen, however, Heath's new answers were found wanting and he was forced to use the state to deal with the developing economic crisis. The Government adopted a Macmillanist approach, relying on the voluntary participation and co–operation of the unions, employers and financial interests to achieve industrial regeneration and bring inflation under control. The centrepiece of this strategy was a package of pay, rent, dividend and price restraint combined with increased public spending on social services. Unfortunately, all three socio-economic groups found something to dislike in Heath's offer and refused to get involved. While employers supported pay restraint, they rejected dividend and price restraint at a time of declining demand and falling profits. Key players in the financial sector were interested in co-operating with the state to deal with the difficulties caused by property speculation, but they refused to countenance rent and dividend restraint. Finally, while the unions were happy to support price, rent and dividend restraint and increased spending on the welfare state, they continued their historic resistance to an incomes policy. The failure of this anti-inflation strategy based on voluntary co-operation led Heath to introduce a statutory incomes policy and government control over prices, rents and dividends. These policies were implemented by a Price Commission and a Pay Board much like the NBPI established under the previous Labour administration.

Despite these elements of compulsion, however, the part of Heath's strategy focusing on industrial regeneration was classically Macmillanist in its reliance on voluntary participation. At the heart of the policy was the 1972 Industry Act, which provided extensive financial incentives for industry to reorganise and relocate in declining regions, but did not compel companies to make use of these funds. Instead, the Government relied on industry to take the initiative and to make a case for the funding of a particular scheme. Heath's post-1972 policy 'U-turn' was, however, not fully Macmillanist, because the state aid made available under the 1972 Industry Act was not complemented by an extensive planning system based on bipartite and tripartite institutions. Heath thus used elements of Macmillanism as a response to an economic crisis, rather than adopting the whole as a means to plan the economy in a rational and comprehensive manner in the way that the previous Labour government had attempted (Young and Lowe, 1974, pp. 131–64).

Although Heath's conversion to Macmillanism was too little too late, it was his compulsory pay policy that ultimately contained the seeds of the Conservative Government's electoral destruction. The unions, which had already been incensed by the provisions of the 1971 Industrial Relations Act, were by now displaying outright hostility to the government's incomes policy. Heath made a number of attempts at conciliation, pointing to increased spending on social services, controls on prices, dividends and rents, and a decision not to apply the 1971 Act as evidence of his good intentions. These appeals were a success in the short term, and the level of strike action fell markedly in 1973, but then came the Arab–Israeli Yom Kippur War. The immediate result of this conflict was a decision by the Organisation of Petroleum-Exporting Countries (OPEC) to restrict the supply of oil to the Western nations, because they had supported the Israelis. This led to a rapid increase in the price of oil which added fuel to the inflationary pressures already operating in the international economy. With the cost of living rapidly increasing in Britain, as everywhere in the developed world, the Government's incomes policy was inevitably put under severe pressure. The policy finally crumbled in the winter of 1973–74 as the miners, one of the largest and most militant sections of the workforce, began a work-to-rule and threatened a national strike if their wage demands were not met. The dispute deepened into a crisis as the work-to-rule led to coal shortages at power stations which, in turn, resulted in power cuts. The Government responded by declaring a state of national emergency and introducing a three-day week in industry to conserve electricity supplies. The dispute dragged on throughout the winter, and by February 1974 Heath lost patience and decided to call a general election to settle the question of 'who runs the country?' He got his answer when the Conservatives lost their overall majority and were replaced by a minority Labour government, which took office with the support of the Liberals (Holmes, 1982, pp. 55–126).

Labour governed in what amounted to a holding pattern between February and October of 1974, putting the finishing touches to their 'Social Contract' with the trade unions. This agreement, which gave the unions a policy-making partnership with the state and promised 'industrial democracy' in return for voluntary wage restraint and improved industrial relations, was a key part of the manifesto on which Labour fought and won the second general election of 1974. However, this victory was by a margin of only three seats, a factor which was crucial in the development of

Labour's approach over the next four and a half years. As was mentioned earlier, the Labour Party's time in opposition had been characterised by a radical shift to the left. Apart from the Social Contract, there were a number of other policy commitments which seemed to indicate that the Labour Government elected in October 1974 was intent on moving progressively towards a socialist, or at least dirigiste, relationship between the state and the market. The manifesto promised an extensive programme of nationalisation, going well beyond the usual targets of inefficient staple industries and the utilities to include profitable manufacturing industries, like aerospace, and key sectors of the financial system. This was to be complemented by state-directed industrial regeneration financed through the National Enterprise Board (NEB) and co-ordinated by sectoral planning agreements (Hatfield, 1978). This process was to be explicitly state-led. As we shall see, however, these commitments were undermined by intra-party conflict and stillborn in the face of deepening economic crisis, and by 1976, like the Conservatives before them, the Labour Government had pragmatically adopted a Macmillanist strategy.

During the winter of 1974–75 it began to become clear that Labour's manifesto commitments would have to be compromised if the Government was to address a range of immediate economic problems. Labour faced the worst balance-of-payments position on record, combined with rapidly declining industrial competitiveness, a poor level of investment and a widening public sector borrowing requirement. In addition, the oil price rise in 1973–74 had given rise to an international economic situation not previously thought possible – stagflation. This refers to a simultaneous increase in both inflation and unemployment. The Government was, therefore, caught on the horns of a dilemma. If it tried to fulfil its manifesto commitments to more extensive state ownership and increased spending on social services, this would result in a sterling crisis caused by the withdrawal of money from Britain by international currency dealers fearful of increased state interference and higher taxation. On the other hand, if the Government did not fulfil these commitments it would lose trade union agreement to wage restraint and, therefore, face even higher inflation and a further erosion of Britain's competitive position in the international economy (Guttmann, 1976, pp. 225–70). The choice between these two policy scenarios was the focus of a bitter struggle within the Labour Party between leading left-wing members of the Cabinet, like Tony Benn (Department of Industry) and Michael Foot (Department of Employment), who argued that the Government should fulfil its commitments to public ownership and state-directed industrial modernisation, and right-wing members of the Cabinet, including Harold Wilson (Prime Minister) and

Denis Healey (Chancellor), who argued that avoiding a sterling crisis was more important. In very broad terms, it can be stated that the left-wing view was in the ascendancy during 1974–75, while the views of the right prevailed after the end of 1975.

Thus, in its first year in office the new Labour Government tried hard to fulfil its manifesto commitments. Public spending on social services was increased, the NEB was set up under the 1975 Industry Act, and legislation to nationalise the aerospace and shipbuilding industries and to repeal the 1971 Industrial Relations Act was introduced. Unfortunately, while Labour showed a willingness to fulfil its part of the 'Social Contract', the trade unions were not willing, or able, to fulfil theirs. As outlined above, the unions had promised to exercise pay restraint in return for a policy-making partnership with state, the improvement of workers' rights and increased spending on the welfare state. The key problem facing this approach was that the miners' strike in the winter of 1973–74 had resulted in massive wage rises in the coal industry. Workers in other industries now argued that they deserved commensurate increases, particularly given the rapidly rising cost of living at this time. Added to this was the fact that the 'Social Contract' was essentially a bargain between the state and union leaders who were unable to exert effective control over their members on the shop floor. This combination of circumstances produced devastating consequences for Labour's strategy. Wage increases averaged 26 per cent, which further undermined Britain's already weak position in international trade. This rampant wage inflation, in combination with increases in public spending and the introduction of pro-union legislation, led directly to a crisis of confidence on the international currency markets. The value of sterling depreciated rapidly, and by the middle of 1975 it was clear that through force of circumstances the views of the right wing of the Labour Party were in the ascendancy (Coates, 1980, pp. 148–201).

By the end of 1975, therefore, Labour had abandoned its attempt to move to a dirigiste relationship between the state and the market. The Government now began to pursue a broadly Macmillanist strategy. Although this policy shift was a response to immediate economic problems, it was given extra force by the conflict at the highest level of the Labour Party, by the Government's tiny parliamentary majority, and by the fact that, as we have emphasised throughout this chapter, extensive state intervention is regarded as illegitimate by Britain's key socio–economic interests and by the mass of the population. A key element of the new approach was a reduction of public spending on social services in order to release resources for industrial investment. Controls on prices, dividends and rents were relaxed in an attempt to win back business confidence and, thus, restore the value of sterling. Swingeing cuts in public expenditure meant that Labour's commitments to nationalise profitable manufacturing industries and key elements of the financial sector had to be shelved, as did proposals for a wealth tax and industrial democracy. Although these changes came before the International Monetary Fund (IMF) loan acquired by Britain in 1976, they were fully supported by the terms under which it was granted (Coates, 1980, pp. 38–43).

Although the main focus of Labour's Macmillanist strategy in the period 1976–79 was to reduce inflation in line with the terms of the IMF loan, the role of the NEB should not be overlooked, because its failure to bring about the hoped-for industrial reorganisation and regeneration represents perfectly the weaknesses of an approach based on voluntary participation and co-operation by the major socio-economic groups. Originally intended as a dirigiste mechanism to help establish and develop strategically important industries, to extend public ownership into profitable manufacturing industries, and to promote industrial democracy, the NEB was hamstrung from its inception by cutbacks in public expenditure. Its limited resources were, thus, targeted almost exclusively on bringing ailing rather than profitable companies into public ownership. These included British Leyland, Ferranti, Alfred Herbert Engineering and Triang. More important, though, was the fact that privately-owned companies were not compelled to take up the state's incentives to reorganise offered under the terms of the 1975 Industry Act. The Act was based on a Macmillanist strategy of voluntary participation, which meant that the state could only impose reorganisation on those companies which were publicly-owned or came to the Government for help because they were in trouble. The NEB, therefore, failed to bring about a fundamental change in the pattern of ownership and control, and instead became a rescue agent for ailing companies (Grant, 1982, pp. 62–73, 101–24).

However, it was over the issue of wage restraint that the Government's Macmillanist strategy proved most damaging. As outlined earlier, the 'Social Contract' drawn up by Labour and the union leaders during the Party's time in opposition was ineffective as a means of containing rampant wage inflation. By the summer of 1975, therefore, the Government realised that if it was to deal with an ever-increasing balance-of-payments deficit, combined with a growing public sector borrowing requirement, then it needed to win voluntary union co-operation with a formal incomes policy. While the call for *voluntary* co-operation was partly a function of Labour's manifesto promise not to impose an incomes policy on the unions, it was also a recognition of the unions' potential to disrupt the smooth running of the economy. Unfortunately, the Government had to try to achieve this aim while reneging on a large part of its commitment to increase public expenditure and improve workers' rights through a programme of industrial democracy. Nevertheless, between 1975 and 1977 this reliance on voluntary wage restraint, backed up by the incorporation of union leaders into the policy-making process, worked surprisingly well. After 1977, however, the unions were either unwilling or unable to maintain this level of co-operation and there was a massive increase in strike activity as the unions demanded wage increases above the agreed guidelines. There were several reasons for this policy failure. Although inflation and unemployment were beginning to be brought under control, they were still high by postwar standards. It was against this background that public expenditure on the 'social wage' (housing, health care and other social services) had been drastically reduced to deal with a ballooning public sector deficit. While these cuts had their greatest impact on the unemployed, low-paid workers were also affected. On top of this, the voluntary incomes policy had significantly eroded wage differentials between skilled and unskilled workers. All sections of the workforce had, therefore, been subject to a relative decline in their living standards which, not surprisingly, led them to strike for higher wages. The final disintegration of voluntary wage restraint came in the infamous 'Winter of Discontent' of 1978–79, when several of the major public sector unions went on strike for wage increases above the norm set by the Government. This proved to be the straw that broke the camel's back. In May 1979, after nearly five years of rising unemployment and falling living standards, the Labour Government lost the general election and was replaced by the Conservative Party under the leadership of Margaret Thatcher (Cox, 1981, pp. 61–99). As the next section will make clear, the election of Thatcher finally seemed to confirm the demise of the postwar consensus built around an active and interventionist role for the state in economic affairs.

LAISSEZ-FAIRISM BY DEGREES (1979–?)

The Conservatives won the general election in May 1979 on a pledge to roll back the frontiers of the state in order to release the full growth potential of private enterprise. In terms of the ideal type categories developed above, therefore, the new Government was intent on creating a laissez-faire relationship between the state and the market. Laissez-fairism refers to a situation in which the pattern of ownership and control in the economy is fundamentally market-based. The state plays a minimal role at the level of the macroeconomy, its key functions being to provide a system of legal guarantees for private property and to maintain a stable business environment by controlling inflation, supporting the value of the currency and defending the nation against internal and external threats. It should be emphasised, however, that laissez-fairism should be seen as an 'end-state' rather than as an ongoing process, because, as the events of the last seventeen years have demonstrated, rolling back the frontiers of the state in the long term may, paradoxically, require increased state activism in the short term (Gamble, 1988, pp. 128–38; Deakin, 1992, pp. 173–4). Thus, the strategy of the Conservatives since 1979 is best thought of as laissez-fairism by degrees, as both Thatcher and Major have used the state to chip away at the foundations of the postwar edifice.

The manifesto on which Margaret Thatcher swept to victory in 1979 had much in common with that presented to the country in 1970 by Edward Heath. Above all, both stressed the need to release the forces of the market if Britain's long-term relative economic decline was to be reversed. Mrs Thatcher was, however, much more deeply convinced that the postwar Keynesian/Macmillanist consensus had directly caused Britain's relative failure and that it needed to be broken once and for all. Indeed, she made something of a virtue of her determination to strike out in new directions, announcing in a pre-election speech: 'I am a conviction politician. The Old Testament prophets did not say "Brothers, I want a consensus". They said "This is my faith. This is what I passionately believe. If you believe it too, then come with me" (quoted in Rose, 1980, p. 4). Of course, both the Conservative Government elected in 1970 and its Labour successor of 1974 had been rhetorically committed to breaking the mould of the postwar political economy, but, as the preceding discussion has revealed, this rhetoric failed to become reality. The difference after 1979 was that the Thatcher strategy was much more in tune with both the popular and the intellectual mood of the time.

From about 1973, controlling inflation rather than maintaining full employment had become the policy priority both in Britain and across the international economy. As we have seen, the response of the Conservative and Labour governments in the 1970s had been to adopt a Macmillanist approach to the problem, relying on the voluntary co-operation of the major socio-economic groups to achieve wage, price, rent and dividend restraint. The perceived failure of this strategy led, by the mid-1970s, to a revival of the classical economic theory that had been successfully challenged by Keynesianism in the 1940s. According to this classical theory, the operation of the economy is best understood, and therefore controlled, in terms of monetary phenomena such as the rate of inflation. The most celebrated exponent of this revival, dubbed 'monetarism', was the American economist Milton Friedman. According to Friedman, inflation can only be controlled by controlling the supply of money in the economy. This follows, because money, like all other commodities, is subject to the laws of supply and demand. If, therefore, the state creates an excessive supply of money by borrowing to meet public spending commitments, then its value will fall and inflation will be the result. The public policy implications of monetarism are that inflation rather than unemployment should be focus of macroeconomic management, and that the extent of state involvement in the economy should be limited in order to bring down public spending and, therefore, reduce the level of borrowing. Mrs Thatcher's conversion to monetarism, soon after she replaced Heath as leader of the Conservative Party in 1975, was complemented by her interest in the ideas of Friedrich von Hayek. In his seminal work, *Road to Serfdom* (1944), he had warned against the threats to personal liberty posed by excessive state interference (Dutton, 1991, pp. 78–80).

By 1979, therefore, the Conservatives had formulated a strategy which aimed to put these ideas into action. Policy then, as now, focused on three key areas: bringing down inflation and keeping it under control; curbing the power of the trade unions in order to create a more 'flexible' labour market; and creating a pattern of ownership and control based on the 'free market' by means of privatisation and liberalisation. While there is an inevitable degree of overlap, in broad terms the Conservatives have taken a step-by-step approach, addressing each of these objectives in turn and following Mrs Thatcher's dictum that 'politics should be the art of the possible'.

The key macroeconomic objective pursued by various means since 1979 has been a low and stable rate of inflation. This represents an explicit rejection of the idea at the heart of the postwar consensus, namely that the state should primarily be responsible for maintaining full employment. Between May 1979 and the autumn of 1985, the Conservatives employed orthodox monetarism in their battle against inflation. The centrepiece of their approach was the Medium Term Financial Strategy (MTFS), which set out annual target ranges for the growth of the money supply. The money supply measure used was 'sterling M3', which consists of all notes and coins in circulation plus all private sector bank deposits denominated in sterling. The choice of this so-called 'broad' money measure was dictated by the fact that its growth was directly linked to the size of the public sector borrowing requirement (PSBR). The counter-inflation policy was thus largely built around a reduction in public spending and, by extension, public borrowing. This link gave the Treasury extra clout in its attempts to rein back public spending, because it was able to warn departmental spending ministers that any relaxation would jeopardise the central aim of macroeconomic policy, low inflation (Smith, 1993, p. 40). The Government argued that an important part of the MTFS would be its impact on inflationary expectations. The view was that the simple existence of a target would go part of the way to convincing the key socio-economic groups that the Government was serious about controlling inflation and would, thus, lead them to revise their wage, price, and rent demands accordingly.

The first real test of the Conservatives' commitment to low inflation rather than to maintaining a high and stable level of employment came in 1980–81. The combined effects of a tight monetary policy, a rapidly appreciating currency, and international stagflation produced by the second oil crisis, had plunged the economy into a deep recession. The choice faced by the Chancellor, Geoffrey Howe, in his 1981 Budget was stark: either continue to bear down on inflation by controlling public spending and maintaining high interest rates, or deal with rising unemployment by using Keynesian techniques to stimulate effective demand. Howe chose the former and the death of the postwar consensus was confirmed. As time went on, however, it became clear that attempting to control the money supply was an ineffective means of bringing down inflation, because it was proving impossible to achieve even the most flexible monetary targets. Constant failure to achieve the stated goals undermined public and business confidence in the Government's ability to create a stable environment for long-term investment, and led to expectational increases in the rate of inflation. There were two main reasons for this failure. First, it was impossible for the Government to fulfil its 1979 manifesto commitment to reduce public expenditure in real terms, because welfare costs were mounting as a result of higher unemployment and an ageing population. This can be seen in the fact that by 1984 policy was merely to contain spending in real terms, while by 1986 it was to ensure that growing public expenditure should decline as a percentage of the faster growing GDP (Dutton, 1991, p. 84). Second, and perhaps more important, the Government was also pursuing policies to liberalize the financial system as part of its broader strategy of freeing market forces. Unfortunately, this liberalisation had the effect of boosting bank lending and increasing the supply of credit, thus making reliable control over sterling M3 almost impossible. As one commentator has put it, this curious combination of policies was an attempt to have 'control without controls' (Smith, 1993, p. 21).

After a temporary suspension in the autumn of 1985, the MTFS was finally shelved by Nigel Lawson in the summer of 1986. From this point until Britain's entry into the European Exchange Rate Mechanism (ERM) in October 1990, counter-inflation policy relied on the short-term manipulation of interest rates by the Treasury and the Bank of England. Although the Chancellor was fulsome in his public support for this more flexible arrangement, it began to become clear that in private he felt that monetary policy had lost its credibility, because it lacked a stable point of reference. The international financial markets seemed to back this judgement, as the value of the pound fell rapidly under intense speculative pressure in July 1984 and January 1985. The effect of this currency depreciation was rising inflation, and all of the Government's hard work in the early 1980s seemed to be being undone. The focus of the battle against inflation, therefore, began to shift onto the role of the exchange rate. A high value for the pound was necessary to keep the inflationary pressure of import prices at a minimum, and interest rates were kept high accordingly. Lawson felt, however, that this could only be a temporary arrangement and that the time had come to formalise this shift in focus by adopting an explicit exchange rate target in the context of the ERM. Although Mrs Thatcher's intransigence over this issue led Lawson to resign in October 1989, the former Chancellor's wishes were ultimately fulfilled when Britain joined the ERM in October 1990. Margaret Thatcher's resignation followed about a month later, again over the issue of European integration. Britain's two-year membership under the new Prime Minister, John Major, was far from successful, in the main because the pound's target parity was set too high. This produced a worsening balance of payments, as British exports were priced out of a world market entering a cyclical downturn. A decline in the balance of payments was followed by predictable pressure on sterling. Despite the deepening recession, the Government remained firmly committed to its new counter-inflationary strategy throughout 1991 and into the early part of 1992. By September 1992, however, the speculators had won and Britain was forced to suspend its membership of the ERM (Smith, 1993, pp. 43–245). Since then, the Government has returned to using interest rates as its main means of controlling inflation.

It is against this broad macroeconomic background that the Conservatives have implemented the two other main strands of their strategy of laissez-fairism by degrees. The first strand has been a programme of legislation to curb the power of the trade unions and to introduce a more democratic and open structure into the way they conduct their affairs. This has been complemented by a complete rejection of the Macmillanist/corporatist idea that the state should formulate policy in partnership with the unions, which Mrs Thatcher in particular saw as 'the epitome of all that was bad about the hated post-war settlement' (Taylor, 1989, p. 23). She thought that by incorporating the unions into policy-making, the Conservative and Labour governments of the 1960s and 1970s had connived in rising inflation. It is argued that this part of the strategy **has** helped to create a more 'flexible' labour market and, thus, to improve the productivity and competitiveness of British industry. Some commentators have, however, pointed out that this 'productivity miracle' is an illusion and is simply the result of many fewer workers producing virtually the same amount of goods and services (Glyn, 1992, pp. 77–88).

In line with their step-by-step approach, the Conservatives began cautiously in their attempt to reform industrial relations, a caution which seems eminently sensible when one considers the impact of the 1971 Industrial Relations Act. Of course, it should be emphasised that the strength of union opposition to these reforms was seriously weakened by the fact that, in the main, they were enacted in a period of high and rising unemployment. The first major piece of legislation was the Employment Act of 1980 which placed restrictions on picketing, weakened the closed shop and curtailed union immunities in relation to secondary strike action. This was followed by the 1982 Employment Act, which further weakened the closed shop, enhanced the rights of individual union members, outlawed politically motivated strikes and exposed union funds to liability for unlawful industrial action. After Mrs Thatcher's second election victory in 1983, the pace of reform quickened with the landmark Trade Union Act of 1984. This required the unions to elect their executive committees by postal ballot every five years, made it mandatory to hold a ballot on the establishment of political funds and on decisions to take strike action, and made it possible for the courts to sequester the assets of a union which had acted unlawfully. That these three pieces of legislation had radically altered the balance of power between workers and employers was confirmed by the defeat of strike action by two of the traditionally most militant unions, the miners in 1984–85 and the print workers a year later. Following this high point of confrontation, the industrial relations reform programme entered a period of consolidation with Employment Acts in 1988 and 1990 building on previous legislation. The 1988 Act provided individual union members with a further set of rights, most significantly by limiting the power of unions to discipline members who refused to obey strike calls, while the 1990 Act extended the range of union responsibility for 'unofficial' strikes and increased employers' powers to dismiss strikers. Since 1990, John Major has demonstrated a firm commitment to the employment policies of his predecessor with proposals for legislation to give individuals greater freedom in choosing a union, to require that all pre-strike ballots are postal and subject to independent security, and to require that at least seven days notice is given before strike action is taken. In addition, he fought hard to win an opt-out from the Social Chapter of the Maastricht Treaty. If introduced, this would have swung the balance of power back towards the unions by requiring companies to establish regular and formalised processes of worker consultation (Deakin, 1992, pp. 173–91).

The third and final element of the Conservatives' strategy since 1979 has been in relation to the ownership and control of finance and industry. When she was first elected, Mrs Thatcher made it clear that she regarded the nationalised industries, particularly the utilities, as the worst expression of all that was wrong with British industry. She argued that they had become an inefficient and unproductive burden on the private sector, because they were being used by the state to pursue primarily socio-economic objectives such as the protection of jobs. It is important to stress, however, that the Conservatives were not elected with a commitment to deal with these weaknesses by transferring large sections of publicly-owned industry into the private sector. Instead, their manifesto mirrored that presented by Heath in 1970; they simply proposed to make the nationalised industries operate on the basis of more stringent commercial criteria (Gamble, 1988, p. 124). It soon became clear, however, that as long as the state retained ownership this task would be politically impossible to achieve. The most obvious impact of introducing market criteria into the operations of these industries would be huge job losses, for which the state, as owner, would be blamed. The electoral consequences of such a course of action did not bear contemplation. The Government, thus, began to consider the idea of privatisation. Yet again the progress of this part of the strategy has been gradual, with the success of one privatisation being used to promote the next.

The first major transfer of state assets to the private sector came in 1980–81, when a large part of the NEB's holdings were either sold off (ICL, Fairey and Ferranti) or liquidated (Alfred Herbert and British Tanners Products). This effectively signalled the end of the Board's useful existence, and it was later merged with the National Research and Development Corporation to become the British Technology Group. Next came the sale of the National Freight Corporation in 1982. However, the programme only really began to gain momentum after the successful sale of British Telecom in 1984. Focusing on the most significant privatizations, this was followed by British Aerospace and Britoil in 1985, British Gas in 1986, British Airways and British Petroleum in 1987, British Steel in 1988, the regional water authorities in 1989, the regional electricity boards and the Central Electricity Generating Board (CEGB) in 1991, and finally the remnants of the coal mining industry in 1994. By the end of the 1980s alone nearly 50 per cent of the concerns owned and run by the state in 1979 had been privatized, and about 800 000 jobs had been transferred from the public to the private sector (Fine and Poletti, 1992, p. 317). Most recently, British Rail was prepared for privatisation in 1996–97 by being decentralized to form Railtrack (the owner and operator of the rail infrastructure) and fifty independent service providers.

The key feature of many of these privatisations, most notably the utilities, is that while ownership has largely been transferred to the private sector, the state has been forced to retain a measure of control over the investment and pricing decisions of the newly created companies, because they enjoy a position of natural or de facto monopoly. Thus, while the Conservatives have been able to achieve a laissez-faire relationship between the state and the market at the level of ownership in the utilities sectors, political and economic realities have prevented them from fully relinquishing control (Fine and Poletti, 1992, pp. 317–19). Elsewhere in the economy, however, the Conservatives have succeeded in creating a much greater degree of market-based ownership *and* control. Key elements of this change included the sale of over one million council houses, the transfer of manpower training to the private sector in the form of the Training and Enterprise Councils (TECs), and the 'contracting-out' of services such as hospital cleaning and refuse collection. Perhaps the most obvious and important example, however, has been the liberalisation of the financial sector. Given the major contribution made by invisible earnings to Britain's balance of payments and the historic influence exerted by financial interests over economic policy-making, it should not be surprising that the extent to which the state has been rolled back here is greater than anywhere else.

Beginning with the abolition of all exchange controls in October 1979, only five months after they were elected, the Conservatives have relentlessly dismantled the framework of financial levers regarded as an essential part of economic management by every other government since the war. The knock-on effect of abolishing exchange controls was to render the controls on bank lending, known as the 'corset', completely ineffective, because banks could now bypass the corset restrictions by lending to their customers from overseas subsidiaries. This situation was formally recognised in June 1980 when the corset was abolished. About a year later, further steps were taken to reduce the level of direct state control over the banking system. Both the reserve asset ratio and the minimum lending rate were abolished. The former had required the banks to hold the equivalent of 12.5 per cent of their sterling liabilities in cash or in a form easily converted to cash, while the latter had been used by the Bank of England to maintain a tight rein on interest rates. The overall effect of these changes was to allow the banks to expand into new areas of business. A particular area of interest was the personal mortgage market, which had previously been the preserve of the building societies. The Government did nothing to discourage this interest, because, as part of its programme for reducing the size of the public sector and increasing home-ownership, local councils were being made to sell off their housing stock. This meant that, while the 'right to buy' legislation offered substantial discounts on market value for tenants, there would still be a significant increase in the demand for mortgage finance. At the same time as the banks entered the market for mortgage lending, changes in the tax system led to a massive increase in the supply of funds for mortgage lending by the building societies. The net effect was not only increased competition, and therefore lower interest rates, but also a massive increase in mortgage lending. For example, between 1980 and 1988 net mortgage lending rose from £7.3 billion to £35.5 billion. Given increased access to funds and in the face of competition from the banks in the mortgage market, the building societies were also keen to expand their lending activities into other areas. Yet again the Conservatives obliged in the form of the 1986 Building Societies Act, which allowed them to issue credit cards and to lend on an unsecured basis for the purchase of holidays, cars and other consumer durables. In other words, they were allowed to behave more like banks (Smith, 1993, pp. 21–35).

Another key part of the Government's programme to liberalise the financial sector came to fruition in the so-called 'Big Bang' of October 1986. This was the culmination of a process which had begun in July 1983, when Cecil Parkinson, the Secretary of State for Trade and Industry, had reached an agreement with the Chairman of the Stock Exchange. The agreement required the Exchange to voluntarily reform and restructure its methods for dealing in equities and bonds in order to introduce greater competition, and in return the Government guaranteed that it would drop the case it was pursuing against the Exchange in the Restrictive Practices Court. The Exchange kept to its part of the bargain and just over three years later, on 27 October 1986, the majority of the agreed changes were introduced. The centrepiece of the reforms was an electronic trading and information system. Traditional practices were abandoned overnight. A particularly important stimulus to competition was the replacement of an agreed framework of minimum commission levels by individually negotiated commissions. The term 'Big Bang' was coined to indicate that this change would occur immediately, rather than over a period of time (Smith, 1993, pp. 35–9).

The effects of this rapid liberalisation of the financial sector were spectacular. Between 1987 and 1990 house prices spiralled upwards in response to the massive increase in mortgage lending, and the economy as a whole experienced a boom as consumers took advantage of cheap and freely available credit and the Stock Exchange witnessed an unprecedented rise in trading activity. This was, of course, stimulated by the creation of many new share owners through the Government's privatisation programme. Unfortunately, the boom turned almost as quickly to bust, as the world economy went into a cyclical downturn and the Government bore down on inflation and supported the value of sterling by raising interest rates. House prices started to tumble and, at the time of writing, the market has yet to recover. This has left millions of people with 'negative equity'. Thus, while the Conservatives' efforts to move to a laissez-faire relationship between the state and the market have proved most successful in the financial sector, the result has been far from satisfactory.

To conclude this section it is important to note that, while the Conservatives have made significant progress towards laissez-fairism in the areas discussed above, the bulk of the state's responsibilities in health, education and the social services still remain. The basic problem for a radical government wanting to cut public expenditure and reduce the size of the state has been that these aspects of the postwar consensus remain extremely popular with the electorate, perhaps because they are generally perceived as a success story. Recognising this fact, the Conservatives have emphasised their commitment to maintain these services within the sphere of the state. At the same time, however, they have tried to ensure that the public money spent in these areas is used as efficiently as possible. Part of this effort has, ironically, involved an accretion of control to central government, as the Conservatives have introduced legislation to allow schools and hospitals to 'opt out' of local authority and regional health authority (RHA) control respectively. Those schools and hospitals which have chosen this course of action are now funded directly by the Exchequer, which means that central government has much more effective control over this element of public spending. However, the policy has only been a limited success, with a substantial number of schools in particular refusing to opt out. Another significant innovation has been the development of the 'internal market' in the NHS. This is an attempt to allocate health care resources more efficiently by allowing GPs to manage their own budgets and introducing an element of 'competition' over patients between RHAs. Nevertheless, education, health care and social services are still regarded as legitimate areas of state responsibility.

CONCLUSION

As this chapter has shown, Britain's politico-economic experience since 1939 has drawn on almost all of the ideal type relationships between the state and the market which are detailed in our continuum. That is not to say, however, that any government has been successful in achieving any of these relationships in its entirety. They may have tried hard, but ultimately politics is about balancing conflicting interests which make ideals impossible to achieve. Nowhere is this more clearly demonstrated than in the resilience of the welfare state, even after seventeen years of Conservative governments fiercely committed to laissez-fairism. While this makes an interesting story in itself, a more important question perhaps is what impact have each of these different approaches had on Britain's economic performance. After all, the one thing that has bound all of the governments since the war together has been a determination to produce high rates of growth and increased material well-being for the electorate. The next chapter tries to provide an answer to this question by examining a range of statistical indicators which give a reasonably objective picture of Britain's relative economic performance since the Second World War.

REFERENCES

Beer, S. (1969), *Modern British Politics* (London: Faber).

Berki, R.N. (1975), *Socialism* (London: J.M. Dent and Sons).

Blackburn, R. (1971), 'The Heath Government: a new course for British capitalism', *New Left Review*, 70, pp. 276–82.

Blank, S. (1973), *Industry and Government in Britain* (Farnborough: Saxon House).

Brittan, S. (1971), *Steering the Economy* (Harmondsworth: Penguin).

Coates, D. (1975), *The Labour Party and the Struggle for Socialism* (Cambridge: Cambridge University Press).

Coates, D. (1980), *Labour in Power?* (London: Longman).

Cox, A. (1981), 'Le mouvement syndical brittanique et la recession economique des annees 70', in Couffignal, G. (ed.), *Les Syndicats Europeens et la Crise* (Grenoble: Grenoble University Press).

Crewe, I. et al. (1977), 'Partisan dealignment in Britain, 1964–70', *British Journal of Political Science*, 7, pp. 120–90.

Crouch, C. (1979), *The Politics of Industrial Relations* (London: Fontana).

Deakin, S. (1992), 'Labour Law and Industrial Relations', in Michie, J. (ed.), *The Economic Legacy 1979–92* (London: Academic Press).

Dutton, D. (1991), *British Politics since 1945: The Rise and Fall of Consensus* (Oxford: Basil Blackwell).

Dyson, K. (1980), *The State Tradition in Western Europe* (London: Martin Robertson).

Fine, B. and C. Poletti (1992), 'Industrial Prospects in the Light of Privatisation', in Michie, J. (ed.), *The Economic Legacy 1979–92* (London: Academic Press).

Finer, S.E. (1975), *Adversary Politics and Electoral Reform* (London: Anthony Wigram).

Gamble, A. (1988), *The Free Economy and the Strong State: The Politics of Thatcherism* (Basingstoke: Macmillan).

Glyn, A. (1992), 'The "Productivity Miracle", Profits and Investment', in Michie, J. (ed.), *The Economic Legacy 1979–92* (London: Academic Press).

Grant, W. (1982), *The Political Economy of Industrial Policy* (London: Butterworths).

Grant, W. (1985), 'Introduction', in Grant, W. (ed.), *The Political Economy of Corporatism* (Basingstoke: Macmillan).

Guttmann, R. (1976), 'State intervention and the economic crisis: the Labour Government's economic policy', *Kapitaliste*, 4–5, pp. 225–70.

Harris, N. (1972), *Competition and the Corporate Society* (London: Methuen).

Hatfield, M. (1978), *The House the Left Built* (London: Gollancz).

Hayward, J.E.S. (1977), 'Institutional inertia and political impetus in France and Britain', *European Journal of Political Science*, 7, pp. 120–90.

Holmes, M. (1982), *Political Pressure and Economic Policy: British Government 1970–74* (London: Butterworths).

Howells, D. (1976), *British Social Democracy* (London: Croom Helm).

Macmillan, H. (1938), *The Middle Way: a Study of the Problem of Economic and Social Progress in a Free and Democratic Society* (London: Macmillan and Co.).

McRae, H. and F. Cairncross (1977), *Capital City* (London: Methuen).

Middlemas, K. (1980), *Politics in Industrial Society* (London: Deutsch).

Pahl, R.E. and J.T. Winkler (1974), 'The coming corporatism', *New Society*, 10 October, pp. 72–6.

Panitch, L. (1976), *Social Democracy and Industrial Militancy* (Cambridge: Cambridge University Press).

Rose, R. (1984), *Do Parties make a Difference?*, 2nd ed. (London: Macmillan).

Shanks, M. (1981), *Planning and Politics* (London: Allen and Unwin).

Smith, D. (1993), *From Boom to Bust: Trial and Error in British Economic Policy* (Harmondsworth: Penguin).

Stewart, M. (1986), *Keynes and After*, 3rd ed. (Harmondsworth: Penguin).

Taylor, R. (1989), 'Mrs Thatcher's impact on the TUC', *Contemporary Record*, 2, pp. 23–6.

Young, S. and A. Lowe (1974), *Intervention in the Mixed Economy* (London: Croom Helm).

2. Britain in Decline? A Statistical Survey of Britain's Relative Economic Performance since 1950

Joe Sanderson

INTRODUCTION

The previous chapter described the various state–market relationships created in Britain since 1939. The constant theme of these different approaches to economic management, particularly after the election of Harold Macmillan in 1959, has been the vexed question of how to halt and reverse Britain's decline. To the casual observer this might seem like a rather curious objective, because there is ample anecdotal evidence that the material well-being of the average Briton is many times greater in 1996 than it was at the beginning of the century, or even at the end of the Second World War. The majority of families have a car and a television set, and most take at least one overseas holiday a year. Nevertheless, there is an abundance of academic texts on the subject of Britain's decline (see, for example, Wiener, 1981; Pollard, 1982; Barnett, 1986; Gamble, 1994), and the subject is at the heart of party political debate on the state of the economy and on Britain's 'place in the world'. The question, therefore, arises: what is meant by the use of the word 'decline'?

As Gamble (1994, p. 14) makes clear, there are two distinct senses in which the word is applied to the British experience. First, 'decline' is often used in politico-military terms to refer to the loss of Britain's status as the leading world power with an empire covering a quarter of the globe. In this sense Britain's decline has been absolute, beginning after the First World War and accelerating since 1945, when the US assumed the mantle of political and military dominance by being the first nation to develop nuclear weapons. Over the next two decades Britain completed the process of dismantling the Empire, and by 1973 its status as a middle-sized regional power was confirmed by its application to join the EEC. Second, and more relevant for our purposes, 'decline' is used in an economic sense. The picture here, however, is much more complex, because in absolute terms the British economy has performed very successfully. There has been a steady improvement in terms of most indicators as the twentieth century has progressed. For example, the average annual growth rate of Gross Domestic Product (GDP) increased from 1.8 per cent between 1873 and 1913 to 2.2 per cent between 1924 and 1937 to 2.8 per cent between 1951 and 1973 (Matthews et al., 1982, p. 22). Britain's economic decline, therefore, only emerges when its performance is *compared* with that of its major industrial competitors. For our purposes, we take these to be the five largest OECD economies – the US, Japan, Germany, France and Italy. The paradox generated by such a comparison – an absolute rise in output combined with relative decline – has been made possible by the unprecedented growth of the international economy in the postwar period. In simple terms, Britain's economic performance has resulted in it winning a smaller slice of a much larger cake.

MEASURING BRITAIN'S RELATIVE ECONOMIC PERFORMANCE

The central aim of this chapter is to examine this relative decline by comparing Britain's economic performance since 1950 with that of the five largest OECD economies. In this context, economic performance is defined and measured with reference to five statistical indicators, all but one of which relate to the operation of the whole economy. The exception is a set of figures showing the percentage shares by value of the world market for manufactures enjoyed by each of the countries in the survey. A 'snap-shot' number is given for the beginning of each decade since 1950. This indicator forms a particularly significant part of the picture, because it was by being first to develop a manufacturing base that Britain came to dominate the world economy in the nineteenth century. It is, therefore, in a rapidly falling share of the world market for manufactures that Britain's relative decline finds its clearest expression.

The four macroeconomic indicators used are: growth of GDP (measured as output); growth of productivity (measured as output per man-hour); the rate of inflation; and the rate of unemployment. The figures for these indicators are presented as annual averages over three periods of time – 1950–73, 1973–79, and 1979–88 for GDP, productivity and inflation, and 1952–73, 1974–79, 1980–89 for unemployment. These time periods have been chosen, because, broadly speaking, they were characterised by a particular set of economic circumstances, both domestic and international. The 1950–73 period witnessed unprecedented growth combined with low inflation and low unemployment, and is generally referred to as the 'golden age'. The next two periods were both initially characterised by 'stagflation', a term which refers to slow growth combined with high inflation and high unemployment, followed by a return to historically respectable rates of growth combined with falling rates of inflation and unemployment. In each case, the stagflation was created, partly at least, by a rapid increase in the price of oil. The value of distinguishing these two very similar periods is that it helps us to see the impact of each of the oil crises in isolation, as well as the effectiveness with which each country responded to the shock. The important point is that the economic performance of any country cannot be properly understood in isolation from developments in the international economy. In other words, the fact that Britain prospered in the period 1950–73 is neither surprising nor particularly interesting, because the world as a whole was experiencing rapid economic growth. What is significant is that Britain did less well across the range of indicators than its main economic rivals.

Before we move on to consider each of the indicators in turn, it should be emphasised that this survey leaves out the five years after the war, because a comparison based on these years would be distorted by the experience of Japan and Germany, and to a lesser extent France and Italy. The problem is that these economies were left physically devastated by the war and, as a result, they grew very rapidly from a low base during these years as the process of reconstruction was carried out (Cairncross, 1990, p. 41).

Gross Domestic Product

Perhaps the most fundamental measure of an economy's success is the rate at which its Gross Domestic Product (GDP) increases. In simple terms, GDP refers to the totality of goods and services produced by the domestic economy, and so it is also known as 'output'. As Table 2.1 shows, Britain's performance as measured by this indicator has either lagged markedly behind that of the other leading OECD economies or, as in more recent years, has reached parity.

In the period 1950–73, all six countries experienced impressive rates of GDP growth as the world economy expanded rapidly. However, Britain's annual average of 3.0 per cent compared unfavourably with the rates achieved by its nearest European rivals, and fell along way below the annual average of 9.7 per cent experienced by the Japanese economy.

Table 2.1: Average annual percentage change in GDP (output) of six largest OECD economies, 1950–88

	1950–73	1973–79	1979–88
US	3.7	2.4	2.6
Japan	9.7	3.6	4.2
Germany	6.0	2.3	1.9
France	5.1	3.0	2.0
Italy	5.5	2.6	2.8
Britain	3.0	1.5	2.3

Sources:
Column 1, Crafts and Woodward (1991)
Column 2, Graham and Seldon (1990)
Column 3, OECD Economic Surveys (1990, 1991) and Johnson (1991).

While Japan's astronomical growth in this period can largely be ignored for the purposes of comparison, because it started from a much lower base level than any of its competitors, it seems clear that Britain was much less effective at taking advantage of favourable economic conditions than Germany, France, Italy and the US. The impact of this relatively slow growth on the prosperity of British citizens was reflected in the fact that between 1961 and 1976 Britain slipped from ninth to eighteenth in the international league of GDP per capita (McKie and Cook cited in Gamble, 1994, pp. 15–16). Between 1973 and 1985 the world economy experienced two prolonged periods of stagflation, which were intensified by the effects of rapid increases in the price of oil in 1974 and 1980. As Table 2.1 shows, the growth rate in all six countries was significantly reduced after 1973. The important point, however, is that Britain's average rate of GDP growth remained by far the lowest in this group of countries between 1973 and 1979. The implication of this is that the British economy recovered much more slowly from the impact of the first oil shock, which is particularly surprising in light of the fact that Britain had become a major producer of oil by the late 1970s. Such was Britain's relative weakness that between 1979 and 1981 the economy actually experienced negative growth and manufacturing output fell to the level of the mid-1960s (Gamble, 1994, p. 13). It was against this background that Mrs Thatcher came to power with a pledge to break the mould of postwar politics and to reverse Britain's relative decline. Although she initially failed to deliver on her promises, between 1983 and 1988 the economy achieved a much more respectable average growth rate of 3.7 per cent. This cannot, however, be taken as evidence that Britain's relative decline had been conclusively reversed, because the other five leading OECD economies were also experiencing average annual growth rates of between 3 and 4 per cent in this period (Johnson, 1991, pp. 11–14). The point is that in order to compensate for decades of relative decline, Britain would have had to grow at a significantly higher rate than its main competitors over a prolonged period of time.

Productivity

The next indicator, shown in Table 2.2, is the average annual growth in productivity. This is measured as output per man-hour. It can immediately be seen, therefore, that the rate of growth of productivity can either be raised by an increase in the output (or GDP) of the economy or by a decrease in the number of people in employment. In reality, an increase in the rate of productivity is likely to brought about by a combination of these two factors. Thus, the key to understanding productivity figures is to consider them in the context of GDP growth and the rate of unemployment, shown here in Tables 2.1 and 2.5.

Britain's productivity performance during the 1950–73 period presents the familiar scenario of an economy failing to take full advantage of favourable conditions. As already noted, Britain's GDP growth performance was relatively poor. When this fact is combined with a unemployment rate close to the average for the six largest OECD economies, it becomes clear that the British worker was simply less productive than his continental European or Japanese counterparts at a time when the international economy was expanding rapidly. This situation persisted throughout the 1973–79 period. Given that Britain's average annual rate of unemployment had risen to 4.2 per cent in the face of international stagflation, it is hardly surprising that the economy was only able to achieve an average GDP growth rate of 1.5 per cent. The significance of the productivity growth rate is emphasised if we consider the experience of Italy in the 1973–79 period. As Table 2.5 shows, Italy had an average annual rate of unemployment some 2.4 per cent higher than

Table 2.2: Average annual percentage change in productivity (output per man-hour) of six largest OECD economies, 1950–88

	1950–73	1973–79	1979–88
US	2.4	0.0	0.8
Japan	7.6	2.9	3.1
Germany	6.0	2.9	1.4
France	5.0	2.7	2.1
Italy	5.5	1.7	2.2
Britain	3.2	1.2	2.5[a]

Note: a. 1980–89

Sources:
Column 1, Crafts and Woodward (1991)
Column 2, Graham and Seldon (1990)
Column 3, OECD Economic Surveys (1990, 1991) and Johnson (1991)

Britain and yet it was able to achieve an average GDP growth rate of 2.6 per cent, almost double that of Britain. The simple answer to this conundrum can be found in Table 2.2; Italy's average productivity growth rate was 1.7 per cent, compared with only 1.2 per cent for Britain. One of the major claims of the Conservative Government elected in 1979 was that they had started to make real progress towards solving the problem of Britain's relatively slow productivity growth. It was argued that legislation to curb the power of trade unions combined with measures to deregulate the labour market had brought about a 'productivity miracle', particularly in manufacturing industry. Taken in isolation, the average productivity growth figures in the 1980–89 period would seem to bear this out. Britain achieved a very respectable 2.5 per cent, which was better than the record of all of its major industrial rivals apart from Japan. As mentioned above, however, productivity growth figures cannot be properly understood unless they are considered in the context of figures showing the average growth of GDP and the average rate of unemployment over a particular period. Looked at from this perspective, Britain's performance becomes slightly less miraculous. The average growth of GDP was only 2.3 per cent and the average rate of unemployment was above 9 per cent, one of the highest amongst the leading OECD nations. As a number of commentators have pointed out, therefore, Britain's 'productivity miracle' can perhaps best be understood in terms of many fewer workers producing only slightly more goods and services (Glyn, 1992, pp. 77–88).

Share of World Trade

Table 2.3: Percentage shares by value of the world market for manufactures, 1950–90

	1950	1960	1970	1980	1990
US	27.3	21.6	18.5	15.9	11.8
Japan	3.4	6.9	11.7	13.6	11.5
Germany	7.3	19.3	19.8	29.8	15.1
France	9.9	9.6	8.7	10.5	7.0
Britain	25.5	16.5	10.8	9.7	6.3

Sources:
Columns 1–4, Gamble (1994, p. 17)
Column 5, OECD Economic Surveys (1993)

One of the most obvious consequences of Britain's relatively slow productivity growth has been a loss of competitiveness and, therefore, a rapidly declining share of world trade. This decline has been particularly marked in Britain's share of the world market for manufactured goods. At the beginning of the twentieth century Britain was the unrivalled leader, commanding about a third of the market. As Table 2.3 shows, however, Britain's share declined precipitously from just above a quarter in 1950 to about 6 per cent in 1990.

This is startling in itself, but the more important point is that Japan and Germany were able to rapidly increase their share of the market up until 1980, while France was able to maintain its share at around 10 per cent. Although the US also experienced a relative decline in its market share, from 27.3 per cent in 1950 to 15.9 per cent in 1980, its position in 1990 showed that its products were still competing effectively with those from Japan and Germany. The fact that all the leading OECD economies had a significantly smaller market share in 1990 is probably best explained by the emergence of countries like South Korea and China as major exporters.

Inflation

Table 2.4: Average annual rate of inflation[a] of six largest OECD economies, 1950–88

	1950–73	1973–79	1979–88
US	2.7	8.0	5.4
Japan	5.2	8.1	1.8
Germany	2.7	4.8	3.1
France	5.0	10.6	7.9
Italy	3.9	17.1	12.5
Britain	4.6	16.0	8.0

Note: a. The GDP Deflator
Sources:
Column 1, Glyn et al. (1991)
Column 2, Graham and Seldon (1990)
Column 3, OECD Economic Surveys (1990, 1991) and Johnson (1991)

In terms of inflation, Britain's record in the 'golden age' was unremarkable. The average annual rate of 4.6 per cent was close to the norm for this group of economies. In the 1973–79 period, however, the fundamental structural weaknesses of the British economy were revealed. That the rate increased markedly is unsurprising given the rampant inflationary pressures operating in the international system. The key point is that, apart from Italy, Britain's rate increased much more than those of its nearest industrial competitors. This had an inevitable impact on the competitiveness of British products and led to a further decline in Britain's share of world trade. Although the early 1980s was the highpoint of Mrs Thatcher's monetarist battle against inflation, Table 2.4 shows that these policies had a relatively limited effect. Britain's inflation performance in the 1979–88 period was still significantly poorer than those of the most successful industrial economies, Germany, Japan and the US. Only Italy, an historically high inflation economy, did worse.

Unemployment

Table 2.5: Average annual rate of unemployment (percentage of total labour force) in six largest OECD economies, 1952–89

	1952–73	1974–79	1980–89
US	4.8	6.7	7.3
Japan	1.6	1.9	2.5
Germany	1.8	3.5	5.6
France	2.1	4.5	9.1
Italy	4.7	6.6	10.3
Britain	2.9	4.2	9.1

Sources:
Column 1, Glyn et al. (1991)
Column 2, Graham and Seldon (1990)
Column 3, OECD Economic Survey (1991) and Johnson (1991)

In terms of unemployment, Britain's record until 1980 was no worse than those of its major competitors. According to Matthews (1968, pp. 556–7), this may have had something to do with the cross-party consensus on the need to maintain a 'high and stable level of employment', but we should not be too hasty to attribute this success solely to the policies of post-war governments. A much more plausible explanation for full employment, he argues, was the high and sustained level of investment by the private sector in the two decades following the Second World War, which had the effect of increasing the supply of capital relative to labour. This led to a situation in which labour became scarce relative to capital. The main implication of this scarcity was that it increased the costs of casual hiring and gave employers an incentive to keep people in work even during cyclical downturns. Full employment was, thus, more or less guaranteed in both good times and bad. Matthews' principal explanation for this private sector investment boom is that the demand for investment was exceptionally high, because the capital stock was at an historically low level following a lack of spending before and during the war. Following an initial wave of investment, the demand was sustained by an expansion and liberalisation of world trade. He does concede that the state played a part in initiating the boom by bringing about a massive increase in the level of economic activity during the war, and in sustaining it by providing tax incentives and grants to industry, but he concludes that full employment was fundamentally a result of private sector investment (Matthews, 1968, pp. 560–8).

The logic of the Matthews' thesis can also be applied to the rapid rise in unemployment in the early 1980s. Government policy, in the shape of Mrs Thatcher's strident renunciation of Keynesian demand management after 1979, may again have had something to do with this increase, but a more convincing explanation is that a combination of recession and rapid inflation in the international economy significantly reduced both the demand for and the supply of private sector investment. Furthermore, industries which had experienced sustained capital investment since the late 1940s suddenly found themselves with surplus capacity, because they were now faced with new sources of competition from Japan and the Newly Industrialized Countries (NICs). The relative scarcity of labour which had supported full employment since the war therefore began to be eroded, and a rise in unemployment to consistently higher levels was the result. As Table 2.5 shows, all of the leading OECD economies experienced a increased rate of unemployment in the 1980–89 period. The significant point, however, is that Britain's performance was once again relatively poor, with only Italy doing worse.

INTERPRETING BRITAIN'S RELATIVE ECONOMIC PERFORMANCE

On the basis of the statistical evidence presented in the previous section there would seem to be no doubt that Britain's postwar economic performance relative to that of its major industrial competitors has been poor, and that we can legitimately talk in terms of a 'decline'. Unfortunately, the notion of decline is not value neutral, but instead forces us to think in terms of the 'success' or 'failure' of an economy. Clearly, the most popular interpretation of decline is that it represents a failure, whether a fall from past glories or a failure to keep pace with the achievements of contemporaries. A problem arises, however, because this interpretation is based on a prior assumption which can, and should, be challenged. The assumption is that a particular country is not realising what is imagined to be its full economic potential, because it has a variety of political, economic, cultural or institutional weaknesses. It is further assumed that by identifying and eliminating these weaknesses, the country can reverse its decline and achieve past levels of performance or overtake its rivals. Decline is, thus, interpreted as a failure, because there is seen to be no *necessary* reason why it should be taking place. This line of reasoning is common to all of the many explanations for Britain's 'failure' to keep pace with its major industrial competitors, whether it be a divisive class system, an anti-industrial culture, the domination of government and industry by the financial interests of the City of London, restrictive labour practices, or an adversarial two-party electoral system. The assumption that relative economic decline is synonymous with failure can be challenged in two main ways. First, there are the insights of the catch-up and convergence hypothesis discussed below, and second, there is the fact that the interpretation of relative economic performance is often politically motivated and, therefore, highly suspect.

The Catch-up and Convergence Hypothesis

A country may be experiencing a relatively poor economic performance not because it has political, economic, cultural or institutional weaknesses, but rather because the countries which are performing more successfully are closing a technological gap, are recovering from an abnormal external shock such as a war, or have transferred a previously idle or low-productivity factor of production into a sector of the economy with higher productivity. For example, the impressive productivity growth achieved by France and Germany in the 'golden age' can largely be explained by the transfer of a pool of underemployed agricultural labour to the manufacturing sector. The British economy, on the other hand, was already substantially dominated by manufacturing industry when the Second World War broke out. It could not hope, therefore, to achieve a productivity growth rate comparable with those prevailing in France and Germany. The important point is that relative economic decline cannot properly be interpreted unless it is placed in the context of the performance which an economy 'should' be capable of achieving (Supple, 1994, p. 319). These insights form the basis of what is commonly called the 'catch-up and convergence' hypothesis, which links initial levels and subsequent rates of growth. This is based on a number of historical studies of the process of development (see, for example, Gerschenkron, 1962; Abramovitz, 1986; Maddison, 1991).

In essence, the catch-up and convergence hypothesis states that a very large part of Britain's relatively poor economic performance in the post-war period can be explained by the lower level of development from which war-devastated countries like France, Germany, Italy and Japan started their advance. The lower level of development or 'backwardness' of these latter countries gave them certain advantages not available to the more highly developed British economy, which they were able to translate into much more impressive economic performances. It was unrealistic, therefore, to expect Britain to match their GDP and productivity growth rates, even in the benign economic circumstances of the 'golden age'. The same reasoning can be used to explain the relatively slow growth of the US economy during the 1950–73 period. That the US did slightly better than Britain was more a function of its large internal market, and hence its smaller dependence on exports, and of its political and military dominance than of any inherent superiority in its institutions, techniques and attitudes.

According to the catch-up and convergence hypothesis, the advantages of relative backwardness fall into three main categories. First, there is the effect which it has on attitudes and institutions. In terms of attitudes, the people of a backward or war-devastated country start on the road to modern economic growth with a powerful desire to work long hours and to forgo present consumption in order to fund the investment necessary to modernise and replace the capital stock. They also demonstrate a willingness to embrace new ideas, technologies and working practices which will facilitate a rapid growth in productivity. All of these attitudes were much in evidence after the war in France, Germany, Italy and Japan, while the people of the victorious countries, particularly Britain, sought an immediate reward for their privations in the form of shorter working hours and comprehensive welfare benefits. As far as institutions were concerned, those in the defeated and occupied countries had either been discredited or destroyed, and there was a concerted effort, supported by Britain and the US, to redesign government agencies, employers' associations, and trade unions. This institutional remodelling also presented an opportunity for new ideas and practices to be introduced. Conversely, Britain and the US were neither occupied nor defeated, and this allowed the old institutional settlement to survive largely unchanged (Feinstein, 1994, p. 119).

The second, and perhaps most important, advantage of backwardness is the chance to 'borrow' from more advanced countries. Relatively backward nations are able to borrow not only the technological know-how and capital equipment developed by those countries operating at the leading edge, but also the economic and social institutions and practices which underpin them. These include property rights and other legal practices, corporate structures and management techniques, financial systems and sources of venture capital, and industrial relations practices. A certain amount of adaptation is inevitably needed to fit these borrowed practices and institutions into the particular socio-economic circumstances of the borrowing country, and the relative success with which this achieved may help to explain the variable rates at which backward countries converge with the leaders. The Japanese, who are renowned for their ability to borrow, adapt and improve upon technology from the West, are a particularly good example of this effect. The key to this advantage is that the high costs and risks of developing state-of-the-art technology fall disproportionately on the leading countries, while the technology borrowed by the followers is largely proven and, therefore, presents much lower costs and risks (Feinstein, 1994, p. 120).

The third and final advantage available to relatively backward countries is that, unlike more highly developed industrial economies, they tend to have a large section of their labour force still employed in the agricultural sector. The implication of this is that agriculture is labour intensive in these countries and, therefore, exhibits relatively low productivity. Thus, the average level of productivity in these economies can be raised rapidly simply by transferring labour from agriculture into more capital-intensive sectors such as manufacturing. Furthermore, as the level of capital investment is raised in the agricultural sector, a labour surplus results. This means that it is possible for relatively backward economies to rapidly increase labour inputs in the manufacturing sector without creating inflationary pressure in the form of higher wage demands (Feinstein, 1994, p. 120).

A key implication of the catch-up and convergence hypothesis is that the leading countries and the relatively backward countries will eventually swap places. This happens because the rapid growth of the followers develops its own momentum, which will carry them beyond the point of catch-up, while the leaders will find it extremely difficult to break out of the vicious cycle of slow growth. When this changeover takes place, the hypothesis proposes that the one-time leaders will begin to recognise that their existing attitudes and institutional arrangements are part of the reason for their relative decline. This recognition implies an acceptance of their relative backwardness and opens the way for new attitudes and institutions to be introduced. Conversely, the newly established leaders will lose the attitudinal and institutional flexibility and the commitment to hard work which characterised their relatively backward phase. In addition, the opportunity to achieve rapid productivity growth by transferring labour from agriculture into manufacturing will have been dissipated. Thus a new, slightly modified, cycle of catch-up and convergence will begin, as many of the advantages of relative backwardness pass from one group of countries to another.

The logic of the catch-up and convergence hypothesis can, thus, go some way towards explaining developments after 1973 in the six countries surveyed here. Firstly, the slowdown in growth which occurred in all of these countries in the period 1973–79 was the inevitable outcome of the convergence towards the broadly similar level of productivity predicted by the hypothesis. This convergence came about as the three major advantages of the relatively backward countries were progressively dissipated. The widespread commitment to hard work, long hours and low levels of consumption could not be sustained as the fruits of growth were translated into higher incomes; there were fewer opportunities to borrow from abroad, because countries like Japan and Germany were now operating on or very close to the technological frontier; and, finally, the process of transferring labour from agriculture into manufacturing had now largely been completed. Secondly, the improvement of Britain's relative economic performance in the 1979–88 period, particularly in terms of its productivity growth, can be partly explained as a function of its acceptance that it had become a relatively backward country. This acceptance provided fertile ground for the radical overhaul of institutions and ideas represented by Thatcherism. Conversely, countries like France, Germany and Italy were suffering from the relatively slow growth in productivity which their new leadership position had made inevitable (Feinstein, 1994, pp. 121–2).

The Politics of Relative Economic Performance

The second important point to bear in mind when interpreting relative economic performance is that it is a highly political issue. On one hand, it may be of significant electoral advantage to an opposition political party to suggest that statistical evidence of relative decline is a sign that the current and previous governments have 'failed' the country. This advantage will be further amplified if the opposition party in question is trying to get elected on the basis of a programme of radical, ideological reforms, which seek to question and replace the fundamental attitudes and institutions supported by those other governments. The key insight here is that the interpretation of relative economic performance as a 'failure' is politically rather than economically motivated. It may allow a party to be elected on the basis of a policy platform which would, if advocated without such a justification, face significant opposition. The election of Margaret Thatcher in 1979 provides perhaps the clearest example of an ideological project gaining political acceptance through the definition of Britain's relative economic performance as a 'failure' and the suggestion that there was no other answer to the 'problem' of decline (Budge, 1993, pp. 17–18).

On the other hand, the party in government may very often use statistical measurements of relative economic performance, particularly the GDP growth rate, to show that its policies are a success. While this may superficially appear to be a quite valid use of statistics, the catch-up and convergence hypothesis discussed in the previous section should alert us to the need to interpret the growth rate of a particular economy very carefully. The key insight here is the need to set growth statistics in the context of what this economy 'should' be capable of achieving given its degree of relative backwardness. If an economy qualifies as relatively backward, the hypothesis would lead us to expect that its growth rate will be impressive irrespective of the policies being pursued by the government of the day. Thus, if we set the Thatcher government's so-called 'growth miracle' of the 1980s in the context of Britain's status as a relatively backward economy, it begins to look slightly less miraculous. Indeed, the British growth rate in the 1980s was the same as the EC average, only 0.2 per cent above Germany's, 0.1 per cent above France's, and some 0.3 per cent lower than Italy's (Johnson, 1991, pp. 13–14).

Further problems inherent in economic data stem from the use of annual growth rates rather than the average growth rate between cyclical peaks. One problem is that a high annual rate of growth can give a distorted picture of an economy's progress if it follows on from a year of low, or even negative, growth. Thus, the fact that the British economy grew by a respectable 1.7 per cent in 1982 disguises the absolute decline in GDP in both 1980 and 1981. Even after the impressive growth rate of 3.8 per cent achieved in 1983, GDP was still only back to its 1979 level (Keegan, 1989, p. 182). Perhaps more significant though is the way in which the annual rate of growth can be boosted by government policy (that is, tax cuts, public spending increases, interest rate cuts) in order to create a favourable impression in the run-up to a general election. It is vital, therefore, to see the use of annual growth statistics by government in the context of the electoral cycle. Thus, although Nigel Lawson's claim in early 1987 that Britain was the fastest growing European economy was supported by figures showing a growth rate of 3.6 per cent for 1986, it should have been taken with a large pinch of salt given that an election was due to be held in June of 1987. As Johnson comments, the Thatcher government's vehement rejection of Keynesian demand management was cast aside in both 1982 and 1986 in order to achieve a growth peak sufficient to ensure its re-election in 1983 and 1987 (Johnson, 1991, p. 13). In light of these problems, a much more realistic impression of Britain's relative growth performance in the 1979–88 period can be gained by looking at the average rate for these years. As the above reference to the EC average demonstrates, this method of measurement puts Britain firmly amongst the crowd and undermines Conservative claims of a 'growth miracle'.

CONCLUSION

As the survey of key statistical indicators in this chapter has shown, Britain's economic performance for most of the postwar period has been characterised by relative decline. Every government elected since 1959 has been committed to reversing this decline and, as the previous chapter revealed, this commitment has been translated into a wide range of differing policy approaches. The evidence presented in this chapter would seem, however, to indicate that none of these different approaches has been particularly effective. While it could be argued that the Conservatives were successful in halting Britain's relative decline in the 1983–88 period, developments since then have demonstrated that many of the underlying weaknesses of the British economy still remain. The increased growth rate of the late 1980s was generated largely by the financial and property sectors of the economy, while the contribution of manufacturing industry to GDP continued to decline. The problem with this improved growth performance was that it was accompanied by a rapidly rising rate of inflation and, as a result, it could not be sustained. The recession which followed could, to some extent, be attributed to a cyclical downturn in the international economy, but as usual Britain's economic downturn was more severe than those of its major industrial rivals.

The key question raised by this survey, therefore, is why has the British state been consistently unable to reverse this long-term relative economic decline? This question has stimulated an intense academic debate which, in turn, has generated a range of contending explanations of British decline. We have already considered one such explanation in our discussion of the catch-up and convergence hypothesis. However, the focus of this hypothesis was not 'why did Britain do so badly?', but rather 'why did Britain's major industrial competitors do so well?'. In the next section, we turn instead to those explanations which try to link the peculiarities of Britain's culture, polity and economy to the question of relative economic decline.

REFERENCES

Abramovitz, M. (1986), 'Catching up, forging ahead, and falling behind', *Journal of Economic History*, 46, 2, pp. 385–406.

Barnett, C. (1986), *The Audit of War* (London: Macmillan).

Budge, I. (1993), 'Relative decline as a political issue: ideological motivations of the politico-economic debate in post-war Britain', *Contemporary Record*, 7, 1, pp. 1–23.

Cairncross, A. (1990), 'The United Kingdom', in Graham, A. and A. Seldon (eds.), *Government and Economies in the Postwar World* (London: Routledge).

Crafts, N.F.R. and N.W.C. Woodward (1991), 'The British Economy since 1945: Introduction and Overview', in Crafts and Woodward (eds.), *The British Economy since 1945* (Oxford: Clarendon Press).

Feinstein, C (1994), 'Success and failure: British economic growth since 1948', in Floud, R. and D. McCloskey (eds.), *The Economic History of Britain since 1700, Vol. 3: 1939–92* (Cambridge: CUP).

Gamble, A. (1994), *Britain in Decline: Economic Policy, Political Strategy and the British State*, 4th ed. (Basingstoke: Macmillan).

Gerschenkron, A. (1962), *Economic Backwardness in Historical Perspective* (Cambridge, MA: MIT Press).

Glyn, A. et al. (1991), 'The Rise and Fall of the Golden Age', in Marglin, S. and J. Schor (eds.), *The Golden Age of Capitalism: Reinterpreting the Postwar Experience* (Oxford: Clarendon Press).

Glyn, A. (1992), 'The "Productivity Miracle", Profits and Investment', in Michie, J. (ed.), *The Economic Legacy 1979–92* (London: Academic Press).

Graham, A. and A. Seldon (eds.) (1990), *Government and Economies in the Postwar World* (London: Routledge).

Johnson, C. (1991), *The Economy Under Mrs Thatcher, 1979–90* (Harmondsworth: Penguin).

Keegan, W. (1989), *Mr Lawson's Gamble* (London: Hodder and Stoughton).

Maddison, A. (1991), *Dynamic Forces in Capitalist Development: A Long-Run Comparative View* (Oxford: OUP).

Matthews, R.C.O. (1968), 'Why has Britain had full employment since the war?', *The Economic Journal*, 78, 3, pp. 555–69.

Matthews, R.C.O., C.H. Feinstein and J.C. Odling-Smee (1982), *British Economic Growth 1856–1973* (Oxford: Clarendon Press)

OECD (1990, 1991 and 1993), *Economic Surveys* (Paris: OECD).

Pollard, S. (1982), *The Wasting of the British Economy* (London: Croom Helm).

Supple, B. (1994), 'British economic decline since 1945', in Floud, R. and D. McCloskey (eds.), *The Economic History of Britain since 1700, Vol. 3: 1939–92* (Cambridge: CUP).

Wiener, M. (1981), *English Culture and the Decline of the Industrial Spirit, 1850–1980* (Cambridge: CUP).

PART B:

Explaining Britain's Relative Economic Performance

3. British Culture and Economic Decline

Simon Lee

INTRODUCTION

Of all the factors that might account for national economic performance, culture remains the most nebulous. Culture has been defined as a 'particular form or type of intellectual development', and the form that the civilization and artistic achievement of a people takes at a certain stage of its historical development (Simpson and Wiener, 1989). In politics, as Kavanagh has suggested, the idea that a culture, spirit, or set of values shapes the conduct of politics in a nation is as old as politics itself (Kavanagh, 1987, p. 446). However, despite the longevity of culture as a political phenomenon, the problem of identifying the relationship between culture and economic performance has remained virtually intractable. Indeed, as Robbins has noted, whilst many commentators would accept that there is some sort of relationship between culture and economic performance, the problem has lain in quantifying and accounting for that relationship (Robbins, 1990, p. 1). Because information about economic performance is frequently gathered at the micro-level of the individual, but culture tends to concern behaviour and attitudes at the collective or macro-level, social scientists have been unable to develop a methodology which would enable the global characteristics of a national culture to be derived from the behaviour and attitudes of individuals without falling foul of what Kavanagh has referred to as 'the "individualistic" fallacy', that is, the tendency to ascribe to the wider community the characteristics of certain individuals (Kavanagh, 1987, p.447).

Irrespective of these conceptual and methodological problems, the damaging effect of British culture upon national economic performance has been one of the most widely posited explanations of British decline. Defying the customary Left–Right ideological divisions, it has been put forward by representatives of the Government (for example, Lilley, 1991; HMSO, 1993), the Opposition (for example, the Labour Party, 1993), parliamentary select committees (for example, House of Lords, 1985,

1991), business leaders (for example, ABCC, 1992; EEF, 1992), and trades unions (for example, MSF, 1992). The universal theme of these particular contributions to the debate about Britain's economic performance has been their assertion that there is something peculiar or exceptional about British culture which has made it hostile to industrial development. This chapter will illustrate how the influence of cultural explanations of Britain's relative economic decline has extended beyond the realm of party politics and industry and commerce to economic historians and political scientists. It will also demonstrate how cultural explanations have been used as political weapons by scientists and engineers when they have sought to justify an elevation in their status in society and a greater share of national resources, especially state resources, to further the interests of their particular industry or profession.

Despite their widespread and enduring popularity, it will be argued that cultural explanations are essentially flawed, not least because they have failed to demonstrate how British culture has been able to continue to transmit values and attitudes which are antagonistic towards science, technology and engineering in the face of sustained relative economic decline and attempts by successive governments to remedy it. The chapter also examines the Thatcherite thesis of the enterprise culture which has been advanced as a reaction to and a critique of earlier explanations of British decline and their policy prescriptions. However, it is suggested that this too is an inherently flawed explanation of British decline as has been evinced by the failure of its policy prescriptions to remedy the poor performance of the national economy during the 1980s and early 1990s. The conclusion drawn is that Britain's relative economic decline should not be attributed to cultural weakness but rather to the outdated institutions of the British state which as Barnett (1994) has suggested are themselves the product of the now defunct British Empire and no longer appropriate for the challenges confronting the British polity and economy in the 1990s.

THE DECLINE OF BRITAIN'S INDUSTRIAL SPIRIT?

Probably the most frequently cited and influential cultural explanation of British decline has been that advanced by the American sociologist, Martin Wiener, in *English Culture and the Decline of the Industrial Spirit 1850– 1980*. Wiener's contention is that Britain's transition to modernity was 'relatively smooth and involved no political upheaval' which meant that the modernization inspired by industrialization was incomplete (Wiener, 1981, p. 7). Existing and antiquated social structures were neither challenged nor replaced by industrialization but were instead able to accommodate modernization without the need for radical change. In mid- and late Victorian England, a conservative revolution took place during which the old, entrenched landed aristocracy contained, accommodated and absorbed the nascent industrial middle classes, thereby creating a new dominant bourgeois culture which bore the imprint of the old aristocracy. The industrialist was in this way gentrified, the prevailing culture became anti-industrial, and modernization was frustrated.

The old industries of the first Industrial Revolution gradually declined but the industries of the second were never properly developed. Industry became conservative, defensive, slow to innovate, and the province of restrictive practices. The entrepreneurial innovation and dynamism of the early Industrial Revolution had been dissipated by what Wiener terms 'a counterrevolution of values' (Wiener, 1981, p. 40). This counterrevolution was led and propagated by the elite education institutions, that is, the public schools and the universities, whose values and practices reflected and propagated 'an anti-industrial bias' (Wiener, 1981, p. 132). The children of entrepreneurs and industrialists were inculcated with the aristocratic ideals of honour and public leadership, in the process discarding the industrial spirit of their parents. 'Englishness' was increasingly defined in terms of the antiquated and romantic image of an essentially rural and traditional England in which modern industrial England was portrayed as a society of 'dark satanic mills' and an illegitimate expression of the English way of life. The English countryside became a weapon to be used as a cultural and social force against industrialism. Thus, after the 'high noon of British technological leadership' at the Great Exhibition of 1851, Britain 'was subjected to 'a century of psychological and intellectual de-industrialization' (Wiener, 1981, pp. 29–30, 157).

Since its publication, Wiener's work has received an almost universally favourable reception. It received early endorsement from another influential foreign commentator on British decline, when the German academic and then Director of the London School of Economics, Ralf Dahrendorf, spoke in his 1982 BBC television series 'On Britain' of the 'vanishing of the industrial spirit'. He also identified a 'missing industrial centre', that is, an absence of a social centre, a core of industrial values radiating throughout British society (Dahrendorf, 1982, p. 47). The thesis of an anti–industrial culture has also been developed in successive parliamentary select committee reports, not least that in the 1985 report, *Overseas Trade* from a specially appointed House of Lords' Select Committee. Its principal theme and recommendation was the need to change national attitudes towards trade and manufacturing in Britain in order to avoid 'a major social and economic crisis in our nation's affairs in the foreseeable future' (House of Lords', 1985, p. 6). This recommendation was subsequently endorsed in 1991 by the report, *Innovation in Manufacturing Industry*, from the House of Lords' Select Committee on Science and Technology, which cited Wiener's work and argued that the most urgent need was for a change in Britain's anti-industrial and anti-manufacturing culture (House of Lords', 1991, pp. 7, 30). More recently, the Engineering Employers' Federation has claimed that 'The UK is an industrial nation with an anti-industrial culture' (EEF, 1992, p. 3), the Association of British Chambers of Commerce has written of 'an attitude of decline' reflective of 'the prevailing attitude towards industry in general' (ABCC, 1992, p. 1), and the Manufacturing, Science and Finance union of the need to construct 'a new industrial culture' in Britain (MSF, 1992, p. 7).

If the initial reception for Wiener's work was favourable, more recent analysis of his thesis by historians has produced a much more critical reaction. Robbins, for example, has pointed to Wiener's failure to explain how Britain was able to become a pioneer of industrial modernization in the face of its supposedly anti-industrial culture (Robbins, 1990, p. 5). Great emphasis is placed by Wiener upon the importance of the decline of 'the industrial spirit' after 1850, and yet not once does Wiener provide his readers with a definition of that spirit or how it might be acquired. In a similar vein, Baxendale's critique of Wiener has focused upon the inadequacies of Wiener's conception of culture, and the flaws in his analysis of the relationship between culture and economic performance. Even if Wiener's depiction of English culture is accepted as an accurate account, Baxendale argues that it would not be satisfactory as an explanation of economic decline because it provides neither a theoretical nor an empirical account of how cultural values are translated into poor economic performance. Indeed, Wiener never clarifies 'whether culture was the cause or the effect of economic decline' (Baxendale, 1986, pp. 171–2).

Baxendale suggests that the problem with all cultural explanations of British decline is how to show that they transmit certain values and attitudes, in this instance values that are hostile to industry, modernity, science, technology, and economic growth, and not others. As an alternative to such a demonstration, Wiener's technique is merely to pile up quote after quote of anti-industrial sentiment without addressing the context in which people gave meaning to those quotes. That context, unfortunately for Wiener, is British culture itself, an analysis of which is conspicuous by its absence from Wiener's work along with a clear definition of what culture is, the forces that shape it, and how it all works

(Baxendale, 1986, p. 173). Baxendale also criticizes Wiener for failing to demonstrate that Britain's culture was in some sense exceptional or unusual, and therefore a departure from the norm of attitudes and values in an industrializing society. Nineteenth century Germany, for example, was also characterized by an industrial bourgeoisie which came under the influence of the pre-industrial values of a landed aristocracy. Even in the United States, where there was no pre-industrial landed aristocracy to undermine the industrial spirit, Baxendale is able to point to the importance in American mythology of the Western which 'celebrates neither industry nor urbanism, but sees the untamed frontier as the most appropriate setting for the American virtues' (Baxendale, 1986, p. 172). Therefore, far from being exceptional in its national culture, Britain may indeed have been conforming to part of a broader pattern of historical development, and it is this broader pattern that requires explanation rather than the supposed uniqueness of British culture.

For Raven, cultural factors have been 'willfully overplayed as explanations for Britain's industrial difficulties' (Raven, 1989, p. 183). Raven's belief is that British decline is 'fundamentally structural in origin' and that therefore our attention would be better focused on the consequences of long term international economic relationships, for example, the constraints imposed by Britain's 'early start' as the first industrial nation, the shortcomings of investment and entrepreneurship in late Victorian manufacturing, and, more recently, unsustainable postwar domestic expansion aggravated by 'the over-extension of Britain's international roles and the repeated failure of political initiatives and economic planning' (Raven, 1989, p. 182). Raven also suggests that, quite apart from failing to explain the relationship between attitudinal change and economic effect, the interpretation of cultural evidence has also been highly unsatisfactory. Advocates of cultural explanations, not least Wiener, have been nothing short of cavalier in their use of literary texts to demonstrate a decline in the industrial spirit when was required was a more careful 'interpretation of their contemporary appeal, reception and popularity, and also of how the means by which they were produced affected the message they carried' (Raven, 1989, pp. 183-4). At the same time, cultural explanations have recklessly overstated the influence of anti-technological and anti-urban imagery in the nineteenth century, and ignored the extent of the positive artistic response to industrial development.

Raven is critical too of the manner in which the vital question of management education and training has been dealt with by cultural explanations of British decline. In particular, he objects to the way in which too many analyses have 'rested content with bland assertions of an aristocratic culture, without enquiring closely into the relationship between education and business management' (Raven, 1989, p. 188). Although dubious about the wisdom of generalizing about national trends from an analysis of a few educational institutions, Raven asserts that most historians have concluded that an interest in industry was not encouraged in public schools and the universities in the late nineteenth century. However, he also suggests that, given the expansion of trade within the British Empire and the emergence during this period of finance capital founded commercial expansion and overseas investment, the elite produced by the public schools may have been precisely what was required to promote the commercial interests of the Empire (Raven, 1989, p. 188). This point has also been developed by Robbins who has emphasized the ease, but also the futility, of looking back on Victorian Britain from a post-imperial era and of criticizing both politicians and educators for ensuring that they produced the elite required to run the Empire (Robbins, 1990, p. 10). In any case, where research has focused more closely on the relationship between attitudes and economic growth, it has found that too great an emphasis has been placed on 'the alleged anti-business influence of British universities' (Raven, 1989, p.188). Not only does Wiener's analysis ignore the important contribution made by Scottish universities to the Industrial Revolution, which is the consequence of his having conflated Scottish, Welsh and Northern Irish cultures with 'English' culture, leaving aside the subtleties of regional cultures within each of these countries. It also contradicts the research of Sanderson who has established that the technology departments of English civic universities enjoyed a 'symbiotic relationship' with industrial firms in the period 1870–1914 (Sanderson, 1972). If there was a problem of insufficient innovation in British industry, it was because of a reluctance on the part of industry to apply the universities' discoveries rather than because of an all pervasive anti-industrial culture in a detached world of academic ivory towers.

Given the force of the critique of his work provided by contemporary historians, it might appear surprising that Wiener's explanation of British decline has remained so influential and widely cited. Harvie has attributed the popularity of Wiener's work amongst the elite in British society to the fact that Wiener addresses it 'in the allusive literary discourse to which it is accustomed and provides it with an analysis which accords with its own interests in a period of worrying political transition' (Harvie, 1985, p. 17). Harvie, however, has joined the ranks of Wiener's critics by raising the question of the meaningfulness of Wiener's focus on the period 1850–1980, and whether it is indeed possible to define how a 'normal' industrial society would have behaved in this period compared with the supposedly 'exceptional' Britain (Harvie, 1985, p. 18). If the benchmark for measuring national performance is that of a society in which a balance has been struck between industrial development, political liberty and a diffused enjoyment of their benefits, then Harvie suggests that Britain compares favorably with its industrial competitors, not least France, Germany and Japan, against whose performance, however measured, Britain is normally portrayed as trailing miserably. After all, who would have swapped the superior economic development of these rival nations for Britain's blend of industrial growth, social stability and increasing affluence (Harvie, 1985, p. 18).

The debate amongst historians about the validity of cultural explanations of Britain's relative economic decline has been given renewed vigor by the publication of W.D.Rubinstein's *Capitalism, Culture and Decline in Britain* in which the author claims to furnish a dissection of what he terms the 'cultural critique' of Britain's performance by laying out 'a detailed and clear-headed analysis of Britain's culture, elite educational system, and fundamental analysis of values' (Rubinstein, 1993, p. 24). Indeed, Rubinstein seeks to show that the 'cultural critique' is not only misconceived but actually a non sequitur which offers an explanation for something that did not actually occur. He begins by attacking the central assumption made by proponents of the 'cultural critique' and many other explanations of British decline, that Britain was an industrial economy whose economic dominance disappeared through decline after 1870. Rubinstein suggests that Britain was never fundamentally an industrial and manufacturing economy but was essentially a commercial, financial, and service-based economy, even at the height of the Industrial Revolution. Britain's comparative advantage had always lain with commerce and finance and therefore its industrial decline should be seen and understood 'as a transfer of resources and entrepreneurial energies into other forms of business life'. This transfer of resources was consequently 'an entirely rational economic response' to market conditions rather than anything concerned with 'any factor in Britain's underlying culture, elite educational system, or fundamental system of values' (Rubinstein, 1993, p. 24).

Having challenged the notion of nineteenth century Britain as an essentially industrial nation, Rubinstein seeks to challenge the proposition that 'British culture was and is anti-business and anti-industrial' by comparing it with the national cultures of Britain's more successful competitors, Germany and the United States, so often posited as the exemplars of industrial modernization (Rubinstein, 1993, p. 44). His contention is that British culture was possibly 'the least hostile to entrepreneurship and business life of any in Europe and perhaps the world' (Rubinstein, 1993, p. 49). By identifying the hostility of German culture towards business in the late nineteenth century, and how despite this German economic development was so rapid, Rubinstein is able to demonstrate the futility of identifying culture as the most crucial causal factor when accounting for variations in patterns of national economic development. Indeed, Rubinstein argues that 'one can search Britain's modern cultural history in vain to find the equivalent –any equivalent –of the extremist critics of capitalism, liberalism, and modernity found almost everywhere else' (Rubinstein, 1993, p. 70).

In his analysis of the British educational system, Rubinstein seeks to refute the notion that the children of successful Victorian entrepreneurs were robbed of their parents' industrial spirit by the public school system. He firstly points to the fact that, since not even 10 per cent of boys were educated at public schools in the latter half of the nineteenth century, it was not a sufficiently common experience to have instilled an anti-industrial spirit in the middle classes as a whole. In any case, the public schools were schools for the sons of the professional middle classes rather than for the sons of entrepreneurs and industrialists. The sons of businessmen, in the majority of cases, became businessmen, and if one quarter was lost to the professions, it was often because they were the fourth, fifth or sixth sons and were therefore superfluous to the needs of the family business (Rubinstein, 1993, p. 121). Therefore, the importance of Britain's public schools in understanding Britain's economic performance had been exaggerated especially in comparison to the importance of Britain's comparative advantage in commercial and financial markets. Rubinstein concludes his dismemberment of the 'cultural critique' by focusing upon the structure of Britain's elites. Here he contends that it is most fruitful to view these elites as being composed of three rival elite groups – the landed elite, the commercial-based London elite together with professionals and administrators also based in London, and the northern manufacturing elites. Rubinstein suggests that the interaction of these three elites with each other and with the rest of society constitutes the substance of modern British history. This in turn can be divided into four periods.

The first period lasted from 1780 to 1832 when the three rival elites were part of a 'unified national system', with the landowners in the ascendancy. The second period lasted from the Reform Bill of 1832 until the Liberal Unionist split in 1886. During this period, the ruling elite was neither consensual nor unified, and there was a series of unsuccessful attempts to create a new national political party and consensus. The third period of modern British history, from 1886 onwards, was characterized by the elites and middle classes of Britain functioning as a system, with both the landed aristocracy in decline and the self-conscious, assertive, ideologically distinctive provincial civic culture being emasculated by the First World War and its aftermath. The old staple industries of the North declined but this was a worldwide trend, and British culture did not in any event prevent the emergence of new industries in London and the Midlands in the interwar years. Rubinstein finds it difficult to locate the end of this third period, suggesting that, although the Suez Crisis in 1956 marked a psychological turning-point for Britain, it was the election of the Wilson Government in October 1964 that marked the demise of the old Tory-Imperial Establishment (Rubinstein, 1993, pp. 140–52).

The election of the first Wilson Government marked the beginning of a period of unprecedented social change during which Britain failed both to resolve its postwar dilemma of whether to align itself with the Commonwealth, the United States or the European Community, and whether to match the economic performance of Germany and Japan. Rubinstein suggests that it was against this background of domestic and foreign policy failure that in the mid-1970s, when apparently virtually every politically feasible approach to remedying national decline had been attempted and failed, creating a crisis in the British psyche, that Thatcherism emerged. He sees Thatcherism at heart as 'the admission, as the centre-piece of government policy, that Britain's comparative advantage in the international economic sphere lay in the services, finance, and commerce, and that deliberate attempts by the government to focus economic policy on the fostering of a truly revivified manufacturing sector were likely to be quixotic and counterproductive' (Rubinstein, 1993, p. 154). However, Rubinstein's is not the only or necessarily the most informative interpretation of Thatcherism. It will be asserted towards the conclusion of this chapter that Thatcherism may also be understood as a reaction to and a critique of the attempts by successive postwar British governments to pursue the very policies of state-led modernization advocated by proponents of the 'cultural critique' of British economic performance. In their place, Thatcherism substituted an alternative 'cultural critique' based on the purported loss and proposed restoration of a British culture of individual entrepreneurial enterprise and innovation.

It should not be thought that all recent contributions to the debate about the relationship between economic performance and culture in Britain have been hostile to the notion that Britain has developed an anti-industrial culture that is damaging for the prospects for future national prosperity. In *The Heritage Industry: Britain in a climate of decline*, Robert Hewison has identified the growth of a new cultural force in Britain which he calls the 'heritage industry' (Hewison, 1987, p. 9). This industry, which manufactures heritage instead of goods, Hewison sees as 'an attempt to dispel this climate of decline by exploiting the economic potential of our culture, and it finds a ready market because the perception of decline includes all sorts of insecurities and doubts (which are more than simply economic) that makes its products especially attractive and reassuring'. Indeed, 'Looking at a Laura Ashley catalogue, it is possible that we imagine ourselves living in a museum already' (Hewison, 1987, pp. 9–10). As a historian himself, it would be odd if Hewison was rejecting the need for a past and for an understanding of national history but that it is not his argument. Hewison sees the potential for nostalgia to have 'an integrative effect by helping us to adjust to change', but the problem is that in Britain 'The growth of a heritage culture has led not only to a distortion of the past, but to a stifling of the culture of the present' (Hewison, 1987, p. 10).

Given relative economic decline and the state of English society, Hewison acknowledges that 'it is not surprising that the past seems a better place', but the past 'is irrecoverable, for we are condemned to live perpetually in the present' (Hewison, 1987, p. 43). Moreover, 'When museums become one of Britain's new growth industries, they are not signs of vitality, but symbols of national decline' (Hewison, 1987, p. 84). Hewison notes that the doubling in the number of museums since 1960 is not a phenomenon unique to Britain, for a similar trend is discernible in Japan, continental Europe and North America. His contention is that elsewhere museums are 'objects of pride and prestige' which 'create a focus for ideas of civic or national identity'. Indeed, 'In the twentieth century museums have taken over the function once exercised by church and ruler, they provide the symbols through which a nation and a culture understands itself' (Hewison, 1987, p. 84). However, in England, 'the paradox of the industrial museum movement is that it is ultimately anti-industrial' (Hewison, 1987, p. 104) because it encourages the belief that heritage offers a universal solution to economic regeneration – England as an open-air theme park. Rather than being a source of education and knowledge that demonstrate that the past was not always so wonderful for most people but that ways and means were found to progress, and that change was an ally, industrial museums have become a testament to economic decline and an obstacle to change and progress.

Hewison draws an important distinction between preservation, which means 'the maintenance of an object or building, or such of it as remains, in a condition defined by its historic context, and in such a form that it can be studied with a view to revealing its original meaning', and conservation, which 'creates a new context and, if only by attracting the attention of members of the public, a new use' (Hewison, 1987, p. 98). His contention is that the economic justification for conservation of the past is often because there is no alternative use or employment for buildings and people in the present. The danger is that such 'a growing obsession with the past', and the Conservative Governments' policy of increasing spending on museums and galleries faster than on the live arts, may prevent the contemporary arts from making a contribution to national culture (Hewison, 1987, p. 107). Present policies may deliver an ill-informed and ill-educated population but Hewison contends that this may have been the Government's intention all along because 'An intellectual culture is also a critical culture, which is not prepared passively to accept the decisions made on its behalf by political appointees who are answerable to no one but themselves' (Hewison, 1987, p. 122).

What Hewison is suggesting is that in the era of the heritage industry, 'A change in cultural perception has taken place which narrows the imagination and cramps the spirit'. Whereas, in the nineteenth century, 'museums were seen as sources of education and improvement' and free, today the heritage industry treats them as 'financial institutions that must pay their way, and therefore charge entrance fees' with the consequence that the arts 'are no longer appreciated as a source of inspiration, of ideas, images or values, they are part of the "leisure business"' (Hewison, 1987, p. 129). The consequence is that 'We have no understanding of history in depth, but instead are offered a contemporary creation, more costume drama and re-enactment than critical discourse' (Hewison, 1987, p. 135). If the English had more faith in themselves, and were more certain of their values, they would have less recourse to the images and monuments of the past. Moreover, rather than being redundant other than as a dion from the present, Hewison asserts that history could become a cultural resource with the ideas and values of the past being the source of inspiration for innovation in the present (Hewison, 1987, p. 139). The way forward lies in the nurturing of a critical culture, the elements of which 'already exist, in the ideas and activities of contemporary artists who have continued to struggle with the material of the present, in spite of their increasing neglect by the institutions of culture'. We must encourage 'art as a process of renewal' not 'works of art that are already achieved, where they can be absorbed as symbols of the general culture the heritage institutions support' (Hewison, 1987, p. 144).

The dangers posed by nostalgia and heritage to questions of national identity and economic performance have also been developed in Patrick Wright's, *On Living in an Old Country: The National Past in Contemporary Britain*. In his 'Afterword', Wright asserts, 'History should be the name of a future-orientated project: history-which-is-to-be-made rather than stately history-which-is-already-made and demands only veneration in what it also dismisses as an abjectly inferior and declining present' (Wright, 1987, p. 255). Unfortunately, in Britain, as Wright argues was vividly demonstrated by Thatcher's exploitation of the Falklands War, history 'is evidently not about the making of the future, unless we understand that process to be a re-enactment of the imagined past − "our" moment of vindication and perpetuation'. Events such as the Falklands War, which summon up memories of great conquest of our imperial past, enable the restoration of 'the essential and grander identity of the "Imaginary Briton" to the modern subject: it is the greatest of contemporary fall-back positions' (Wright, 1987, p. 165).

In sharp contrast to Hewison and Wright's contention that English heritage has become part of a self-fulfilling culture of national decline, in *Theatres of Memory* (1995), Raphael Samuel has argued that heritage does not impose a conservative view of the past on us but is in fact 'part of a change in attitudes which has left any unified view of the past − liberal, radical or conservative − in tatters'. For Samuel, heritage is culturally pluralist and 'far from simply domesticating or sanitising the past, it often makes a great point of its strangeness, of the brute contrast between now and then' (*Independent on Sunday*, 12 February, 1995). He also asserts that some historians who criticise 'heritage' are engaged in 'a favourite conceit of the aesthete that the masses, if left to their own devices, are moronic; that their pleasures are unthinking and their tastes cheap and nasty'. After all, the public following of heritage can be measured in hundreds of thousands whereas audiences for academic lectures can frequently be numbered in single figures. Samuel may be correct in his assertion that theme parks do have a constructive role to play in the future development of the economy but there nevertheless remains the danger, identified by Wright, that they will contribute more to 'the strategies of contemporary Conservatism [which] acknowledge, even thrive on, the extent to which history itself has become utopian in terms of a public culture which has substantial difficulty in conceiving a future at all' (Wright, 1987, p. 185).

AN ANTI-ENGINEERING CULTURE?

We have already seen in the chapter on the state and industrial policy how a technocratic, state-led programme of industrial modernization has been one of the consistent policy prescriptions of commentators on British decline throughout the twentieth century. One of the explanations for the failure of British industry to modernize has been the absence in the higher echelons of Westminster and Whitehall of the requisite technical expertise to design and implement a modernization programme. Freeman, for example, has identified the avoidance of a complete underestimation of the role of scientists and engineers as one of his seven 'essential features' of an effective 'national system of innovation' (Freeman, 1987, pp. 99–100). His contention is that Britain has failed to recognize and properly reward the expertise of the engineer. However, a far more exhaustive analysis of the technocratic deficiencies of the British state has been provided by the historian Peter Hennessy. In his lengthy exploration of Whitehall, Hennessy devotes a chapter to what he terms 'The Missed Opportunity', that is, the period at the end of the Second World War when the state, in the form of both politicians and senior civil servants, failed to retain the technical expertise of the army of scientists, engineers and managers who had been forced upon Whitehall by the threat to national survival posed by Hitler (Hennessy, 1989, pp. 120–168). Rather than being disbanded, this wartime technocratic elite could and should have stayed in government to win the peace, but the British civil service did not replicate the postwar brilliance of the French and Japanese state bureaucracies on 'economic and industrial fronts' because it was not designed to do so. Within six months of the end of the war, Whitehall had abandoned its wartime role of 'thinker doer' and 'world-beating bureaucracy' to resume its status as a 'largely hands-off institution', characterized by a 'failure-avoidance culture' and a 'waterfall of negativism' (Hennessy, 1989, p. 125). More recently, Hennessy has suggested that the absence of technical expertise within Whitehall has meant that successive postwar British governments have come and gone but an anti-industrial culture has remained (Hennessy and Anstey 1991, p. 53).

Some commentators on British decline have not confined their criticisms to the absence of technical expertise in government. They have contended instead that British society and culture as a whole has not granted sufficient status or resources to particular technical professions specifically engineers and scientists. For example, in his *Anatomy of Britain*, Anthony Sampson asserted that whilst the average British engineer was as well trained as his continental European peers, he or she lacked the equivalent of the demanding five year course for French 'polytechniciens' which provided a route for engineers to play a major role in government and industry in France (Sampson, 1962, p. 517). Three decades on, Sampson has urged British society to 'Stop doing the dirty on Britain's engineers' (Sampson, 1993, p. 30). It was not always thus, he claims, for in the early nineteenth century, British engineers such as Brunel were able to undertake engineering projects on an heroic scale. Engineers were seen as the agents of progress, efficiency and modernity but whereas Germany and France trained their engineers as a distinct elite with the capacity to administer, British engineers developed beyond government patronage, and thus were denied the sort of education and training that might have made them into a technocratic elite (Sampson, 1993, p. 32).

A similar thesis has been developed by Correlli Barnett, notably in *The Audit of War*, where he contends that from 1870 to 1940, during Britain's formative period as an industrial society, a combination of 'the cult of the "practical man"; romantic idealism; and the profound British dislike of coherent organisation, especially if centrally administered, especially if under the aegis of the state' denied Britain the national system of modern technical education and training which would have enabled the engineer to occupy his rightful place in the vanguard of society (Barnett, 1986, p. 209). For Barnett and many others (for example, Child et al., 1983, 1986; Hutton and Lawrence, 1981), the principal country for comparison of the treatment of engineers has been Germany because, as Smith has demonstrated, their objective is the Germanification of the occupational structure of British management and the technical education of engineers (Smith, 1990, p. 459). For them, Germany is the model because it is a society dominated by the 'third culture' of 'Technik', or the art of manufacture, which guarantees that German engineers are locked in to a virtuous circle of high pay and high status (Freeman, 1987, p. 100; Smith, 1990, p. 461). The absence of this culture of 'Technik' from Britain is exemplified for Barnett by the fact that the English language does not have an equivalent word for 'Technik'.

Smith, however, has taken issue not only with the uncritical acceptance of the characterization of British and German management practices implicit in the analysis of historians like Barnett, but also with the fact that the political agencies capable of implementing modernization programmes are never specified. Smith emphasizes the weakness of an essentially a historical model of German engineering which passes over the political conflicts behind the social formation of German engineers. He also criticizes the failure to disaggregate the causes of German economic success, for example, the close relationship between banking and industry, and the huge use of migrant labour which has not been educated or trained in German institutions. Many of the practices which German engineers have benefited from, such as greater job stability than in Britain and social partnership between employer and employee, have been general features of the German economy and not specific to engineering. Furthermore, in their enthusiasm to bemoan the absence of engineers from management in manufacturing industry in Britain, historians like Barnett have overlooked the dominance of engineers in other sectors of the economy, notably electricity, gas, mining and construction (Smith, 1990, p. 463).

It could also be argued that British engineers may not have been the unfortunate victims of a hostile culture or indifferent society but may instead have been subject to self-inflicted wounds. Engineers in Britain have not been gathered together under a single professional institution, but have preferred to be members of a plethora of engineering organizations. Incapable of speaking with a single voice, such political divisions amongst engineers may offer a more credible explanation of their status within industry and influence on government than any cultural explanation of British decline. The damage done to the engineering profession over a period of decades by its internal divisions was recently and vividly demonstrated in the profession's response to the 1980 report produced by the Finniston Committee's inquiry into the engineering profession. The Committee had been commissioned in July 1977 by the Callaghan Government because of its concern about a number of disturbing industrial and educational trends, not least the fact 'that between 1967 and 1973 the number of engineering students had increased by only 5 per cent while student numbers in sociology increased by 38 per cent, in theology by 51 per cent, and in general arts by 169 per cent' (Donoughue, 1987, p. 111).

The very fact of the Finniston Committee's formation reflected a wider assumption that a greater supply of engineers was an essential precondition of industrial recovery. Having initially been intended as an inquiry purely into the engineering profession, at the last minute the Secretary of State for Industry, Eric Varley, was persuaded to broaden the Committee's inquiry into an examination of the needs of manufacturing industry for skilled engineering manpower. There has indeed been a tendency for cultural explanations of British decline, and in particular those focused upon engineering to equate wealth creation with manufacturing, and therefore to believe that manufacturing is a uniquely valuable form of economic activity (Jordan, 1992, p. 57). In this regard, the Finniston Report was therefore typical in its examination of the decline of manufacturing in Britain and associating that poor performance with deficiencies in the 'engineering dimension', that is, 'the effective priority accorded to engineering as a system for translating engineering expertise into the production and marketing of competitive products through efficient production processes' (HMSO, 1980, p. 22). The Report attributed low morale in the engineering profession to a lack of status for professional engineers, and accounted for Britain's industrial decline in terms of a shortage of engineering skills in the national economy. However, as Jordan has shown, one of the problems for the Finniston Committee was the fact that much of the evidence it gathered and analysed did not sustain the assumption that British engineers were suffering from a lower status than engineers in competitor economies. A major survey of more than 5 000 engineers commissioned by the Committee from the Policy Studies Institute revealed little evidence to sustain the assumption that engineers were underpaid. Indeed, a second survey discovered that science graduates possessed both higher academic entrance qualifications and lower salaries than engineers (Jordan, 1992, pp. 49–51). In any case, Britain could hardly be regarded as a society that was indifferent to the importance of engineering when the first edition of 9 000 copies of the Finniston Report sold out in only ten days, and around 25 000 copies were sold in the first year after publication.

The engineering institutions' attitude towards both the inquiry and report from the Finniston Committee was mixed. Most professional engineering bodies did not see the need for an inquiry, including the Council of Engineering Institutions, the umbrella organization for the profession. After all, fragmentation in the engineering profession could be traced back to the mid-nineteenth century when new organizations like the Institute of Mechanical Engineers (established in 1847) sought to provide status for those engineers excluded by the existing institutional arrangements (Jordan, 1992, p. 67). The fragmentation of the engineering profession stemmed in part from the lack of status granted to some of its members by fellow engineering organizations. Despite a number of amalgamations, in 1979 there were no less than 19 chartered engineering institutions. Indeed, in 1982 the Department of Industry was able to identify 72 engineering institutions of relevance to the Finniston Report. This fragmentation acted as a strong stimulus for the Report to recommend the creation of a single statutory Engineering Authority, capable of knocking into shape the engineering profession with the sort of central administrative intervention advocated by Barnett and those other historians wishing to Germanify British institutions.

Political divisions within the engineering profession spilled over into the Finniston Committee itself. It took no less than six drafts and the threat of a dissenting minority report before the final version of the Finniston Report was agreed to and published in January 1980. To surmount 'the national undervaluation of engineering', the Report advocated the establishment of a new statutory Engineering Authority with the 'strategic objective of correcting the historic neglect of the engineering dimension' (HMSO, 1980, pp. 151–3). The Committee chairman, Sir Monty Finniston, assumed that the failure of successive previous inquiries into engineering in Britain during the previous 138 years could be attributed to the absence of a 'champion for change'. The Engineering Authority would act as that champion. However, as Jordan's exhaustive analysis of the post-Finniston Report's negotiations has shown, the commitment to a statutory authority was abandoned by the Department of Industry in August 1980 after six months of intense and on occasions bitter political debate within the engineering profession (Jordan, 1992, p. 143). In its place was created the

Engineering Council, a non-statutory, royal-charter based organization. The notion that the deficiencies in Britain's 'engineering dimension' should be addressed by the introduction of a statutory authority was rejected. As Jordan has suggested, the reaction of the engineering profession to institutional reform appears to confirm Mancur Olson's view (Olson, 1982) that one of the principal causes of slow economic growth in mature societies such as Britain is the capacity of well-entrenched interest groups to oppose change in their policy field (Jordan, 1992, p. 147). The decision to proceed with an Engineering Council operating with the approval and assistance of the existing engineering institutions, was criticized amongst others by Ken Gill, the General Secretary of the trade union TASS., because it appeared to leave the fate of the profession in the hands of the very leadership whose inadequacies in defending and promoting the interests of engineering had helped to inspire the Finniston inquiry in the first place (Jordan, 1992, p. 192).

The fate of the Finniston Report demonstrates that any lack of status for engineers has as much to do with divisions within the engineering profession as with any lack of appreciation of engineering's value to wealth creation in wider British society. If engineers have been used and valued differently in Britain than in France or Germany, it is because of identifiable economic, political and social factors rather than because of some all pervasive anti-engineering cultural malaise. In the case of manufacturing industry in general and engineering in particular, cultural explanations of their decline are no substitute for rigorous political analysis of the sort provided by Jordan in his study of the Finniston inquiry, which has revealed the detail and complexity of the multitude of political, economic and social factors that influence national economic performance. Eltis, Fraser and Ip have pointed to the divergent performance of different sectors of the engineering industry in Britain during the postwar period (Eltis, Fraser and Ip, 1992, pp. 25–51). If it is indeed the case that Britain has been affected by a societal and cultural antipathy towards engineering, some new explanation would have to be advanced to explain why it is that some engineering sectors have declined but many others flourished.

Ten years after the publication of the Finniston Report, the Director General of the Engineering Council, Denis Filer, took part in a debate about the engineering profession in which he assessed the progress of the Council and the profession during the 1980s. Although he was able to identify some progress in raising public awareness of the importance of engineers, Filer nonetheless believed that Britain remained 'an anti-industry, anti-engineering culture' (Filer, 1992, p. 4). However, the very next speaker in the debate amply illustrated through his contribution the continuing sterility of the debate within the engineering profession about how to raise its status. Dr A.E. Moulton retreated into the familiar exhortations about the necessity of 'a fundamental change in our national attitudes towards the manufacturing industry, which in turn depends on engineers' (Moulton, 1993, p. 8). He proceeded to lambast the short-termism of the City of London whilst conveniently ignoring the huge number of software engineers whose careers had benefited from the rapid expansion of financial services in London during the deregulation of the 1980s. Such narrowness of vision should ensure that similar debates will continue to be conducted within the engineering profession in Britain for the foreseeable future with little action for change resulting.

AN ANTI-SCIENTIFIC CULTURE?

Together with engineers, scientists are the other profession whom proponents of technocratic remedies for British decline have identified most frequently as an undervalued and under-resourced national asset. This is perhaps not particularly surprising for as Edgerton has suggested, 'the connections between science and technology and business are central to theoretical accounts of "industrial" and "capitalist" society' (Edgerton, 1987, p. 84). A failure to effectively develop and exploit science and technology in Britain might therefore go a long way towards explaining British decline. Both Roderick and Stephens, and Hobsbawm have identified the increasing role of pure and applied science as the most profound aspect of the second industrial revolution of the late nineteenth century (Roderick and Stephens, 1981, p. 234; 1982, p. 3; Hobsbawm, 1969, pp. 169–72). For these historians, for national economies to remain competitive in the two major new growth markets in the world economy – that is, the electrical and chemical industries – scientific research had to be organized, rational, and systematic, depending on a close working relationship with manufacturing industry. However, whilst German industry developed a systematic, national approach to research and development, British industry has been portrayed as remaining too fragmented to sustain a similar effort. Lost markets in growth industries and industrial decline has been seen as the inevitable consequence.

To account for British decline, frequent reference has been made to C.P. Snow's 'two cultures' thesis in which he contended that there was a literary cultural and a separate scientific culture in British society, and that these two cultures were divided by a 'gulf of mutual incomprehension' (Snow, 1965, p. 4).

Although Snow believed that these cultures could be identified throughout the West, the gulf was most pronounced in England because of its 'fanatical belief in educational specialization', and because of the slow pace of change in British institutions which had acted to deepen the cultural divide (Snow, 1965, p. 19). Furthermore, a division had arisen within British science between pure science on the one hand, and applied science and engineering on the other. Too many pure scientists had become profoundly ignorant of manufacturing industry and regarded applied science as a second rate occupation. Whatever the effect of the 'two cultures' upon Britain's economic performance, it is evident that they did not prevent the Macmillan Government from appointing the then Quintin Hogg (latterly Lord Hailsham) as Minister for Science (admittedly Hogg was a lawyer by profession), nor Harold Wilson from reviving the Labour Party's political fortunes in Opposition by embracing the 'white heat' of the scientific revolution during the run-up to the 1964 General Election campaign, and subsequently creating the Ministry of Technology once in power.

At the forefront of more recent debates for greater funding and recognition for scientists has been Save British Science, a pressure group formed from scientists. In January 1986, Save British Science placed an advertisement in The Times exhorting the Secretary of State for Education and Science to undertake immediate action to protect Britain's science base. Led by Denis Noble, the eminent Professor of Cardiovascular Physiology at Oxford University, Save British Science sought to highlight low morale in the scientific profession as a consequence of inadequate funding, and advocated a substantial increase in state and private sector resources for civil science (for example, Save British Science, 1990). In his 1987 Lloyd-Roberts Lecture, Noble defended the view that science, culture and industry are linked, and contended that the only way to ensure the long term health of science is to continue to attract bright recruits into the profession by creating and maintaining a culture in which young scientists respond to intellectual challenges (Noble, 1987, p. 1). For Noble, in policy terms, the creation and maintenance of this culture meant an increase of £3 billion per year in Britain's expenditure on civil R&D by government and industry if Britain was to match the spending of its principal industrial competitors. Noble advocated that Britain should seek to catch up its competitors over a period of five to ten years (Noble, 1987, p. 2).

Save British Science's demands reflected the views of many within academia and industry, and a large number of politicians too. Trying to revive Harold Wilson's themes of the early 1960s, Neil Kinnock spoke of 'living in the science society and the science economy', and argued that the presence, or in Britain's case the absence, of sustained investment in a long term strategy for science was a major determinant of economic performance in a 'modern' economy (Kinnock, 1990, pp. 84–5). Indeed, a constant theme of the Labour Party's Policy Review following its 1987 General Election defeat was the need for greater investment in Britain in civil science and technology, an attempt seemingly to replicate Wilson's 'white heat' modernization strategy (Labour Party, 1989, pp. 11–12; 1990, p. 14; 1991, pp. 15–17; 1992, p. 12; 1993, pp. 9–10). Parliament expressed its support for greater investment in science and technology through a series of select committee reports from both Houses. For example, in 1986 the House of Lords' Select Committee on Science and Technology produced a report, *Civil Research and Development*, which pointed to low morale in the scientific community, pessimism in industry, and the alarming shrinkage in the UK's manufacturing base. The Committee asserted that long term industrial recovery required national success in science and technology, and that the Government had the responsibility of providing leadership (House of Lords, 1986, p. 12). Reiterating the conclusions of its previous reports and anticipating the conclusions of its subsequent inquiries (House of Lords, 1982; 1983; 1987; 1991), the Committee advocated the necessity of a 'recognized policy for the public support of R&D' in general, and an increase in and redirection of DTI support for industrial R&D in particular (House of Lords, 1986, pp. 12, 41).

In its official response to *Civil Research and Development*, as with its response to so many select committee reports of both Houses of Parliament during the 1980s, the Government emphasized the benefits to be derived from the more 'effective management' of resources in the public sector, and did not accept the need for the sort of 'recognized policy for the public support of R&D' advocated by the Lords' Committee (DTI, 1987, p. 1). On the contrary, with profitability returning to many sectors of manufacturing industry in Britain, the Government was adamant that industry must increase the level of R&D that it funded. That there would not be an expansion in the DTI's support for industrial R&D was confirmed in the 1988 White Paper, *DTI – The Department for Enterprise*, which identified firms as the best judges of 'the commercial risks and rewards of financing R&D and innovation' (DTI, 1988, p. 33). In her 1989 lecture to celebrate the fiftieth anniversary of the establishment of the Parliamentary and Scientific Committee, the Prime Minister pointed to a 25 per cent increase in real terms in the science budget since 1979 (Thatcher, 1990, p. 3). At the same time, she argued that Britain could perform only a small percentage of the world's research, and that politicians could not decide in any case which areas of basic science should be funded because the eventual economic rewards were unpredictable. More importantly, Thatcher emphasized that, whilst the intellectual capacity of Britain might be judged by the number of its Nobel Prizes and scientific publications, the wealth of Britain would be determined by the speed at which scientific discoveries could be translated into industrial and commercial products (Thatcher, 1990, p. 3). The message for Britain's scientists could not have been clearer. With 95 per cent of scientific research being conducted overseas, the future performance of the British economy would be as much if not more dependent on the ability of British companies to purchase and apply science and technology from abroad as it would be on domestic sources. By increasingly emphasizing not only the application of technology, from whatever source, rather than its domestic production, but also collaboration amongst firms rather than single company projects, government policy and funding, especially at the DTI, had long since reflected the message of Thatcher's lecture.

As with the engineering profession, the political competence of scientists has to be called into question. For example, Save British Science was formed by scientists at Oxford University, the very institution which had previously refused to award the Prime Minister an honorary degree. Having so publicly snubbed its leader, could the same scientists at Oxford really have imagined that they were going to influence a government which in any case was not sympathetic to demands for higher public spending from most interest groups. It was, moreover, a source of great frustration to Save British Science that Thatcher appeared unsympathetic to their demands when she herself had been an undergraduate scientist at Oxford, and begun her career as an industrial chemist. She had been acclaimed as the first scientist to become Prime Minister but what was all too easily forgotten, especially by the scientists, was that she had subsequently abandoned industry for a more lucrative career in the legal profession. More importantly, Thatcher's actions as Conservative Party leader and Prime Minister had made it abundantly clear that she was a politician in the first, second, and third place. Scientists, like engineers, were important to her but only where they assisted in her great political project by behaving entrepreneurially and thereby assisted the recreation of an enterprise culture in Britain.

Some scientists thought that they had been reprieved by a sudden and hitherto undetected change of direction in government policy towards science in the autumn of 1988 when, in a series of speeches to the Royal Society, Conservative Party Conference, and the United Nations' General Assembly, Thatcher spoke about the need to address global environmental destruction. She claimed that 'No generation has a freehold on this Earth. All we have is a life tenancy – with a full repairing lease. And this Government intends to meet the terms of that lease in full' (Thatcher,

1990, p. 274). However, whilst some saw this as a genuine desire to embrace Green politics, with hindsight it appears that Thatcher's concern was less with the potential for British science to help to save the depletion of the ozone layer and tropical rainforests, and more to do with two other, more mundane political considerations. In the first place, at this time Ronald Reagan was coming to the end of his second and final term as US President, and therefore Thatcher could now arguably project herself as the senior statesman of the Western world, especially if she could see off President Mitterrand, her one rival, by addressing global issues on prominent international stages such as the United Nations. The environment appeared to be an issue which would enable Thatcher to serve this purpose. At the same time, and more importantly, the Government was facing considerable domestic opposition to its plans to privatize the electricity and water industries. Many Opposition politicians and members of the public could not identify any legitimate justification for these policies. By using the issue of concern about the environment to emphasize the costs of cleaning up Britain's power stations, rivers and beaches, and by simultaneously pointing to the very poor investment record of the electricity and water industries as nationalized, public sector utilities, Thatcher could provide an environmental justification for privatization. She could argue that it would only be when these industries were privatized and had access to large amounts of private capital that they would be in a position to make the huge investments that would enable them to meet existing and future EC environmental standards. As with their other policies towards science, what motivated the Thatcher Governments' conduct of policy were immediate political and economic factors and not the indeterminate influence of an anti-scientific culture in Britain.

Whilst most of the literature on the contribution of science to economic performance has tended to be hostile towards government policy during the 1980s (for example, Walker and Sharp, 1991a; 1991b) and sympathetic to the demands of Save British Science (for example, Ince, 1988), this mainstream position has been challenged by Terence Kealey, a Conservative commentator on science policy. Kealey has branded as 'science fiction' the claim by Save British Science that British science is in decline as a consequence of inadequate government funding, which is in turn harming Britain's present and future economic performance. Kealey's contention is that the reality of contemporary British science is that it is thriving, that academic science is dependent on economic growth rather than the contrary, and that British scientific institutions will benefit from greater exposure to market forces (Kealey, 1989, p. 4). Refuting the usually unsubstantiated but nevertheless commonsensical belief that there is a positive correlation between scientific output and national economic performance, Kealey also rejects the idea that national salvation lies through an expansion in the numbers of scientists and engineers graduating from our universities. As an alternative basis for science policy, he endorses the Thatcherite contention that economic decline can be stemmed by the restoration of an enterprise culture in Britain where a once again commercially minded people will look towards entrepreneur-led innovation and initiative rather than government intervention as the primary agency of economic and social progress.

To demonstrate his thesis concerning the dependence of science for its well-being upon commerce and industry's capacity to create wealth, Kealey points to the fact that most of the major technological innovations of the first Industrial Revolution predated the foundation of England's great civic universities. A similar experience has more recently occurred in Japan where major technological breakthroughs were brought about by its companies before the establishment of a modern university system (Kealey, 1989, p. 24). Kealey asserts that in both Britain and Japan, the universities' expansion was founded on the private wealth of industrialists and not government funding, and whilst successive postwar British governments had consistently increased their expenditure on the universities up until 1970, Britain's relative economic decline had continued inexorably (Kealey, 1989, p. 32). Therefore, for Kealey, the expansion in government-funded universities education during the 1960s which was pursued as a consequence of bipartisan acceptance of the recommendations of the 1963 *Robbins Report* (HMSO, 1963), was a major mistake. There was little evidence of an unfulfilled demand for places at university to study technology, or indeed that industry wanted to employ more technologists. The inevitable consequences of this ultimately unnecessary expansion were that academic standards for admission to degrees had to be lowered, and that an expansion occurred in the arts and social sciences' degree programmes where the demand for places was inevitably strong given the generous levels of government funding.

Kealey accepts that in more recent years Britain has fallen behind the United States and Canada in terms of both the quantity and quality of its national scientific output, although it remains ahead of Germany, France and Japan (Kealey, 1989, p. 7). However, whilst British science may have experienced the greatest relative rate of decline amongst the major science nations, Kealey argues that this is understandable given the 'spectacularly high base' from which it has begun (Kealey, 1989, p. 31). The true way to save British science is simply to abolish the Universities' Funding Council's research budget, allocate it instead to the research councils, and thereby encourage greater competition for resources amongst scientists for research. This would enable the most productive and efficient university science departments to thrive and allow the many surplus, unproductive and parasitic departments to wither and die (Kealey, 1989, pp. 38–51). Whilst many of Kealey's policy recommendations may have been ignored in the 1993 White Paper, *Realizing our Potential: A Strategy for Science, Engineering and Technology*, it is clear that the Major Government, like its immediate Conservative predecessors, has identified greater exposure of science to market forces as the most effective remedy for the anti-scientific culture which it acknowledges still exists in Britain (HMSO, 1993, p. 53).

One important policy to strengthen science in Britain that was implemented by the Thatcher Government during its third term was the introduction of the national curriculum in state education, with science and mathematics as compulsory elements to be taught until the age of 16. However, there is as yet little evidence that the new curriculum is persuading more British teenagers to consider studying science as an A-level subject, let alone reading it at university and then employing the resulting scientific skills at the workplace. In fact, the A-level results for the UK in 1994 suggest that the trend is if anything away from subjects traditionally regarded as a prerequisite to a science-based career. Compared with a year earlier, the number of students sitting examinations at A-level in physics fell by 5.6 per cent (after a 9.6 per cent decline in the previous year), and in mathematics by 6 per cent (following a 10.6 per cent decline in 1993). Social science A-levels, by way of comparison, enjoyed a 7.6 per cent increase in examination entrants. One encouraging trend for science and industry was an increase in the numbers taking technology subjects, which increased by 18.5 per cent, but this increase nevertheless meant that only 10,931 entrants had sat technology exams compared with 75,716 entrants for social science subjects (*The Guardian*, 18 August, 1994). As a consequence, the British secondary education system appears to be caught in a self-perpetuating spiral of decline in which the falling numbers of science students at school is leading to fewer science graduates from universities and fewer trainee science teachers, which in turn will deliver an even smaller number of pupils studying science at school.

It might be tempting to regard this disturbing trend as the clearest possible demonstration of Britain's anti-scientific culture. On the contrary, pupils' selection of subjects at A-level and university, and their subsequent career choices, can largely be attributed to a secondary education system which forces them to choose between sciences, arts and social sciences at too early an age. They have thereby been denied the choice of a more balanced curriculum up to the age of 18 when they might be deemed sufficiently mature to be able to decide whether they want to specialize in a particular discipline. And if at present too many undergraduates opt for arts and social sciences in pursuit of careers in the law or financial services professions, and too few for sciences and careers in manufacturing, it is because that is the choice they are almost bound to make in a society whose manufacturing accounts for a rapidly diminishing number of relatively poorly paid career opportunities. and whose governments since 1979 have chosen to create a taxation system that encourages and rewards investment in non-scientific, and non-industrial commercial activities. These policies for the most part have been the deliberate political and economic choices of governments concerned about the presence of an anti-enterprise, and not an anti-scientific culture in Britain.

AN ANTI-ENTERPRISE CULTURE?

The true value and danger of cultural explanations of British decline, as Harvie has suggested of Wiener's work, lies not in the provision of a proper explanation for none is provided, but in their use as 'an ideological weapon' which 'lies there, unexploded, ticking away' (Harvie, 1985, p. 18). Furthermore, as Raven has contended, it is where these dormant cultural explanations have been seized upon and revived by party politicians that they have been most powerfully articulated and given the greatest practical effect (Raven, 1989, p. 195). The potency of the political influence that a cultural explanation of British decline may have upon the conduct of government has been most vividly illustrated by the way in which Thatcherites, notably the former Cabinet ministers Sir Keith (latterly Lord) Joseph and Lord Young, used their thesis of the restoration of an enterprise culture in Britain as the remedy for national decline to justify in particular their governments' industrial policies. The Thatcherite think-tank, the Centre for Policy Studies, has defined an enterprise culture as 'the full set of conditions that promote high and rising levels of achievement in a country's economic activity, politics and government, arts and sciences, and also the distinctively private lives of the inhabitants' (Morris, 1991, p. 23). However, as with a number of studies of the concept of the enterprise culture by social scientists (for example, Keat and Abercrombie, 1991; Heelas and Morris, 1992), this definition attaches insufficient importance to the notion of entrepreneurship which holds the key to understanding this particular cultural explanation of British decline.

For Thatcherites such as Sir Keith Joseph and Lord Young, Britain led the world during the Industrial Revolution and its aftermath in the nineteenth century because of the heroic efforts of entrepreneurs. However, their heroism was not confined merely to commerce and industry. It also extended to all other facets of Victorian society. The capacity of entrepreneurs to develop new ideas and to take risks stemmed from the freedom given to them by open markets characterized by a minimum of state intervention. The profits that they derived from their innovations in turn enabled them to become philanthropic patrons of the arts, science and architecture in Britain. In striking contrast to this Golden Age of British entrepreneurship from 1770 to 1870, Thatcherites point to the postwar era as years characterized by the loss of the entrepreneurial spirit in Britain. British business and society became overdependent on the interventions of and subsidies from a bloated and inefficient state machinery which had displaced the entrepreneur as the prime agency of social change. For Thatcherites, by 1979 the damage inflicted upon the entrepreneurial spirit by the policies of successive Labour and Conservative governments had bequeathed to the nation the legacy of a society overburdened with bureaucracy, regulation, direct taxation and uncontrolled trades' union power. National decline could only be remedied by a rolling back of the frontiers of the state to restore to the entrepreneur the opportunity to enjoy the freedom provided by open markets to innovate, to take risks, and to create wealth.

The centrality of the enterprise culture thesis to the Thatcher Government's longer-term ambitions, if not to the immediate conduct of policy, was emphasized in Thatcher and Joseph's first inaugural speeches to the House of Commons' as Prime Minister and Secretary of State for Industry respectively. Thatcher asserted that the choice confronting the electorate in 1979 had been to 'take further strides in the direction of the corporatist all-powerful State or to restore the balance in favour of the individual'. Where enterprise and opportunity had become 'dirty words in the Labour Party', her Government would restore 'the economic balance of society ... and choice', and 'do everything possible to encourage free enterprise, particularly the small business sector, which is the source of genuine new jobs' (Official Record, 'Debate on the Address', 15 May 1979, c. 75–8). However, it was Sir Keith Joseph who at the outset most clearly articulated the Thatcher Government's belief that it brought with it 'a different analysis and a different set of policies' (Official Record, 'Industrial Policy and Employment', 21 May 1979, c. 706). There were 'six main obstacles to full employment and prosperity' that Joseph identified, although he did not specify that they should be addressed in any particular order of priority. These obstacles were high state spending, high direct taxation, egalitarianism, nationalization, a Luddite trades' union movement, and an anti-enterprise culture. The key to the restoration of an enterprise culture, and thereby to the stemming of British decline, lay in the replacement of the postwar culture of state subsidies and intervention by a culture in which entrepreneurial innovation and risk-taking were once again to the fore.

Whilst the Thatcher Governments may have been underpinned throughout by a very clear analysis of the causes and remedies for British decline, the clarity of its ideology was not generally reflected in its conduct of policy during the first term of office. As with all its predecessors, this government did not start with a clean sheet of paper on which to transcribe its manifesto commitments. For the policies and institutions appropriate for an enterprise culture to be restored to Britain, the institutions of the postwar British dependency culture had first to be reformed or dismantled. In this regard, Sir Keith Joseph's experience during his tenure at the Department of Industry (DOI) is particularly instructive. On taking office at the DOI, Joseph was asked by his senior officials to clarify his approach to industrial policy. He did so by circulating a reading list of 29 texts (*The Economist*, May 19, 1979). Apart from a speech on DOI policy to the Conservative Bow Group, Joseph declined to define his department's industrial strategy because he did not believe that it should have one. Greater clarification of the likely direction of future policy was however provided in November 1979 by Sir Peter Carey, the Permanent Secretary and most senior civil servant at the DOI, when he delivered the sixty-sixth Thomas Hawksley Lecture on the theme of 'UK Industry in the 1980s'. Carey pointed towards the need for a restoration of the primacy of wealth creation, in the face of the 'undoubted increased dependency of many individuals on the state', and the subordination of wealth creation to 'the pursuit of egalitarian social ideals' (Carey, 1980, p. 445). Addressing an audience of engineers, Carey stressed that 'It is within the wider industrial community that the engineer must search for his role in an "enterprise culture" ... the engineer must assert himself as, in a way, an entrepreneur, "a man who shows enterprise". Within that general revival of the entrepreneurial spirit in large and small firms which I believe to be necessary, there must equally be a revival of the enterprising engineer' (Carey, 1980, p. 446).

The rhetorical commitment of Sir Keith Joseph and his Permanent Secretary to the restoration of the entrepreneur through the disengagement of industry from state subsidies and intervention was at least partly fulfilled through the DOI's disposal of the Government's stake in Cable and Wireless and part of British Aerospace. During his tenure at the DOI, Joseph also managed to separate the telecommunications system from the Post Office, which paved the way for the later privatization of British Telecom. However, what is equally apparent is that the ambition to dismantle the postwar dependency culture of state subsidies had to be subordinated to the more pressing need to save major parts of British manufacturing from the recession of 1979–82. Thus, in March 1981, Joseph steered the Iron and Steel Bill through the House of Commons which wrote off £3.5 billion of British Steel's past losses and extended the corporation's future borrowing powers from £1.5 billion to £3.5 billion. At the same time, Joseph provided a two-year, £200 million guarantee to the troubled state-owned computer manufacturer, International Computers Limited (ICL).

The acid test of how far the first Thatcher Government was prepared to apply its ideas about the remedies for British decline to its industrial policies arose when it was faced with a request from the beleaguered state-owned vehicle manufacturer British Leyland (BL) for further financial assistance. Sir Keith Joseph initially permitted his officials to circulate a paper to his Cabinet colleagues in which it was argued that assistance should be granted to avoid the possibility of the company collapsing, which would in turn have serious industrial ramifications for the West Midlands and serious political implications for the Government in an area of marginal constituencies which had been instrumental in its General Election victory in 1979. Subsequently, however, when a Cabinet committee met to discuss the DOI's paper on BL, Joseph spoke against it, stating 'Prime Minister, I am afraid that after much reflection I have to disagree with the arguments of my own department, and urge you not to let this go through' (Keegan, 1984, p. 176). Despite offering what Joseph later described as 'a very strong lead' for a 'desubsidising policy' (Joseph, 1987, p. 30), the Cabinet was more persuaded by the DOI's arguments about the political implications of BL's collapse, and thus the company was saved with an injection of almost £1 billion of taxpayers' money. Joseph has latterly conceded his lack of resolve at the time to adhere to his convictions concerning the entrepreneur-driven, enterprise culture solution to British decline, admitting that 'The test was Leyland: I didn't have the conviction and moral courage to assume that, had I put successfully the argument to desubsidise, the investment and risk-taking to absorb many of the jobs would have been forthcoming. That's the reason for the half-heartedness of my policy' (Joseph, 1987, p. 30).

Given that the first Thatcher Government's industrial policies were preoccupied with firefighting in the nationalized industries, and the second Thatcher Government's industrial policies preoccupied with the privatization of some of these industries, notably British Telecom and British Gas, it was not until the third term of office that the highwater mark of the enterprise culture in industrial policy arrived with the appointment of Lord Young as Secretary of State at the Department of Trade and Industry (DTI). Young had already served as a part-time industrial advisor to Joseph at the DOI, helping to launch the Loan Guarantee Scheme which had initially provided loans of up to £5 000 to entrepreneurs unable to secure finance from the banks. He had subsequently served as Chairman of the

Manpower Services Commission, as Minister without Portfolio, and as Secretary of State for Employment. In each of these roles, Young had attempted to promote enterprise but using government resources. Ironically, when Young had first met Joseph at a fund-raising lunch in 1976 and volunteered to assist him, Joseph had tartly replied 'Why? ... you don't believe'. Nevertheless, despite his many schemes and policy initiatives, Young claimed to be a believer in Joseph's 'simple truth' that 'The state creates nothing but the climate for enterprise' (Young, 1990, p. 29).

Of all Thatcher's Cabinet ministers after Sir Keith Joseph, Lord Young provided the clearest articulation of the key role of the entrepreneur in the Thatcherite cultural explanation of British decline. In an address to a Conservative Political Centre meeting at the 1985 Conservative Party Conference, he spoke on the theme of 'Enterprise Regained' by focusing on 'the role of Enterprise, and those who practice it, the Entrepreneurs' (Young, 1985, p. 3). Young's contention was that Britain had 'voluntarily left the garden of enterprise' but should return. The accomplishment of this mission would be dependent on a prior understanding of British history since 1776. Entrepreneurs had been the cause and effect of the Industrial Revolution during what Young termed 'The Hundred Years of Enterprise' from 1776 to 1876. Unlike Sir Keith Joseph who had bemoaned the foreign origins of the term 'entrepreneur', Lord Young celebrated the fact that the word could at least 'be traced back in our language to the early fifteenth century'. The new entrepreneurs of the Industrial Revolution had been drawn from every social class and from all parts of Britain. As the source of innovation, their particular skill had lain in drawing together different factors of production and in being 'as much organisers as risk-takers'. Indeed, 'staggering progress was achieved by the small men – not the vast Corporations' (Young, 1985, p. 4).

But then came 'The Hundred Years of Empire' from 1876 to 1976, a period characterized by the 'antithesis of enterprise – typified by the disdain for "trade"' and the development of 'the gentrified corporate cosseted state'. Like Wiener and Barnett, Lord Young focuses on the expansion of the professions, Empire, civil servants, and the public schools which educated them as the actors which served to submerge the 'urge for enterprise ... in a search for stability' (Young, 1985, p. 5). Business was openly disparaged in popular fiction, 'there would be no profession of Entrepreneur', and unlike Germany, Britain would not develop 'systematic education in science and technology' to foster competitiveness in the technologies of the second industrial revolution. Instead, Britain developed cartel-forming professions and trade associations which encouraged the creation of a culture that fostered 'security at the expense of efficiency, the status quo at the expense of innovation' (Young, 1985, p. 7). The whole structure of the British economy therefore acted against individual entrepreneurial initiative for more than a century until the denouement under a Labour Government in 1976 of a sterling crisis and the lesson of monetary discipline 'carried by the IMF' (Young,. 1985, p. 9).

To remedy Britain's anti-enterprise culture, Lord Young identified 'four conditions as vital to individual enterprise – stability in decision making, pro-enterprise attitudes, clear incentives, and less bureaucracy'. These prerequisites formed part of what he termed his 'strategic vision' for the restoration of an enterprise culture. At the same time, Young rejected 'the idea of an industrial strategy because of what that language implies', that is, the possession by government of some special ability to pick which industries should be chosen for development and how they then be developed. His strategic vision would fill the vacuum in government industrial policy created by the absence of an industrial strategy. On arrival at that the DTI, Lord Young announced to the media that he wanted his department to become the 'Department of Wealth Creation' and, as he later admitted in his memoirs, he would soon become 'obsessed with the reorganisation of the DTI and could think of little else than how best to accomplish it (Young, 1990, p. 254). Indeed, Young regarded his tenure at the DTI as an adventure (Young, 1990, p. 321). His plans for the DTI and strategic vision for restoring enterprise in Britain were crystallized in January 1988 in the White Paper, *DTI – The Department for Enterprise*. This document achieved, in industrial policy terms, many of the political objectives which Sir Keith Joseph had been unable to advance beyond rhetoric during his tenure as Secretary of State at the DOI.

The White Paper repeated Lord Young's earlier belief that since 1870 an absence of enterprise had played a major role in the relative economic decline of Britain, largely because of the distortion of the process of entrepreneurial decision-making by the ill-conceived interventions of successive postwar governments (DTI, 1988, p. 1). However, the turning point for Britain had occurred in 1979, with the election of a government committed to the control of inflation and the encouragement of enterprise. In future, the keynote of DTI policies would be enterprise, combating the 'past anti-enterprise bias of British culture' through open markets and individuals (DTI, 1988, pp. 2–3). The DTI would 'champion all the people who make it happen, rather than just individual sectors, industries or companies' (DTI, 1988, p. ii). It would also no longer provide innovation grant assistance to individual companies, or provide large-scale assistance for the information technology and space industries, despite the demands for strategies for both these sectors from interested industrial parties and select committee reports. As an alternative, Lord Young launched the

DTI's Enterprise Initiative, a package of consultancy schemes for companies with a maximum of 500 employees, to assist their development in fields such as marketing, business development, design and quality. Young's passion for using the DTI's budget as a vehicle for promoting the restoration of an enterprise culture in Britain was not to be shared by either of his immediate successors at the DTI. Both Nicholas Ridley and Peter Lilley were to demonstrate their belief that the best way to promote entrepreneurship was to further roll back the frontiers of state intervention, including those of the DTI. On his appointment, for example, Ridley acidly commented, 'Damn all to do and 20 000 civil servants to help me' (*The Independent on Sunday*, 7 March, 1993). He may have overestimated the number of civil servants in his employ but no one was left in any doubt as to Ridley's intentions.

Whilst the notion of the enterprise culture may have resonated through many Government policies during the 1980s, there is little evidence to suggest that it has succeeded in its objective of stemming British decline. The Thatcher Governments claimed that they would create a stable economic climate in which entrepreneurs would be able to invest in new and existing business ventures with confidence. In reality, the domestic economy moved from deep recession to an unsustainable consumer and property-led economic boom and then back to a further and even deeper recession within the space of only eleven years. Thus, for example, although new company formations increased from 96 190 in 1983 to 130 748 in 1989, as the severest recession in the postwar period took its full toll of entrepreneurs, company formations fell back to 107 375 in 1992 (*Financial Times*, 11 January, 1993). It was naive in the extreme to expect small businesses to be able to generate sufficient jobs to be able to cut unemployment when large manufacturing companies were 'hollowing out' their workforces at the rate of many tens of thousands per year. At the same time, the Thatcher Governments' policies of privatization, financial deregulation, and an open market for takeovers, mergers and management buy-outs, ensured that the safest and easiest investments would tend to be in established companies rather than in new innovative businesses where the degree of risk and uncertainty for investors would be much greater.

Whilst it was wholly realistic to expect redundant workers to set up their own businesses in the services or construction sectors, it was entirely unrealistic to expect them to be the source of a wave of innovations that would enable Britain to re-enter lost markets for manufactures and thereby reduce the growing balance of payments deficit at the end of the 1980s. The failure of the Thatcher Governments to match even the wretched record for long-term growth of industrial output of their predecessors suggests that fault may have lain with the whole notion of the enterprise culture as an explanation of the causes of British decline. Perhaps the central problem with the thesis of the enterprise culture which has never yet been either satisfactorily explored or accounted for is that of the missing years between 1870 and 1945. For whilst the thesis has been able to identify an ideal 'Golden Age' of British entrepreneurship from 1770 to 1870, and a period of national decline from 1945 to 1979 caused by a culture of over dependency of individuals and businesses on state subsidies and intervention, the Thatcherite analysis of the development of the modern British economy has never provided a satisfactory explanation of developments in between these two eras. However, for many economic historians the period between 1870 and 1914, known as the climacteric, is the most important for understanding the origins of British decline.

There is far from agreement amongst historians that a deficiency in entrepreneurship was the root cause of British decline before the First World War. In his seminal account of this period, the eminent economic historian Sidney Pollard has concluded that the debate about entrepreneurship amongst economic historians has been fundamentally misconceived in many cases because Britain was not a backward country in the late nineteenth century. For Pollard, traditionalism did not obstruct the wholehearted pursuit of profitable business opportunities by entrepreneurs in Britain. On the contrary, Britain was the most advanced industrial nation in the world because of the very weakness of traditionalism and the strength of the indigenous commercial spirit. Britain remained the world leader in many of the most important industrial and service markets up until the outbreak of the First World War, and if there was economic or industrial failure in specific contexts in certain sectors, it was because of weakness in British society rather than a failure of entrepreneurship (Pollard, 1989, p. 265). Peter Payne's evaluation of the causes of British decline in the late nineteenth century is that 'British entrepreneurs did not fail, but that there was a failure of industrial entrepreneurship'. Whilst individual businessmen could not be condemned for the manner in which they managed their own businesses, Payne suggests that as a whole British industry failed to develop sufficient new technologies and industries with the potential for high levels of productivity (Payne, 1990, p. 42).

Simply omitting a detailed consideration of the seventy-five years of British economic history between 1870 and 1945, including the impact on the role of the state and public attitudes and expectations of two devastating world wars, does not in itself resolve the difficulty of determining the contribution of entrepreneurship to national economic decline relative to other contributory factors. The fact that Thatcherism had avoided such historical, theoretical and practical complexities was belatedly acknowledged by Lord Joseph after he had left the second Thatcher

Government. He conceded that he was not aware of any 'research work emphasising the connection between entrepreneurship, good management and productivity on the one hand and jobs, prosperity and the money available for public services on the other (Joseph, 1989, p. 14). In a similar vein, there appears to be nothing in the public domain that demonstrates that there was a thorough prepatory analysis by the DTI of the condition of entrepreneurship in Britain prior to the launch of *DTI – The Department for Enterprise* and Lord Young's Enterprise Initiative. This serves merely to confirm that both the critique of state intervention developed at the Centre for Policy Studies during the late 1970s, which underlay the enterprise culture thesis, and a great deal of the subsequent economic and industrial policy of the 1980s, were founded upon an incomplete and, at the very least, highly contentious interpretation of modern British history. At the same time, it reveals the importance of ideas for political economy, and how, in contemporary Britain, a political ideology based as much upon instinct and whim as carefully considered analysis can have a major influence upon the conduct of public policy.

A DOMESTIC IMPERIAL CULTURE?

The performance of the British economy in the period since the demise of Margaret Thatcher as Prime Minister and leader of the Conservative Party in November 1990, has demonstrated that her attempts to recreate an enterprise culture in Britain have not bequeathed to her successors a strong, entrepreneur-driven economy or a stable political settlement. On the contrary, the almost continual state of political crisis that has beset the Major Governments during their first four years in office, and the virtual elimination of Conservative parliamentary representation in Scotland, Wales, and now, after the recent local elections, of Conservative local authorities in many English regions, has raised the question of the very viability of the constitution of the United Kingdom itself. John Major has seen political advantage for his party and government in terms of a passionate defence of the Union and the state structures that sustain it. Michael Portillo, the Secretary of State for Employment, however, has seen attacks upon the integrity of the United Kingdom as evidence of the development of a new and damaging culture in Britain. In 'The New British Disease', his President's Lecture to the Conservative Way Forward Group on the 14th January 1994, Portillo identified what he claimed is 'one of the greatest threats that has ever confronted the British nation', that is, 'the New British Disease – the self-destructive sickness of national cynicism ... spread by the so-called opinion formers' (Portillo, 1994, p. 30). He claimed that this internal threat to Britain has sought to undermine 'our institutions', namely the monarchy, Parliament and Church and that there was a need 'to assert the value and the quality of the British way of life, and of British institutions' because this is what most Britons are proud of (Portillo, 1994, p. 36). Without the assertion of these values and institutions, Portillo has suggested that great damage might be inflicted upon Britain's future political and economic prospects.

The value of Portillo's lecture, as the Charter 88 activist Anthony Barnett has suggested, is that it has clarified the argument between those such as Portillo who believe that the institutions of the British state are vital to national well-being and capable of restoring prosperity, and that traditions such as tolerance must be sacrificed to preserve them, and those such as Barnett who believe that 'to conserve positive British traditions, of tolerance, probity, freedom, fairness and successful enterprise', institutional reform must be undertaken (Barnett, 1994, p. 18). Barnett has coined the term, the 'Empire State' to denote the 'arch of institutions, financial, commercial and military, that spanned the world' to govern the British Empire (Barnett, 1994, p. 11). In this arch, the monarchy, and ceremonies such as the State Opening of Parliament, became for the Victorians 'a dramatic and novel means of expressing British purpose and prowess, of claiming a world role' (Barnett, 1994, p. 11). Thus, 'The Empire State is systemic, its anachronisms a formidable set of institutions linked by their procedures to each other ... an exceptionally concentrated system of sovereignty, whose power is symbolized but not exercised by the monarchy' (Barnett, 1994, p.34). As Barnett suggests, 'We have inherited an Empire State and having lost the empire and entered Europe, we are in urgent need of a non-Empire State' (Barnett, 1994, p. 35).

Barnett contends that 'what may once have been a modern machine, republican in spirit behind the royal decoration, is no more. Today, the decoration has become flesh' (Barnett, 1994, p. 30). The Empire State was built by the 'gentlemanly capitalists' of the City of London and during the latter half of the nineteenth century was extended to incorporate a reformed civil service and local government, with the public schools and the clubs of Pall Mall acting as guardians of 'the culture and behaviour of the political elite of gentlemanly capitalists'. However, the central instruments of the Empire State were remade from the traditional material of the monarchy and the Palace of Westminster such that 'Everything else – army, church, judiciary, broadcasting, industry and foreign policy – would be subordinated to it' (Barnett, 1994, p. 32). In this regard, Barnett cites the work of Bulpitt (Bulpitt, 1983), who has asserted that the framework for local government in Britain was modeled on the practice of colonial indirect rule, where 'The centre, Whitehall and Westminster, in true imperial fashion jealously guarded high politics, such as overall fiscal control, and relations between the parts' and 'The locals did not consider policy, whether in energy, transport or housing. Their task was the time consuming "low" detail of handling the natives face to face' (Barnett, 1994, p. 33).

In the post-war period, so many governing structures of British colonialism have been dismantled externally but the question of whether mere administrative reorganization of the centralized, imperial British state might be insufficient in itself to remedy national decline has rarely penetrated debates in mainstream party politics. Above all else, the assumption has remained that irrespective of the modernization strategy being proposed, it should be implemented within the parameters of Westminster and Whitehall. Their political and administrative sovereignty has remained largely unchallenged, but as Barnett has correctly pointed out, 'We all inhabit a Union in Britain, a union forged in empire. In the aftermath of the Empire the Union will have to be renegotiated if cohabitation is to continue' (Barnett, 1994, p. 44). Furthermore, he has concluded that 'The key issue is not the royals it is the system, what I have called the Empire State' which 'is not a matter of history. It is Britain's constitution. Immensely powerful and successful in its time, its time is up' (Barnett, 1994, pp. 51, 53). For Barnett, the relative economic decline of Britain is not a matter of cultural weakness as Wiener has suggested but rather the product of the institutions of the Empire State, 'a machinery of rule, a machinery that governs the way we are governed' (Barnett, 1994, p. 53).

The most discernible product of the Empire State for the governance of Britain has been the growth in the number of quangos (quasi-autonomous non-governmental organizations). In their democratic audit of the United Kingdom, Weir and Hall have identified no fewer than 5,521 non-elected executive bodies (EGO's) in the UK of which 443 operate at the national level, 355 at regional level, and 4,723 at local level. In 1992–93, these EGO's. spent £46.65 billion (£48.1 billion at 1994 prices) of taxpayers' money, which represents a 24 per cent increase in real terms over the £35.20 billion spent (in constant 1992–93 prices) in 1978–79 at the time when the first Thatcher government was campaigning and being elected on the platform of a promise to roll back the frontiers of the quango state (Weir and Hall, 1994, p. 9). Weir and Hall note that this means that EGO's now spend around one-third of total central government public expenditure without being directly responsible to the public through effective mechanisms of accountability. More recently, the Major Government's own statistics for quangos, which vastly underestimate the extent of quangoland by failing to acknowledge most local quangos, have revealed that funding for quangos has doubled in real terms since the election of the first Thatcher Government. Moreover, 1994 witnessed the largest annual rise in the budgets for executive bodies since 1979, with spending increasing from £15.4 billion in 1993 to £18.3 billion in 1994. These figures do not include National Health Service or other appointed bodies, such as Training and Enterprise Councils, which spend large amounts of public money. Nevertheless, it does demonstrate that the government is now spending almost half as much as the total grant to elected local government in England. At the same time, the number of appointees to these bodies has increased from 41 011 in 1993 to 42 876 in 1994 (*Financial Times*, 7 February, 1995).

As Foster has recently suggested, the quango state in England has taken on the shape and culture of a colonial government. The ten senior civil servants who act as directors of Whitehall's regional offices have been described by Peter Kilfoyle, the Labour MP for Liverpool Walton, as 'a viceroy appointed by a far-away power, with little or no regard for local opinion or democratic rights' (*Independent on Sunday*, 5 February, 1995). These regional viceroys possess sole responsibility for implementing at the regional level most of the policies of four Whitehall departments, namely Employment, Environment, Transport and DTI, and also administer the £1.4 billion Single Regeneration Budget. The message from London to the regions of England is clear. The people of England are not to be trusted or permitted to govern themselves if that means locally or regionally accountable government. As the frontiers of the democratic state have been rolled back during the 1980s and 1990s, the frontiers of the unaccountable, appointed administrative state have been rolled forward. Nowhere is there a clearer expression of the tensions since 1979 between the Conservative Governments' enthusiasm for unleashing the full force of a deregulated market and their enduring commitment to the preservation of national sovereignty over the levers of economic policy. However, David Hunt, the Minister for Public Service, has ruled out any major reforms to the quangos and other unelected bodies that govern England, and has also rejected Opposition claims that such appointments have disproportionately benefited supporters of the Conservative Party. Given the enduring unpopularity of the Major Government in which he serves, Hunt is risking a further acceleration in the development of a political culture in Britain in which the legitimacy of the existing institutions of the state is increasingly called into question by a sceptical and disillusioned electorate. The culture of national cynicism is not necessarily confined, as Portillo has suggested, to an unrepresentative elite of opinion-formers amongst the chattering classes. It may well reflect the prevalence of a much deeper-seated attitude amongst the British people about the capacity of their existing political institutions to address even the symptoms let alone the causes of national decline. For the nations of Britain, the threat to their future economic prosperity may reside less with the consequences of greater political union within the European Union, as asserted by the Conservatives, and more with the stifling effect on their enterprise and initiative of the outmoded domestic political union that is the United Kingdom.

CONCLUSION

It should therefore not be assumed that the debate about constitutional reform in Britain is irrelevant or of no more than marginal importance to the debate about how to remedy Britain's relative economic decline (even though the connection between the two debates has too rarely been established by advocates of constitutional reform). The structure of political and administrative institutions that governs the market in any particular national economy will have a major influence on the sort of business culture that is created for the generation of wealth. There is, for example, considerable evidence to suggest that a federal and decentralized system of government, such as that practised in Germany during the postwar period, has often been mirrored by a parallel decentralization of financial and economic power. This tendency for financial power to follow political and administrative power has been particularly beneficial for the financing of small and medium-sized companies in Germany by regional development banks (Mullineux, 1994; Hutton, 1995). Given that the idea of decentralization runs counter to the Thatcher and Major Governments' defence and accentuation of centralized political sovereignty in Westminster and Whitehall, the prospects for constitutional change before the next General Election appear remote. However, it is the very refusal to contemplate the notion of even limited constitutional reform in the short term which may guarantee more fundamental constitutional change in Britain in the longer term.

What is more likely is that, despite their frequently dubious empirical and theoretical basis, and the fact, most notably in the case of the Thatcherite enterprise culture, that they tend to gloss over the great complexity of modern British history, explanations of Britain's relative economic decline which invoke the damaging impact of national culture will remain attractive. Their enduring popularity is largely attributable, as Robbins has suggested, to the fact that cultural explanations offer monocausal simplicity both in their analysis of, and their prescriptions for remedying, British decline (Robbins, 1990, p. 85). Their simplistic conclusion that Britain needs an immediate and fundamental change in its attitudes towards its scientists, engineers or entrepreneurs ignores the profound difficulty in bringing about   peacetime revolutions when operating within the constraints of a liberal democracy. Unfortunately, this same argument applies to those advocating constitutional reform in Britain, especially given the fact that reform of one key institution is likely to invite reform of others, thereby setting in motion a political domino effect which may well distract and divert governmental attention and resources from less ambitious but more effective means of improving national economic performance.

The fact that successive British Social Attitudes surveys during the late 1980s revealed a recurrent reluctence of the British people to jettison their widespread support for the institutions of the postwar welfare state demonstrates that not even the most determined use of legislation and other forms of state intervention over more than a decade can guarantee that a government will bring about attitudinal change, let alone in the direction that it intended. If the economic historian was seeking to explain absolute decline then, as Edgerton has contended, cultural explanations might be appropriate (Edgerton, 1987, p. 85). But given that Britain's economic decline is at least for the present relative rather than absolute, the key task for political economy in contemporary Britain lies in the more subtle and more demanding process of being able to account for the differences in economic performance between Britain and its more successful competitors. In this regard, monocausal cultural explanations have only limited utility. However, as Robbins has concluded, they should not yet be dismissed out of hand because there is a need for the cultural thesis to be explored comparatively (Robbins, 1990, p. 21). They may yet contribute more to the debate about Britain's decline than the provision of a convenient and seductive analytical short-cut for politicians, business leaders, and select committees seeking to blanket their respective technocratic remedies for British decline behind an ideological smokescreen.

REFERENCES

ABCC (1992), *A Basis for an Industrial Policy* (London: Association of British Chambers of Commerce).

Barnett, A. (1994), 'The Empire State' in Barnett, A. (ed.), *Power and the Throne: The Monarchy Debate* (London: Vintage).

Barnett, C. (1986), *The Audit of War: The Illusion and Reality of Britain as a Great Nation* (London: Macmillan).

Baxendale, J. (1986), 'Review. Martin Wiener: English Culture and the Decline of the Industrial Spirit, 1850–1980', *History Workshop Journal*, 21, pp. 171–4.

Bulpitt, J. (1983), *Territory and Power in the United Kingdom: an Interpretation,* (Manchester: Manchester University Press).

Carey, P. (1980), 'UK industry in the 1980s', *Proceedings of the Institute of Mechanical Engineers*, 193, pp. 439–46.

Child, J., M. Fores, I. Glover and P. Lawrence (1983), 'A price to pay? Professionalism and work organisation in Britain and West Germany', *Sociology*, 17, 1, pp. 63–78.

Child, J., M. Fores, I. Glover and P. Lawrence (1986), 'Professionalism and work organisation: reply to McCormick', *Sociology*, 20, 4, pp. 607–13.

Dahrendorf, R. (1982), *On Britain* (London: British Broadcasting Corporation).

DTI (1987), *Civil Research and Development,* Government Response to the First Report of the House of Lords Select Committee on Science and Technology, 1986–87 Session, Cmnd 185 (London: HMSO).

DTI (1988), *DTI – The Department for Enterprise* (London: HMSO).

Donoughue, B. (1987), *Prime Minister: The Conduct of Policy under Harold Wilson and James Callaghan* (London: Jonathan Cape).

Edgerton, D. (1987), 'Science and technology in British business history', *Business History*, 29, 4, pp. 84–99.

EEF (1992), *Industrial Strategy: Proposals for Recovery and Sustained Growth* (London: Engineering Employers Federation).

Eltis, W., D. Fraser and J. Ip (1992), 'The Engineering Challenge' in Keating, G. (ed.), *The State of the Economy 1992* (London: Institute of Economic Affairs).

Filer, D. (1992), 'Public perception of the entrepreneur', *Technology, Innovation and Society*, pp. 3–6.

Freeman, C. (1987), *Technology Policy and Economic Performance* (London: Pinter).

Harvie, C. (1985), 'Liturgies of national decadence: Wiener, Dahrendorf and the British crisis', *Cencrastus*, 21, pp. 17–23.

Heelas, P. and P. Morris (eds.) (1992), *The Values of the Enterprise Culture: The Moral Debate* (London: Routledge).

Hennessy, P. (1989), *Whitehall* (London: Collins).

Hennessy, P. and C. Anstey (1991), *From Clogs to Clogs? Britain's Relative Economic Decline since 1851* (Glasgow: Strathclyde Papers on Government and Politics in association with 'Analysis', BBC News and Current Affairs).

Hewison, R. (1987), *The Heritage Industry: Britain in a climate of decline* (London: Methuen).

HMSO (1963), *Report of the Committee on Higher Education*, Cmnd 2171 (London: HMSO).

HMSO (1980), *Engineering our Future,* Report of the Committee of Inquiry into the Engineering Profession, Cmnd 7794 (London: HMSO).

HMSO (1993), *Realising our Potential: A Strategy for Science, Engineering and Technology,* Cmnd 2250 (London: HMSO).

Hobsbawm, E. (1969), *Industry and Empire: From 1750 to the Present Day* (Harmondsworth: Penguin).

House of Lords (1982), *Science and Government,* Report of the House of Lords Select Committee on Science and Technology, 1981–82 Session, HL20–1 (London: HMSO).

House of Lords (1983), *Engineering Research and Development,* Report of the House of Lords Select Committee on Science and Technology, 1982–83 Session, HL89 (London: HMSO).

House of Lords (1985), *Overseas Trade,* Report of the House of Lords Select Committee, 1984–85 Session, HL238–1 (London: HMSO).

House of Lords (1986), *Civil Research and Development,* Report of the House of Lords Select Committee on Science and Technology, 1986–87 Session, HL20–1 (London: HMSO).

House of Lords (1987), *UK Space Policy,* Report of the Select Committee on Science and Technology, 1987–88 Session, HL41–2 (London: HMSO).

House of Lords (1991), *Innovation in Manufacturing Industry,* Report of the House of Lords Select Committee on Science and Technology, 1990–91 Session, HL18–19 (London: HMSO).

Hutton, S. and P. Lawrence (1981), *German Engineers: The Anatomy of a Profession* (Oxford: Clarendon).

Hutton, W. (1995), *The State We're In* (London: Jonathan Cape).

Ince, M. (1988), 'Politics and money in British science', *Higher Education Quarterly*, 42, 1, pp. 4–19.

Jordan, G. (1992), *Engineers and Professional Self-Regulation: From the Finniston Committee to the Engineering Council* (Oxford: Clarendon Press).

Joseph, K. (1987), Escaping the Chrysalis of Statism', Contemporary Record, Spring, pp. 26–30.

Joseph, K. (1989), 'One-eyed vision', *Policy Studies*, 10, 2, pp. 12–14.

Kavanagh, D. (1987), 'Political Culture' in Bogdanor, V. (ed.), *Blackwell Encyclopedia of Political Institutions* (Oxford: Basil Blackwell).

Kealey, T. (1989), *Science Fiction and the True Way to Save British Science* (London: Centre for Policy Studies).

Keat, R. and N. Abercrombie (eds.) (1991), *Enterprise Culture* (London: Routledge).

Keegan, W. (1984), *Mrs Thatcher's Economic Experiment* (Harmondsworth: Penguin).

Kinnock, N. (1990), 'Science and our future', *Science in Parliament*, 47, 2, pp. 84–6.

Labour Party (1989), *Meet the Challenge Make the Change: A New Agenda for Britain* (London: The Labour Party).

Labour Party (1990), *Looking to the Future* (London: The Labour Party).

Labour Party (1991), *Modern Manufacturing Strength* (London: The Labour Party).

Labour Party (1992), *It's Time to Get Britain Working Again: Labour's Election Manifesto* (London: The Labour Party).

Labour Party (1993), *Making Britain's Future* (London: The Labour Party).

Lilley, P. (1991), 'Innovation, Competition and Culture', speech delivered by the Secretary of State for Trade and Industry at the University of Warwick, 21 May (London: Department of Trade and Industry).

Morris, P. (1991), 'Freeing the Spirit of Enterprise: The Genesis and Development of the Concept of the Enterprise Culture', in Keat, R. and N. Abercrombie (eds.), *Enterprise Culture* (London: Routledge).

Moulton, A. (1993), 'Public perception of the engineer', *Technology, Innovation and Society*, pp. 7–9.

MSF (1992), *Manufacturing Matters: The Need for a National Industrial Strategy* (London: Manufacturing, Science, Finance Union).

Mullineux, A. (1994), *Small and Medium-sized Enterprise (SME) Financing in the UK: Lessons from Germany* (London: Anglo-German Foundation).

Noble, D. (1987), *Science, Culture and Wealth: The 1987 Lloyd-Roberts Lecture* (Oxford: Save British Science).

Olson, M. (1982), *The Rise and Decline of Nations* (New Haven, Connecticut: Yale University Press).

Payne, P. (1990), 'Entrepreneurship and British Economic Decline', in Collins, B. and K. Robbins (eds.), *British Culture and Economic Decline* (London: Weidenfeld and Nicolson).

Pollard, S. (1989), *Britain's Prime and Britain's Decline: The British Economy 1870–1914* (London: Edward Arnold).

Portillo, M. (1994), *Clear Blue Water: A Compendium of Speeches and Interviews given by the Rt. Hon. Michael Portillo MP* (London: Conservative Way Forward).

Raven, J. (1989), 'British history and the enterprise culture', *Past and Present*, 123, pp. 178–204.

Robbins, K. (1990), 'British Culture versus British Industry', in Collins, B. and K. Robbins (eds.), *British Culture and Economic Decline* (London: Weidenfeld and Nicolson).

Roderick, G. and M. Stephens (eds.) (1981), *Where did we go Wrong? Industrial Performance, Education and the Economy in Victorian Britain* (Lewes: The Falmer Press).

Roderick, G. and M. Stephens (eds.) (1982), *The British Malaise: Industrial Performance, Education and Training in Britain Today* (Lewes: The Falmer Press).

Rubinstein, W.D. (1993), *Capitalism, Culture and Decline in Britain, 1750–1990* (London: Routledge).

Sampson, A. (1962), *Anatomy of Britain* (London: Hodder and Stoughton).

Sampson, A. (1993), 'Stop doing the dirty on Britain's engineers', *Management Today*, February, pp. 30–6.

Samuel, R. (1995), *Theatres of Memory* (London: Verso).

Sanderson, M. (1972), *The Universities and British Industry, 1850–1980* (London: Routledge).

Save British Science (1990), *British Science: Benchmarks for the Year 2000* (Oxford: Save British Science).

Simpson, J. and E. Wiener (1989), *The Oxford English Dictionary: Volume IV* (Oxford: Clarendon Press).

Smith, C. (1990), 'How are engineers formed? Professionals, nation and class politics', *Work, Employment and Society*, 3, 4, pp. 451–70.

Snow, C.P. (1965), *The Two Cultures and a Second Look* (Cambridge: Cambridge University Press).

Thatcher, M. (1990), '50th Anniversary Lecture', *Science in Parliament*, 47, 1, pp. 2–5.

Walker, W. and M. Sharp (1991a), 'Thatcherism and technical advance: reform without progress? Part I: The historical background', *Political Quarterly*, 62, 2, pp. 262–72.

Walker, W. and M. Sharp (1991b), 'Thatcherism and technical advance: reform without progress? Part II: The Thatcher legacy', *Political Quarterly*, 62, 3, pp. 318–29.

Weir, S. and W. Hall (eds.), *Ego Trip: Extra-governmental Organisations in the United Kingdom and their Accountability* (London: The Charter 88 Trust).

Wiener, M. (1981), *English Culture and the Decline of the Industrial Spirit, 1850–1980* (Harmondsworth: Penguin).

Wigley, J. and C. Lipman (1992), *The Enterprise Economy* (London: Macmillan).

Wright, P. (1985), *On Living in an Old Country: The National Past in Contemporary Britain* (London: Verso).

Young, Lord (1985), *Enterprise Regained* (London: Conservative Political Centre).

Young, Lord (1990), *The Enterprise Years: A Businessman in the Cabinet* (London: Headline).

4. Industrial Policy and British Decline

Simon Lee

INTRODUCTION

The influential American industrial policy analyst, Chalmers Johnson, has defined industrial policy as 'a summary term for the activities of government that are intended to develop or retrench various industries in a national economy in order to maintain global competitiveness' (Johnson, 1984, p. 7). For Johnson, and for many advocates of state-led industrial modernization programmes, industrial policy forms the third side of an economic policy triangle. The two other sides of the industrial policy triangle are composed of a government's monetary policies, that is, its policies with regard to the control of the money supply, the rate of inflation, the level of interest and exchange rates, and its fiscal policies, that is, its policies with regard to public expenditure and the level of direct and indirect taxation. In the specific instance of Britain, it has been widely asserted that successive governments, whether Labour or Conservative, have operated economic policies without the industrial policy side of the economic policy triangle. Thus, for example, Cowling and Sugden have contended that British economic policy during the twentieth century 'has been characterized by the absence of a coherent industrial strategy' (Cowling and Sugden, 1993, p. 83). Furthermore, when industrial policies have been initiated, it has been suggested that they have been sacrificed or subordinated to the demands of monetary and fiscal policies and that, consequently, industrial modernization in Britain has been frustrated (Newton and Porter, 1988).

The literature on industrial policy has also widely portrayed Britain's political and administrative elites as characteristically anti-industrial and myopic in their attitudes towards industrial development. These elites have also been depicted as operating against the backdrop of a political process whose essentially dogmatic and short-term orientation has mitigated against the longer term perspective on economic development which advocates of proactive industrial policies have held to be a prerequisite of effective state intervention. For example, in the aftermath of Margaret Thatcher's resignation as Prime Minister, Leadbeater identified 'a tacit conspiracy between the Labour and Conservative leaderships to return British politics to a dull, uninspiring, unambitious pragmatism – a kind of realistic defeatism in the face of the scale of Britain's difficulties' (Leadbeater, 1991, p. 15). Like many others, Leadbeater's remedy for Britain's 'difficulties' is the urgent creation of a strategic modernizing consensus with long-term ambitions to transform Britain's institutions, customs and culture. However, this chapter will seek to demonstrate that this modernization agenda is inherently flawed, not least because it never identifies how the deeply divided, ideologically riven British political culture which it despises is to be suddenly transformed into a united force which places modernization unequivocally at the top of the domestic political agenda.

Leadbeater may have portrayed the contemporary British political elite as being characterized by a 'dull, uninspiring, unambitious pragmatism' but this chapter will contend instead that his prescriptions and those of his fellow industrial modernizers have been laced with another form of pragmatism. 'Technocratic pragmatism' is a concept that was originally applied by the Russian Marxist commentator, Kagarlitsky, to the politics of the declining Soviet empire (Kagarlitsky, 1990). However, the suggestion here is that technocratic pragmatism is a concept that may also be gainfully employed to characterize the politics of another declining imperial power, namely Britain. Such is the pervasiveness of technocratic pragmatism that it has underpinned many of the prescriptions for industrial renewal of the non-Thatcherite Right, the social democratic Centre, and the Marxist and non-Marxist Left. It has also enveloped a considerable number of academics and business leaders of indeterminate party political affiliation. What has been common to all is a belief that the problems of British decline can be surmounted if only politicians will cast aside their ideological differences, sit down together around the conference table or in some form of industrial forum, and rationally discuss how industrial modernization can best be achieved.

This chapter asserts that the technocratic pragmatists' modernization agenda is at best a forlorn hope, and at worst, a crude betrayal of the wider population. A brief history of postwar industrial policy in Britain is also provided to illustrate that it is wrong for the technocratic pragmatists to suggest that Britain has been characterized by the absence of an industrial strategy. On the contrary, whilst it is true that Britain's political and administrative elites have failed to deliver the technocratic blueprint for civil industries that the technocratic pragmatists have demanded, postwar

British history has been littered with attempts by successive governments to implement various industrial modernization strategies. Indeed, Thatcherism itself should be understood as a reaction to, and a critique of, these very strategies. At the same time, it will be suggested that by virtue of their attachment to an ideology of 'liberal militarism' (Edgerton, 1991a), which has been based upon the defence of British interests through the development of high-technology weaponry, British governments have pursued a technocratic industrial policy to support defence manufacturers. During the tenure of the Thatcher and Major Governments in particular, this continuing bias towards defence industries has not only resulted in the payment of huge subsidies in the form of export credits to autocratic regimes but also has generated a series of political scandals that has brought the British political system into disrepute. This chapter therefore seeks to contrast two important but contending theses in the literature on industrial policy and relative economic decline. The first is the long-standing thesis, put forward by technocratic pragmatism in its various conceptual guises, concerning the absence from Britain of the personnel and institutions required to implement a technocratic modernization strategy. The second is the more recent, and arguably more enlightening, thesis of liberal militarism which challenges the assumptions about the historiography of the British state underlying technocratic pragmatism, and which instead identifies the structures and institutions of a technocratic, modernizing state, but in the sphere primarily of defence rather than civil industries. The conclusion drawn is that the pursuit of liberal militarism has sustained an order of priorities that has severely damaged Britain's long-term industrial performance. Above all else, it has enabled the maintenance of the myth of Britain as a Great Power to be projected overseas even though the reality of domestic deindustrialization and social division has demanded an urgent programme of industrial and social renewal.

TECHNOCRATIC PRAGMATISM

Technocracy has been defined as 'a system of governance in which technically trained experts rule by virtue of their specialist knowledge and position in dominant political and economic institutions' (Fischer, 1990, pp. 17–18). However, Fischer has asserted that technocracy 'is more than expertise per se' and constitutes a reference to 'the adaptation of expertise to the tasks of government' such that technical solutions to political problems are promoted and expertise regarded as the dominant basis for organizing political power (Fischer, 1990, p. 18). As it exists, the pattern of largely incremental policy making in contemporary liberal democracies has been regarded by technocrats as 'a nightmare of irrationality – a system of government perpetually generating ineffective policies that mainly compound the very problems they seek to solve'. Politics has been a problem rather than a solution to societal problems, but one which 'may be surmounted by redefining political issues in scientific and technical terms', a role for technically trained experts standing above the debilitating cancer of adversarial party politics (Fischer, 1990, p. 22). When this technocratic conception of politics has been applied to remedies for British decline, the assumption has been that national industrial salvation, in the form of a proactive industrial policy, would soon follow if only the British state was to be controlled and manipulated by a technically-trained elite rather than by successive governments of partisan and essentially anti-industrial politicians lacking the requisite knowledge and political will to engineer industrial modernization.

The conception of the state that has arisen from this 'emphasis on the rational coordination of institutional processes to the functional requirements of the productive system' is, as Fischer has contended, 'uniquely administrative or managerial'. The state has been viewed 'as a positive instrument in the pursuit of economic and social progress' because it is 'the only institution capable of engaging in comprehensive systemwide planning and management' (Fischer, 1990, p. 25). At the same time, this administrative conception of the state has been located by the technocrat within a systems approach to politics, where the search is for overarching concepts and 'general laws' that govern all systems, and where the technical side of economic problems is emphasized over their social and political dimensions. In the industrial policy literature, the three most common overarching concepts that have been put forward are the 'coherent industrial strategy', the 'developmental state' and the 'national system of innovation'. It has also been a characteristic of such systems thinking that, as the system evolves, one of its parts emerges as a central and controlling agent for the system as a whole. In the specific instance of industrial policy in Britain, the Department of Trade and Industry (DTI) has most consistently been identified as the central and controlling agent in the policy process, not least because of its failure to measure up to the effectiveness of controlling agents in other national economies, most notably the Commissariat General du Plan (CGP) in France and the Ministry of International Trade and Industry (MITI) in Japan.

It was perhaps inevitable, given their concern with the improvement of national economic performance, that advocates of state-led industrial modernization should have looked to the examples provided by more successful national economies, in which the state is understood to have played a leading role, for their blueprint for Britain. Since the mid-nineteenth century, Germany has featured prominently in such blueprints, although academics and politicians alike have more recently enthused about aspects of French state policies and institutions in the 1960s, aspects of the Italian state in the 1970s, and aspects of the Japanese and other East Asian states in the 1980s. In sharp contrast, relatively few comparisons have been drawn between the performance of the British economy and that of the US, which until recently has been the most successful economy of the twentieth century. Indeed, a report from the CBI Manufacturing Advisory Group in 1991 pointed out that whilst UK manufacturing productivity was still some 30 per cent lower than in West Germany overall, and 35 per cent lower than in Japan, it was around 45 per cent lower than in the US (CBI, 1991, p. 5). Because of their peculiar conception of politics, which has reduced politics to a matter of technical control and manipulation of administrative structures, technocratic pragmatism has tended to regard Britain and the US as being precluded from strategic interventions because of their tradition of liberal political economy in general and their belief, at least rhetorically, in free (that is, free from state intervention) markets and the benefits of unfettered competition and entrepreneurship in particular.

A COHERENT NATIONAL INDUSTRIAL STRATEGY

The most common conceptual framework within which the technocratic agenda for industrial modernization has been clothed is that of the coherent national industrial strategy. The prefix 'coherent' is important because it expresses, on the one hand, the belief that previous state intervention has been poorly coordinated and therefore incoherent because of the presence of party political dogma and the absence of technical understanding of industry amongst governmental and administrative elites. On the other hand, the prefix 'coherent' expresses the self-confidence of the technocratic pragmatist that rational, well coordinated administration will be able to surmount the normal constraints of the policy process once ideology is cast aside. Although examples of the demand for a coherent national industrial strategy are legion, the assumptions that this approach to industrial modernization engenders are well illustrated in Keith Smith's *The British Economic Crisis* (Smith, 1984). Smith's concern is to escape what he regards as simplistic explanations of British decline and the panaceas for recovery that have been built upon them. He contends that Britain's political parties have concentrated on economic issues that are peripheral to Britain's 'real and urgent problems'. National recovery is dependent on a revival of manufacturing but there are two essential difficulties confronting 'policies for industrial reconstruction' that must be overcome. These are, firstly, economic problems associated with Britain's 'low and poorly directed R & D activity, and low industrial investment', and, secondly, problems concerning the choice of policy instruments to direct the economy. Smith asserts that Britain has not had experience of policies for reviving manufacturing, concentrating instead on the other two sides of Johnson's economic policy triangle, that is, monetary and fiscal policy, when what has been needed is 'a specific policy instrument to enhance the supply potential of the manufacturing sector: an industrial policy' (Smith, 1984, pp. 200–7).

Smith does not argue that Britain has never had an industrial policy for it has had 'some sort of industrial policy for many years'. What Britain has never embraced, although its economic crisis has so clearly demanded, has been the kind of industrial policy, for which he has a very clear blueprint, with four characteristics. It must be an industrial policy 'to which all other government policy requirements are subordinated, which possesses 'clearly articulated objectives for reconstruction', which is 'adequately funded and staffed', and which has 'powers sufficient to attain the objectives which are set for it' (Smith, 1984, p. 206). This is not an argument for 'a central planning agency on the East European model' for he has utter confidence in the capacity of the state to massively extend its powers without disrupting the normal workings of a modern liberal democracy. Given the depth of Britain's economic crisis, what could be more common-sensical, practical, hard-headed and rational? The central problem with this prescription, as with all agendas for remedying British decline which are rooted in a technocratic conception of politics, is that it completely ignores the fact that governments in liberal democracies find it difficult to deflect let alone insulate themselves from the constraints exerted upon their actions by the demands of a plethora of vested interests both within and outwith government itself. The technocratic pragmatist appears to assume that somehow the revelation of the depth of the British economic crisis will suddenly and so profoundly affect the attitudes and behaviour of all the competing interests within society that they will immediately and unconditionally accept that all else has to be subordinated to the task of industrial modernization. This assumption appears naive in the extreme but is the inevitable outcome of a reductionist conception of politics which chooses to bypass those aspects of liberal democracy which it finds dysfunctional.

Smith's first stipulation that industrial policy must be accorded clear primacy in governmental priorities echoes Pollard's concern about the Treasury's 'contempt for production' and the subordination of the 'real' quantities in the economy, such as goods and services, to 'symbolic' figures and quantities, such as prices, exchange rates and the balance of payments (Pollard, 1982, p. 72). In historical terms, the clearest example of such misguided priorities was the abandonment of the National Plan by the Wilson Government in 1965, and its sacrificing of the Department of Economic Affairs (DEA) on the altar of the Treasury's monetary orthodoxy and currency devaluation. The central problem with Smith's argument is that at no point does it address the critical question facing any incoming government, especially a Labour government, of how the inevitable and powerful constraints on economic policy exerted by the City of London and international markets are to be deflected or subordinated to the singular policy priority of industrial modernization. In a similar vein, Smith's second stipulation in his industrial policy blueprint is the need for clearly articulated objectives for reconstruction. However, there is no guarantee on past evidence that an agenda for reconstruction would be self-evident to all the powerful interests operating in the British economy. It unfortunately appears highly unlikely that the City of London, the CBI, the Institute of Directors (IOD), the trades unions, and the political parties themselves, would suddenly abandon their political differences for the sake of national reconstruction. The history of two world wars has shown that not even the sobering influence of total warfare has been sufficient to persuade some interests within British society to jettison their cherished political and economic objectives.

The third stipulation, that industrial policy must be adequately funded and staffed, is also problematic because adequacy itself is not a self-evident concept. Given the reluctance on the part of business and individuals to pay more tax, and given the difficulty that previous governments have encountered in seeking to cut or to reorient their spending away from existing programmes towards new priorities, the resources which might be available to a modernizing government might be less than what Smith might regard as adequate. A budget measured even in several tens of billions of pounds would be seeking to influence a national economy whose GDP is measured in several hundreds of billions. At the same time, private sector finance has shown itself to be extremely reluctant to become involved with government schemes unless it has been underwritten by government or guaranteed a high return. Furthermore, to attract top personnel from the private sector, with the requisite technical skills demanded by technocrats, would entail considerable expense and likely political controversy given the salaries paid to contemporary executives. Smith's final stipulation is that any industrial policy should have powers sufficient to attain its set objectives, but this leaves unresolved the crucial issue of the means by which these objectives would be secured. Britain is now a relatively small national economy operating in a much larger global market. Even if a domestic consensus about modernization was possible, it is extremely doubtful whether government possesses the policy instruments capable of changing the attitudes and performance of multinational corporations. At the same time, the legislative framework provided by Britain's membership of the European Union (EU) and international trade agreements, most notably the General Agreement on Tariffs and Trade (GATT), place major limitations on the forms of state intervention that are permissible in an era of liberalization and deregulation. Such constraints on policy may be regrettable but they cannot be ignored.

The first task of the industrial policy that Smith would introduce to Britain would be to stave off the collapse of the economy because of its attendant and disastrous implications for the financing of public services and the welfare state. To avert disaster, Smith identifies the development of a nucleus of dynamic, export-orientated manufacturing industries as the prerequisite for economic recovery. To implement this agenda, a national reconstruction agency would be created whose central function would be the coordination and, where necessary, the direction of a major programme of R & D in an integrated range of products. For Smith, this would avoid the mistakes of past industrial policy in Britain, namely the concentration of substantial economic support on essentially declining industries together with the founding of crucial decisions on 'fantasies about Britain's economic and political place in the world, rather than according to commercial and economic criteria' (Smith, 1984, pp. 207–11). The reason that this agenda might work in Britain is the fact that it has worked in Japan whose economy, Smith maintains, is in many respects similar to that of Britain. The basis of the similarity resides in both countries being small, heavily populated islands, with resource bases inadequate for industrial production (overlooking Britain's considerable fossil fuel reserves), and a consequent need to import food and raw materials. Both Britain and Japan have been heavily dependent on their export of manufactures, but only Japan has succeeded in exporting successfully (Smith, 1984, p. 211).

The major problem that arises at this juncture concerns the transferability of institutions from one national context to another. Smith claims that Japan's economic success is unique as indeed are the policy methods and institutions that it has used to address its problems. He concedes that a major problem lies in the separation of transplantable policies and institutions from culturally specific traits, but despite this uniqueness Smith is adamant that one essential lesson can and should be learned from Japan's postwar economic success. That lesson is the management and guidance of the Japanese economy by the state 'to a degree unparalleled in modern capitalism'. If anything is to be learned from Japan, 'it must be from its techniques of industrial policy' (Smith, 1984, pp. 214–5). In focusing on the role of the Japanese state, Smith asserts that it is difficult to exaggerate the importance of the Ministry of International Trade and Industry (MITI) to Japan's economic success. It is on MITI that Smith wishes to model his reconstruction agency because he sees MITI as having played the coordinating and developmental role that for him is the prerequisite for remedying industrial decline. He readily concedes that MITI is not omnipotent, but his depiction of MITI illustrates that it has fulfilled the four stipulations required of an effective industrial policy. MITI has helped create and sustain new industries, coordinated programmes of industrial modernization, controlled industrial capacity and prevented excessive investment in particular industries, and subsidized the phasing out and rationalization of older industries (Smith, 1984, pp. 221–4). There has in fact been a 'MITI formula' of restricted competition for nascent industries, major financial assistance, and the use of technology from many sources (Smith, 1984, p. 228).

One of the many difficulties of applying this 'MITI formula' to the contemporary British context is that its expiry date may long since have passed. It may have been acceptable in the post-war Bretton Woods era of unprecedented worldwide economic boom sustained by a seemingly unchallengeable American hegemony and largesse for tariff and especially non-tariff barriers to be erected to protect infant industries. In the current context of pressures for increasing liberalization of the world economy and the removal of state subsidies to industry, the political let alone the economic viability for Britain of the 'MITI formula' would appear limited and likely to attract the attention of the European Commissioner responsible for competition policy as soon as it was attempted. Smith also notes that the Japanese economy is 'research intensive', with comparatively few resources being devoted to military R & D, and considerable resources, which mostly originate from the private sector, being allocated to applied process and product development rather than basic science (Smith, 1984, p. 229). In Britain, the pattern and principal sources of R & D expenditure have been markedly different. Because of the state's pursuit of liberal militarism, until recently at least half of national expenditure on R & D has been devoted to the defence sector, and even during boom conditions, such as those of the late 1980s, the private sector in Britain has in general failed to match the level of R & D spending sustained by its principal competitors. Moreover, Japan has recently begun to invest heavily in basic science creating the danger that large Japanese companies may seek to privatize any major advances in science, and thereby exclude their industrial competitors from entry into certain lucrative, high-technology markets. Consequently, the past Japanese strategy of licensing modern technologies from other advanced economies and subsequently upgrading them through successive product and process innovations may not be open to British companies even if they were attentive to the possibilities of licensing. Where licensing is permitted in future, the technology licensed may well be either prohibitively expensive or outdated, thereby ensuring that obsolescence is built into the products of competitors to the Japanese.

In concluding his analysis of the Japanese economic miracle, Smith concedes that 'it is by no means the case that an economy like Britain either could or should imitate Japan'. Japanese economic growth, after all, 'occurred on the basis of a very poor society which completely lacked a welfare framework'. Nevertheless, Smith maintains that 'we should draw the appropriate conclusions', amongst which the most important is that 'MITI is simply the most extreme example of a phenomenon which is found in all of the most successful advanced economies, namely a coordinating mechanism which promotes innovation and investment across industries, and reduces the risks associated with such activity' (Smith, 1984, pp. 231–3). Smith cites Dore's contention that the unusual features of Japanese industrial policy are derived from the capacity of the bureaucracy, with its close links with industry, to 'generate a consensus around particular interpretations of the national interest'. Smith then argues that such a consensus is impossible 'without a framework of discussion, debate and bargaining' to establish objectives and means of achieving them through powerful policy instruments. Indeed, he suggests that consensus in Japan may be more of an effect of a successful economy than a cause (Smith, 1984, p. 233).

Irrespective of whether consensus or economic success is accorded primacy in the cause/effect equation in explanations of Japanese industrial performance, Smith is adamant that the 'appropriate conclusions' should be drawn for and about Britain. Recovery is dependent on overcoming the core economic problems surrounding R & D and more general investment in Britain (Smith, 1984, p. 236). Some succour may be taken from the Thatcher Governments because they had the great merit of at least recognizing the need for 'some kind of transformation of the British economy', but simultaneously the great demerit of relying on a laissez-faire policy of demand inflation rather than supply-side reconstruction. Smith's conclusion (admittedly, he was writing in the early 1980s) is quite upbeat about Britain in that he contends that the problem in Britain is 'not the principle of government activity in industrial development, but its scale'. All that is absent is effective coordination and purpose amongst leading sectors of British government, and government that takes the problem of industry seriously and makes the surmounting of these problems its core priority in economic policy. Fortunately, these issues are 'of course well known and accepted by most businesses and by all the sector working parties of the National Economic Development Council'. Furthermore, the requisite expertise is present within the existing structure and machinery of the British state and all that is lacking, once again, is intervention on a sufficient scale, with greater powers, and a sense of clearly articulated strategic direction (Smith, 1984, pp. 238–9).

British recovery for Smith is ultimately a matter of 'political imagination and commitment, and public acceptance of the costs involved' (Smith, 1984, pp. 239–40). This single phrase demonstrates most vividly all that is deficient when political economy is based on a narrow, technocratic conception of politics. It singularly fails to acknowledge the revolution in popular attitudes and expectations that would be required throughout British politics and society for the Japanese experience to be replicated in Britain. After all, even with all the benefits of a booming rather than recession-prone world economy and a highly deferential and compliant population motivated by the national humiliation and destruction wrought by the Second World War, it took Japan a quarter of a century to achieve its economic miracle. The absence of a welfare state in Japan, the irreconcilable differences in national cultures and temperament, from which institutions and practices that may be unique to that culture have been developed, are all mentioned by Smith but ultimately swept aside because his conception of politics reduces politics to the manipulation and control of administrative structures such as MITI and defines the underlying societal problem as a lack of political will at the centre of goverment to implement what to any rational, non-dogmatic individual should be a self-evident agenda for industrial revival. The conflicting priorities and absence of coordination in the political agenda that is often served up by liberal democracies may be a source of frustration and may ultimately deliver a less than optimal implementation of government policies, but the state can only be insulated from these pressures if democracy is abandoned altogether or they are not identified as constraints on policy. Since the former option is deemed unacceptable, the latter has too frequently been chosen by advocates of industrial modernization.

More recent examples of the advocacy of a national industrial strategy have been provided in the work of Cowling and Sugden. Their work is of importance beyond the realm of academia because both have participated in the Industrial Strategy Group, a group of academics and researchers established in 1986 which has made detailed submissions to the Labour Party's Policy Review process and advised Opposition spokesmen for Trade and Industry. In its *A New Economic Policy for Britain: Essays on the Development of Industry*, the Industrial Strategy Group seeks to provide 'readable, non-technical yet fully supported analyses' outlining the Group's remedies for British decline (Cowling, 1990, p. vi). However, Cowling's argument concerning 'The strategic approach to economic and industrial policy' is far from being 'fully supported' (Cowling, 1990, pp. 6–34). Whilst he claims that it is based on an identification of 'systemic deficiencies within the market', in practice Cowling's argument is founded on the same reductionist and ahistorical analysis of the Japanese state and its undiluted application to the British context as Smith's. Cowling also claims to be providing a 'distinctively British approach' to industrial policy because he has not ventured into 'the detail of Japanese planning, its various instruments, institutions and mechanisms' for these 'are a product of its own history and culture' which, in any case, he admits are incapable of transplantation to 'quite different historical and cultural circumstances' (Cowling, 1990, p. 18). It seems therefore that Cowling's strategic approach is derived from an alien context that he readily acknowledges is immeasurably different from Britain and which he does not pretend to have explored fully, let alone understood. As a basis for future Labour government policy, this does not appear an altogether sound foundation.

Whatever his reservations about his lack of knowledge of Japan, Cowling soon casts them aside to distill his strategic approach from the Japanese experience, the essential lesson of which he holds to be the importance of 'proper organisation' (Cowling, 1990, p. 18). In this way, Cowling seeks to fill what he regards as a lacuna in mainstream economics which he claims does not 'identify a central role for a coherent industrial strategy within economic policy' and has consequently reduced industrial policy to an afterthought in British economic policy (Cowling, 1990, p. 6). His complaint is that it is usually industrialists and political scientists rather than economists who have explored 'the unfamiliar territory of industrial strategy', but this assertion can only be based on a highly selective reading of the industrial policy literature, or the application of eccentric criteria to his definition of an economist. This definition would have to exclude the work of, amongst others, Smith (1984), Rothwell and Zegveld (1985), Pavitt (1980), Henderson (1986), Freeman (1987), and Godley (1988), most of whom have been fellow proponents of the necessity of a coherent industrial strategy for Britain.

Cowling's remedy for British decline is to pursue the Japanese 'strategic approach' to industrial policy and to create a MITI-like 'small entrepreneurial team' dedicated to strategic thinking and equipped with 'the independent capability of implementing the strategy which evolves from the process of wide consultation with industry'. Intervention should and would be based on a 'programme of industrial modelling' and would be restricted to 'those industries, both old and new, which appear viable and indeed strategically important in a long-term perspective' (Cowling,

1990, pp. 19–20). As is customary with technocratic prescriptions for industrial policy, the criteria for picking these industrial winners remain unspecified. Nevertheless, by such measures, the 'continuity, consistency and commitment to economic development', which has been absent from the reactive adhocery of past interventions would be instilled in the British state as it was transformed into a 'catalytic and entrepreneurial' rather than 'negative and bureaucratic' proactive agency (Cowling, 1990, p. 28). Under Cowling's technocratic schema, planning would by some unspecified administrative miracle achieve the elusive standard of being coherent without being comprehensive, directed by a strong institutional core which nonetheless would avoid centralization.

Beyond the realm of technocracy, Cowling's faith in institutional engineering might appear remarkable, but located within the tradition of technocratic pragmatism, it is merely typical. How the state is to be insulated from the normal impediments of democratic politics in general, and the demands of powerful economic interests in particular, when selecting which industries to support is never clarified. Cowling points to the importance of securing a 'democratic structure of intervention and development', and where he has elsewhere extended his industrial strategy to encompass the whole of Europe, to meet the imperatives of 'modern economic conditions', he has written of 'the essence of democracy – the ability of people and their communities to allocate resources in the way they choose' (Cowling, 1989, p. 26). This creates a clear and fundamental tension between the imperatives of democratic participation and accountability and the disciplines of industrial development, but Cowling surmounts this tension by confining his notion of participation to the involvement of a technocratic elite. Moreover, when referring on several occasions to 'wide-ranging consultation within science and technology and industry', Cowling never addresses the crucial issue of who is to speak for science, technology and industry (Cowling, 1990, p. 22). The assumption appears to be that the only legitimate voice of these interests will be that which will accord with his technocratic modernization agenda.

THE DEVELOPMENTAL STATE

The central importance to the technocratic vision of locating political power in the hands of a technical elite possibly explains the attraction of the developmental state model to advocates of a more proactive industrial policy for remedying British decline. The developmental state model has been most influentially developed in *MITI and the Japanese Miracle*,

Chalmers Johnson's seminal work on the role of the state and industrial policy in Japan's economic success, and, more recently, in Wade's analysis of patterns of East Asian industrialization (Johnson, 1982; Wade, 1990). The fact that such eminent political commentators as the historian Hennessy and the former Labour Shadow Cabinet member Bryan Gould have wrongly attributed the concept of the developmental state to the political scientist Marquand should not come as an undue surprise because abstracting models of foreign polities and misapplying them undiluted as remedies for British decline is a central trait of technocratic pragmatism (Hennessy, 1989, p. 728; Gould, 1989, p. 106). Indeed, the application of a model derived from the very different context of East Asian industrialization as a remedy for British decline parallels the way in which the theory of economic backwardness developed by Gerschenkron (Gerschenkron, 1966) has also been used by some historians to generate a deterministic model of development, not merely for late industrializers but also for national economies in need of modernization, despite the fact, as Friedman has noted, that Gerschenkron's objective was to avoid such determinism by demonstrating that economic and political diversity are characteristics of industrial development (Friedman, 1988, p. 231).

The four key elements of the developmental state that have been identified by Johnson are 'the existence of a small, inexpensive, but elite bureaucracy staffed by the best managerial talent available in the system', a 'political system in which the bureaucracy is given sufficient scope to take initiatives and operate effectively', the 'perfection of market-conforming methods of state intervention', and the existence of a 'pilot organization like MITI' (Johnson, 1982, pp. 315–19). Therefore, the developmental state model rests, as Onis has suggested, on the presence of 'a strong and autonomous state, providing directional thrust to the operation of the market mechanism' as the key to rapid industrialization for late developers (Onis, 1991, p. 110). However, as Onis has also asserted, there are at the very least three major obstacles to the application of this East Asian model of industrialization to the context of a mature liberal democracy such as Britain. Firstly, the developmental state model demands 'single minded adherence to growth and competitiveness at the expense of other objectives' (Onis, 1991, p. 120). Whilst developmental states like South Korea and Japan have not been burdened by responsibility for welfare provision, in Britain the competing demands of the welfare state for resources cannot be ignored. Secondly, the developmental state in East Asia has enjoyed an 'unusual degree of bureaucratic autonomy and capacity' by being insulated from the political tensions of an industrializing society through 'the destruction of the left and curtailment of the power or organized labour plus other popular groups' (Onis, 1991, p. 114). Whilst the Thatcher

Governments may have shared similar objectives to these in their attempts to discipline the trades unions in Britain, it is difficult to envisage the use of political repression on a similar systematic basis in a mature parliamentary democracy. Thirdly, East Asian developmental states have been characterized by an 'equally unique and unusual degree of public-private cooperation' although this cooperation in practice has depended upon a significant element of compulsion and the 'extraordinary degrees of monopoly and control exercised by the state conglomerates on bank finance' (Onis, 1991, p. 116). Since it would require intervention on an heroic and previously unprecedented scale in peacetime to reorient the investment priorities of the City of London and the British banking system away from commerce and property and more towards manufacturing industry, this facet of the developmental state appears incapable of transference to Britain.

It is 'unambiguously clear' as Onis suggests that the East Asian developmental state is 'inconsistent with the vision of a pluralistic form of democracy' of the British type (Onis, 1991, p. 119). In the specific instance of Japan, Onis notes that democratic institutions and the developmental state have been reconciled, more because of the 'unique features and structural imperatives of Japan as distinct from an inherent capability' (Onis, 1991, p. 121). Indeed, in the conclusion of his analysis of MITI's role in Japanese industrial success, Johnson clearly indicates that he regards his particular conception of the developmental state as 'only a model, and a sketchy one at that' (Johnson, 1982, p. 320). Japan's high-growth system could not be reduced to a specific device or institution having been 'the product of one of the most painful passages to modernity' that any nation has ever had to endure (Johnson, 1982, pp. 306–7). Rather than seeking to emulate Japan's achievements, other nations would be better advised 'to fabricate the institutions of their own developmental states from local materials'. In the case of the US (and the same lesson would appear to apply to Britain), this would entail the unleashing of 'the private, competitive impulses of its citizens' rather than adding 'still another layer to its already burdensome regulatory bureaucracy' (Johnson, 1982, p. 323). It could therefore be argued that the Thatcher Governments' use of dirigiste state intervention during the 1980s in an attempt to recreate an enterprise culture in Britain, where the expression of private individual entrepreneurial initiative in open markets was intended to become the prime agency of social change, was tantamount to the reconstruction of an authentic British developmental state precisely because it sought to exploit the 'private, competitive impulses' of British citizens and also sought to fashion institutions from 'local materials'.

Despite the seemingly insurmountable obstacles that both Onis and Johnson have identified to prevent the undiluted institutional transference of the East Asian developmental state to Britain, it has been seized upon as a remedy for British decline by a number of influential commentators, most notably Peter Hennessy. In both *Whitehall*, his lengthy description of the history of the British civil service, and *From Clogs to Clogs?*, the transcript of his BBC radio series about British decline, Hennessy has advocated the introduction of the principles of a developmental state to Britain's unprincipled society (Hennessy, 1989; Hennessy and Anstey 1991). In *Whitehall*, Hennessy devotes an entire chapter to what he terms 'The Missed Opportunity', that is the failure at the end of the Second World War to sustain into peacetime the technocratic elite which had been incorporated into government during wartime. This 'irregular' elite had transformed Whitehall into a 'thinker-doer' and 'world-beating bureaucracy' but with the end of the war came the disbandment of the technocrats and the resumption of Whitehall's traditional 'failure-avoidance culture' and 'waterfall of negativism'. In this way, Britain was denied the opportunity, in what Hennessy claims were comparable circumstances to those in France and Germany, to replicate the industrial policies that were to be instrumental in the latter's superior postwar economic performance (Hennessy, 1989, p. 125).

In *From Clogs to Clogs?*, Hennessy attributes the failure of the nightwatchman British state to play a more developmental role to the fact that it 'simply wasn't considered' for 'Britain really was the do-nothing state'. It has never pursued a long term modernization programme because 'From Gladstone to Major we remain the alibi society – can't take on the City; can't buck the market; can't force industry to modernize; can't get technical education into every classroom' (Hennessy and Anstey, 1991, p. 16). For Hennessy, 'Those are the weasel words', but it is not as he suggests a matter of alibis. The explanations for British decline do not lie in a series of excuses, in state inaction backed by apologies. On the contrary, if industrial modernization is to occur in Britain, then a continuous battle of ideas and interests is unavoidable. The problem is that Hennessy and his fellow technocratic pragmatists refuse to recognize the necessity of that battle, let alone to engage in it themselves. They perceive their role, being rational, pragmatic people as one of standing aside from unnecessary and time-consuming irrelevances, so that they may prophesize and exhort what would be self-evident truths to those who actually govern and administer, had they the necessary political will and technocratic skills. Hennessy asserts that, after the First World War, 'a new cultural fixation' took hold in Britain, that is, 'all those theological debates, which still obsess us, about the public/private divide'. Indeed, he continues, 'For an allegedly unideological people, we've taken to the political barricades about the power of the state in a way the French and the Germans never have' (Hennessy and Anstey, 1991, p. 18). This assertion can only be upheld if the odd continental European revolution and war is overlooked and, in any case, who is it other than Hennessy who has claimed that the British are 'unideological'? This unattributed claim could only be put forward by a pragmatist who fails to see that disputes over the respective roles for the state, the market and the individual are not obsessive 'theological debates', but the very essence of democratic politics.

NATIONAL SYSTEMS OF INNOVATION

It was the English economist John Maynard Keynes who most memorably drew attention to the influence of ideas upon policy when he wrote in his most famous work, *The General Theory of Employment, Interest and Money*, that the world was ruled by little else than ideas and that even 'practical men' were 'usually the slaves of some defunct economist' (Keynes, 1936, pp. 383–4). Keynes's statement has never been better illustrated than by the way in which some of the most influential work on industrial policy and its implications for British decline has been shaped by the ideas of an early nineteenth-century German economist, Friedrich List. In particular, Christopher Freeman, the founding Director of the Science Policy Research Unit (SPRU) at Sussex University, itself a monument to the Wilson Government's attempts to modernize Britain in the late 1960s, has developed the concept of 'national systems of innovation' directly from List's most influential work, *The National System of Political Economy* (List, 1928), which was published in 1841 (Freeman, 1987). In his analysis of the nature of national industrial development, List asserted that the world was characterized by independent, competitive sovereign states which could intervene to develop their 'productive powers', that is, their national scientific, technological, educational and transport infrastructure, together with their systems of public administration, law and order, and self-government. Implicit in this analysis is the notion of industrial convergence, that is, 'the idea that firms, industries, and national economies will tend over time to become more and more similar'. As Friedman has suggested, industrial convergence 'is premised on the belief that there is one, most efficient solution to the problem of organizing individuals, capital, and raw materials to produce goods'. Domestic and international competition would create 'a Darwinian struggle between companies and nations in which the most efficient producers triumph over the rest'. But, just as 'Other manufacturers need first to emulate and then to surpass the most efficient producers in order to survive', in List's national political economy, laggard industrial states would be required replicate the administrative blueprint of more successful competitor national economies (Friedman, 1988, p. 7). Despite the passage of 150 years, this is a blueprint for modernization which some technocratic pragmatists believe to be wholly appropriate for the Britain of the 1990s.

The developmental agenda that flows from List's notion of 'productive powers' is manifest in a substantial part of the industrial policy literature but is writ largest in Freeman's *Technology Policy and Economic Performance: Lessons from Japan* (Freeman, 1987). Freeman initially claims to be 'following Schumpeter' in asserting that 'technological capacity is the main source of the competitive strength of firms and nations' (Freeman, 1987, p. 1). He implies that Schumpeter placed technical innovation at the centre of his economics whereas Schumpeter's theory of capitalism actually identifies entrepreneurship as the prime agency of social change (Freeman, 1990, pp. 17–38). Freeman does not define his understanding of 'technological capacity' but instead seeks to develop the Listian notion of 'national systems of innovation'. He asserts that List's 'concern to identify the essential feature of a national "catching-up" strategy' was the earliest articulation of a national technology policy, and that List could have legitimately given his most important work the alternative title of *The National System of Innovation* (Freeman, 1987, p. 98). The concept of a national system of innovation denotes 'The network of institutions in the public and private sectors whose activities and interactions initiate, import, modify and diffuse new technologies'. This 'network of institutions' in turn refers not only to 'those scientific and technical activities which are intended to promote the flow of technical and organizational innovations and their diffusion' but also to 'national education and training systems' (Freeman, 1987, p. 1). Indeed, Freeman subsequently extends the concept of national systems to the possibility of a 'national science and technology system' (Freeman, 1987, p. 30).

For Freeman, national systems of innovation offer the key to understanding both national economic success, as exemplified by Japan, and national economic decline, as exemplified by Britain. This is because there are seven 'fundamental points in List's advocacy of national technology strategies', notably the avoidance of a complete underestimation of 'the role of scientists, engineers and designers', the importance of a 'very long-term historical view' on 'the development of manufacturing and of the appropriate institutions and "mental capital" to enable manufacturing to flourish', and a very strong emphasis on 'the importance of an active national policy in order to promote long-term development'

(Freeman, 1987, pp. 99–100). According to Freeman, all seven 'essential features' are to be found in Japan but none are to be found in Britain. Therefore, the lesson from Japan that those seeking to remedy British decline should understand is the necessity of engineering a national system of innovation in Britain. This is precisely what Freeman proceeds to undertake by assembling all the elements of a state-led modernization programme, including the means to educate and accord proper status to a technocratic elite.

Freeman contrasts the 'amateurish' dominant management tradition in Britain, with its 'system of "practical" training on the job' and emphasis on 'accountancy considerations on a short-term basis' with the foundations of the German national system of innovation, namely 'thorough and deliberate professional development' and 'recognition of Technik – design and engineering – as a "third culture" of the greatest importance for the general "management culture" in German industry'. In the absence of a suitably trained and rewarded technocratic elite, Freeman contends that Britain has been denied 'The type of long-term strategic thinking necessary for long-term success with new technologies ... as well as an insistence on high quality and design on the technical side' which is 'more characteristic of German industry' and 'even more true of German firms' (Freeman, 1987, p. 100). Furthermore, the German technocratic elite has not been confined merely to industry but has also been 'extremely important in government (for example, in the finance of research and education, as well as in measures to promote strategic industries) and in financial institutions'. The all encompassing nature of this rival elite is made to appear all the more damaging for the prospects of state-led modernization in Britain by Freeman's citing of the failure of the British state to act upon 'successive inquiries and Royal Commissions which pointed to the widening gap between British standards of education and training and those of its industrial competitors, particularly Germany' (Freeman, 1987, pp. 129–30).

There is a tendency throughout Freeman's analysis to assume that certain industrial policy prescriptions should be self-evident to the reader, not least the necessity for state-led modernization, and consequently a concomitant practice of riding roughshod over vital and complex historical detail. This is merely indicative of the political, historical, social and cultural vacuum in which technocratic pragmatism tends to operate. Indeed, neglect of the constraints upon industrial policy imposed by the surrounding political and broader societal context has enabled the process of implementation of a modernization programme to be reduced to the status of an exogenous, 'black box' phenomenon. Thus, for example, in his earlier analysis of government policy, Freeman had asserted that the implementation of his highly ambitious modernization programme would be accomplished 'somehow or other' (Freeman, 1980, p. 310). It transpired that this 'somehow or other' involved nothing less than a rekindling of the wartime Dunkirk spirit for 'once the diagnosis is correctly made and widely understood at all levels in British society', the same resilience which had made it possible for Britain to stand alone against the Nazi threat in 1940 would now inspire economic revival (Freeman, 1980, p. 313). Freeman sustains a deafening silence over how this understanding would be communicated to all levels of British society, and appears to neglect the fact that whilst his diagnosis may have been appropriate to the Britain of 1940, the body politic has undergone some major surgery in the subsequent decades which may have rendered the original diagnosis obscolescent. Responsibility is duly abdicated for providing a 'detailed blueprint' for implementation of his policy prescriptions because Freeman contends that politics and industry are dynamic contexts for policy, he is ignorant of the machinery of government, and, in any case, a surfeit of reorganizations of the machinery of British government has demonstrated that the selection of policy instruments is of secondary importance to a long-term governmental commitment to industrial policy (Freeman, 1980, pp. 315–16). Evidently, ignorance of the personnel and structures of implementation, which might be expected to fatally undermine the effectiveness of modernization policies, is not to be regarded as an obstacle that should obstruct the advocacy of ambitious remedies for British decline.

The concept of national innovation systems has been explored at greater length in a more recent cross-national analysis of industrial policy. Ironically, perhaps because they are conscious of the antiquity of his writings, in 541 pages none of the authors of *National Innovation Systems* (Nelson and Rosenberg, 1993) acknowledges their debt to List. One of the central purposes of this text is to fill the vacuum which the editors believe has been caused by 'the absence of a well-articulated and verified analytic framework linking institutional arrangements to technological and economic performance' (Nelson and Rosenberg, 1993, p .4). The question arises, however, as to whether List's national political economy, or a modern derivative of it, is an appropriate conceptual tool for understanding the context of industrial policy in an era of internationalization and globalization of production. This is an especially pertinent question given that Nelson et al. not only interpret the term 'innovation' very broadly 'to encompass the processes by which firms master and get into practice product designs and manufacturing processes that are new to them, if not to the universe or even to the nation', but also define the term 'system' not as 'something that is consciously designed and built' but as 'a set of institutions whose interactions determine the innovative performance, in the sense above, of national firms' (Nelson and Rosenberg, 1993, p. 4). Furthermore, the editors acknowledge that the concept of the 'national' system may be both too broad, in missing the different systems of innovation across industries, and too narrow, given the transnational nature of institutions in modern innovation systems (Nelson and Rosenberg, 1993, p. 5). With such a diluted conception of innovation, system and an a priori sense of the limitations of the nation state, the usefulness of 'national innovation systems' as a tool for understanding the modern industrial economy appears dubious.

It is significant for those who have contended that state intervention has been a key determinant of national economic performance that Nelson's conclusion to *National Innovation Systems* is that its studies 'play down the existence of active coherent industrial policies'. Moreover, in the case of European countries known to possess what technocratic pragmatists would regard as a coherent industrial policy, Nelson points to the fact that in these countries, policy is highly decentralized and, with the exception of the Airbus project, government programs account for only a very small fraction of industrial R & D (Nelson and Rosenberg, 1993, p. 515). Thus, 'government leverage has been exaggerated and that where strong policies have been executed, they as often lead to failure as to success' (Nelson and Rosenberg, 1993, p. 515). At the same time, the importance of high R & D intensity for innovation is downgraded by Nelson since 'there does not seem to be strong empirical support for the proposition that national economies are broadly advantaged if their firms are especially strong in high tech and disadvantaged if they are not' (Nelson and Rosenberg, 1993, p. 517). Whilst the usefulness of the concept of national innovation systems as an analytical framework for linking institutional arrangements, especially those of the state, to economic and technological performance may have been undermined by Nelson et al.'s analysis, their conclusions nevertheless have important implications for future British industrial policy especially when they are linked to other recent work on industrial policy.

In *The Future of UK Competitiveness and the Role of Industrial Policy*, Kirstie Hughes and Ian Christie raise some important questions about the extent to which the internationalization of capital and production has created transnational firms that are perfectly footloose and over which national, regional or local governments therefore have no leverage (Hughes and Christie, 1993, pp. 171–4). At the same time, David Edgerton further punctures the widely-held assumption that a technocratic, centralized industrial strategy, with a strong emphasis on higher R & D spending, offers the most effective route to an improvement in manufacturing performance (Edgerton, 1993a, pp. 40–54). In his analysis of 'Research, development and competitiveness', Edgerton departs from the conventional approach to the analysis of R & D statistics by focusing on absolute quantities of R & D rather than proportions (measured in terms of GDP, industrial production, or national R & D totals). As a consequence, he contends that from 1950 through to the mid-1960s, British industry was second only to the US in its spending on R & D in absolute terms. Indeed, even as it was in the process of being overtaken by German and Japanese industry in the late 1960s, British industry still maintained the highest private research intensity in the world (Edgerton, 1993a, pp. 41–2).

Whilst there was a catastrophic decline in British industrial R & D during the 1970s, Edgerton notes that the 'outstanding feature of British industrially funded R & D in the 1980s was its remarkable growth' (Edgerton, 1993a, p. 45). State R & D funding may have declined but private industrial R & D has been characterized by its increasing internationalization and concentration, with the top five private R & D spenders accounting for nearly 40 per cent of the total national R & D spend in 1992. This is hardly a new phenomenon since about 30 per cent of total R & D employment in Britain in 1938 was accounted for by the seven largest R & D spenders (Edgerton, 1993a, p. 46). However, given that British decline has continued unabated during periods of rising and declining R & D intensity, it is clear that R & D is not necessarily the key to remedying national decline as has been suggested in so many select committee reports (for example, House of Lords, 1985, 1986, 1991; House of Commons, 1993) and strategy documents from business (EEF, 1992; CBI, 1991, 1992), the trades unions (MSF, 1992) and the Labour Party (1991, 1993). Furthermore, as Edgerton suggests, since no clear principles of policy appear to operate with regard to the role that Government should play in supporting industrial R & D, thereby denying the many commentators who aspire to the implementation of a coherent national strategy in this regard, there is a strong case for public funding of R & D on a whole variety of non-industrial and non-economic grounds, as has been the practice to a large degree with defence R & D (Edgerton, 1993a, pp. 52–3).

AN AUDIT OF CORRELLI BARNETT

The debate about the significance of Britain's defence industrial policy, and the lessons that may be derived from it for civil industrial policy, was given renewed vigour in 1986 with the publication of *The Audit of War: The Illusion and Reality of Britain as a Great Nation* in which Correlli Barnett sought to challenge some of the central assumptions concerning post-war

British decline by analysing the role of the state during wartime. Barnett's work was also interesting because it constituted only the latest contribution to a longstanding tradition of admiration for the performance of the German economy. Writing shortly after the Great Exhibition of 1851, which had been intended as a celebratory showcase for British technology and engineering, Dr. Lyon Playfair had warned that continental European industry would move ahead of British industry if Britain did not amend radically its industrial outlook and methods (Playfair, 1852). A whole succession of reports from parliamentary and other committees of inquiry reiterated Playfair's warning during the latter half of the nineteenth century culminating in the publication in 1896 of E.E. Williams' best-seller, *Made in Germany*, in which he warned of the threat from 'the German Industrial State' (Williams, 1896, p. 164). Williams outlined an agenda for the state and individual businesses in Britain that might make national economic salvation feasible. Amongst his recommendations for the British state were policies of discriminatory and protective tariffs on imports, the overhauling of the British Consular system abroad to make the promotion of British trade and commerce its primary objective, and the expansion and upgrading of technical education in the face of what he saw as the collapse of the apprenticeship system. This last policy recommendation anticipated by some 85 years the criticisms of the reform of technical education by the first Thatcher Government. Amongst his recommendations for individual businesses, Williams exhorted manufacturers to be more attentive to their customers, to deploy a sales staff with knowledge of foreign languages, to pay greater attention to detail, and to invest in modern equipment for their workshops (Williams, 1896, pp. 164–75).

The desire to Germanify part or all of the structure and institutions of both the state and industry in Britain has remained a feature of the twentieth-century historiography of British decline. *In The Audit of War*, as Harris has suggested, 'the long-drawn-out structural and cultural superiority of Germany at all stages of nineteenth- and twentieth-century British history' is one of the subsidiary themes of Barnett's thesis about British decline. His thesis is based on the twin assumptions that a nation's industrial strength is the essential basis of both its power and its material well-being, and that 'total war submits nations to a ruthless audit of resources, talents and failings: human, social, cultural, political and technological no less than military' (Barnett, 1986, p. xi). Since industrial institutions are for Barnett 'expressions of their parent national society and its culture', the explanations for British industrial decline must be sought in 'the nature of British society itself, its attitudes and its values' (Barnett, 1986, p. 183). By auditing Britain's industrial performance during the

Second World War, Barnett seeks to locate and to identify the causes of Britain's postwar decline.

Barnett's contention is that even when they were confronted by the ultimate challenge of total warfare, both the state and industry in Britain were incapable of surmounting the forces in British culture and society that had frustrated industrial modernization during peacetime. British industrial performance was to be equally inferior during wartime, compared to both its American allies and German enemies. Far from being a triumph for British industry, the Second World War had merely served to demonstrate 'the classic symptoms of what was later to be dubbed the "British disease"' (Barnett, 1986, p. 51). British management was inept in all industries and at all levels, providing weak leadership to its workforce. This in turn had exacerbated the obstructiveness of the trades unions and accentuated the constraints on productivity caused by the absence of commitment amongst the workforce. A cripplingly narrow base in high-technology industries and skills was revealed, caused by the gulf between groups of world-class scientists and inept industrialists operating inferior and inefficient industrial plant and machinery. Above all, total warfare was to demonstrate that, from machine-room to the boardroom, Britons had been educated for national economic decline.

Britain had emerged from the Second World War in a self-congratulatory mood, neglecting the fact that 'its impressive figures of war production had only been possible because Lend Lease and Sterling Area credit had relieved Britain of the need to earn her own way through exports' (Barnett, 1986, p. 51). Governmental plans for the postwar reconstruction of Britain had been riven by a conflict of priorities between industrial reconstruction, which should have been the overriding concern given Britain's underlying industrial weakness, and the construction of a new social order, or what Barnett terms 'The Dream of New Jerusalem' (Barnett, 1986, p. 11). This New Jerusalem of 'an open-ended social security scheme and free national health service, full employment, and a colossal house-building programme' was for Barnett the dream, above all, of a soft, sentimental, liberal, Christian, anti-industrial and anti-militaristic middle class governing elite, 'a motley collection of idealistic do-gooders, of which Sir William Beveridge is the most famous and certainly the most influential' (Barnett, 1986, p. 15). What was desperately required in 1945 was a massive state-led programme of industrial reform, reconstruction and modernization, embracing a huge national commitment to and investment in plant and machinery, education and training, and the national transport infrastructure. Such a programme demanded 'a compact and highly talented planning staff under a director of outstanding calibre ... rich in the best available industrial, commercial and engineering talent'. What

Britain's struggling industries got instead, after being routed in the struggle for resources by the 'prevailing contagion of New Jerusalemism' was 'Tinkering as Industrial Strategy' (Barnett, 1986, pp. 265–75). Britain's manufacturers were exposed to 'neither the scruff-of-the-neck intervention in industrial change later practised by the French or Japanese; nor the reliance on free-market competition under a favourable financial regime in the American or postwar West German style' (Barnett, 1986, p. 268). Barnett's deeply pessimistic and emotive conclusion is that the ultimate consequence of the subordination of industrial modernization to New Jerusalemism has been 'a dream turned to a dank reality of a segregated, subliterate, unskilled, unhealthy and institutionalised proletariat hanging on the nipple of state maternalism' (Barnett, 1986, p. 304).

Barnett's work is particularly noteworthy because of the way in which it has influenced thinkers and politicians on both the Conservative New Right and the Marxist Left. The New Right has been attracted by Barnett's scathing critique of the postwar British welfare state, and the Left by his advocacy of a proactive, dirigiste state-led industrial modernization programme. Thus, for example, Nigel Lawson, when Chancellor of the Exchequer, acknowledged that 'Correlli's book' had been a major source of authority for his fiscal and social policies (Harris, 1990, p. 177). In a similar vein, the Marxist historian Anderson has contended that *The Audit of War* 'is composed at a ... depth that makes previous treatments seem indulgent sketches by comparison' (Anderson, 1987, p. 47). Barnett's thesis is also important because, as Edgerton has noted, of the broadly sympathetic response that it has attracted from a plethora of eminent economic historians, almost all of whom have singularly failed to identify Barnett's peculiar ideological perspective in their commentaries on his work (Edgerton, 1991c, p. 362). Only Addison has appropriately described Barnett as 'probably the only modern British historian whose creed is Bismarckian nationalism', although even his review of *The Audit of War* suggested that Barnett's 'demonstration of the inefficiency of major industries in wartime would be hard to refute' (Addison, 1986, p. 7).

Fortunately, not all historians have been taken in by Barnett's arguments. His thesis has been audited critically on two fronts by Harris and Edgerton. Harris has furnished a critique of Barnett's contention concerning the allegedly debilitating effects of the welfare state on Britain's postwar economic performance. Indeed, Harris has used the issue of whether the relative decline of the British economy was synonymous with the rise of the welfare state to explore the wider question of whether welfare states in general enhance or subvert national economic performance. Harris' own assertion is that the generalized case for the existence of a parasitic welfare state that has crippled the performance of the British economy relative to its competitors appears weak (Harris, 1990, p. 181). For example, even in 1950, when much of Western Europe had only recently benefited from the first injection of funds from the Marshall Plan, combined spending on social insurance and health care as a proportion of GDP was already greater in West Germany than in Britain. Britain's welfare spending as a proportion of GDP was also overtaken in the early 1950s by that of Austria, Belgium, Denmark and Sweden (Harris, 1990, p. 180). Indeed, by the early 1970s, Britain's combined expenditure on health and pensions was lower than that of any other European country. However, whilst Britain's industrial economy was not unduly burdened by its social security expenditure relative to competitor economies, Harris does contend that the welfare state in Britain has been different from others in that its non-economic objectives, that is, the unconditional relief of poverty and equal access for all citizens, notably to health care, have been accorded much higher priority than elsewhere in Western Europe where welfare systems have been more directly concerned with contractual entitlement and the promotion of industrial efficiency (Harris, 1990, pp. 183–4).

Harris also contests Barnett's depiction of the Beveridge inspired wartime reconstruction movement, and specifically the image of Beveridge as 'the veritable incarnation of that "Victorian", sentimental, Christian, pacificistic, classical, public school, Oxbridge culture which he believes to be the Achilles heel of British public life over the previous century' (Harris, 1990, p. 184). Harris notes that Beveridge himself was never a Christian, nor a pacifist, and throughout his eighteen years as director of the London School of Economics remained a strong advocate of the business, vocational and practical education that Barnett claims has been lacking in Britain. Furthermore, during his service at the Board of Trade during the First World War, Beveridge had been one of the earliest advocates of the argument that modern public administration demanded technocrats and managers rather than classicists and philosophers in the civil service (Harris, 1990, pp. 185–6). If postwar British welfare expenditure did become out of control by the mid 1960s, Harris suggests that this should not be regarded as the institutionalization of Victorian sentimentality and egalitarianism, but rather as the product of the global trend towards an aging population and the expansion of the welfare state beyond a minimalist safety net. As for Barnett's assertion that it was the all pervasive influence of Christianity which undermined postwar industrial modernization in Britain, through its relentless pursuit of the New Jerusalem, Harris notes that although there were individual Christians and groups of Christians in the social reconstruction movement, some of whom were undoubtedly 'tender-minded, leftist-inclined, enterprise-despising, liberated utopians of the kind that Barnett finds most abhorrent', they were very much in the minority. Indeed, the activities of one of the Christian groups which advised the wartime Secretary of State for Education were far from being anti-industrial, since this particular group recommended a programme for reform of education which embraced a state-led takeover of the public schools, compulsory technical and vocational training for all 14-18 year olds, and the replacement of classics by science and technology in the national curriculum. In this way, Britain might be prepared for the challenge posed by competitor economies in the postwar period. Harris records that this programme was defeated at the 1942 Conservative Party Central Council meeting, not by the machinations of a sentimental anti-industrial Christian elite, but by the massed ranks of ordinary party members (Harris, 1990, pp. 191–2).

LIBERAL MILITARISM AND POSTWAR INDUSTRIAL POLICY

A more important contribution to the debate about the role of the state in British decline, and an even stronger critique of Barnett's portrayal of Britain's governing elites, has been provided by David Edgerton. Challenging the widespread assumption that the British state has failed to measure up to the technocratic blueprint sought by Barnett, Edgerton has contended that 'the central bodies of the state, including the Treasury, have pursued a policy of "liberal militarism" which has required the creation of "technocratic" departments of state'. However, because liberal militarism has meant centrally-directed state intervention primarily in military rather than civil industries, historians of Britain's post-war relative economic decline, especially those adherents to technocratic pragmatism who have sought the creation of technocratic departments of state for the civil economy, have tended to overlook Britain's defence-led developmental state, national system of innovation and industrial strategy. Indeed, Edgerton suggests that the history of postwar Britain is the history of successive Labour and Conservative governments pursuing 'an expensive strategy of keeping Britain's military industries at the leading edge' (Edgerton, 1991b, pp. 140–1). Britain has been 'essentially an economic, industrial and commercial power', the preservation of which has necessitated armed force. Excessive defence expenditure would have undermined Britain's 'essential' power so the British elite has sought to avoid this problem by taking advantage of Britain's 'relative strengths most notably in science and technology and specific classes of industrial expertise' (Edgerton, 1991b, p. 149).

Edgerton identifies four key features of liberal militarism. Firstly, it does not entail the use of mass conscription armies and therefore, secondly, compensates for this deficiency in manpower by reliance on technology and professionals. Thirdly, Britain's armed forces have been directed not only at enemy armies but also at their civil populations and economic capacity. Fourthly, liberal militarism has been advanced 'under the banner of its own universalist ideology', initially the Pax Britannica and latterly the postwar Pax American (Edgerton, 1991b, p. 141). In its infancy, from the defeat of Napoleon at the Battle of Waterloo in 1815 to the outbreak of the First World War, Edgerton contends that liberal militarism found expression in the protection and projection of Britain's commercial interests through unrivalled naval power. In the interwar years and during the Second World War, British strategy switched from 'navalism' to 'airforceism' through the deployment of a large strategic bomber. The threat of its use to destroy enemies' civilian populations and industries was seen as an effective means of protecting British interests (Edgerton, 1991b, pp. 143–4). In the postwar period, Edgerton asserts that airforceism was replaced by 'nuclearism' as the British state identified nuclear power as a more effective instrument for projecting British power than expensive conventional armed forces. More recently, he suggests that the Gulf War demonstrates how liberal militarism may have entered a new phase with Britain playing an active but minor role in a new 'Pax Technologica', under which nuclear weapons are supplemented by the deployment of a new generation of weaponry based on advanced electronic technologies which only a few nations possess the economic and industrial capacity to develop (Edgerton, 1991b, p. 148).

Because liberal militarism has necessitated the procurement of high-technology weapons that could only be supplied domestically through selective intervention in manufacturing industry, the British state has not been able to pursue a liberal, non-interventionist industrial policy in the defence sector. However, Edgerton suggests that this tradition has generally been overlooked by the industrial policy literature because it has tended to regard defence industrial policy as somehow different from civil industrial policy, without specifying, in historical and empirical terms, how this difference arises (Edgerton, 1991b, p. 153). Therefore, the historiography of British industrial policy has tended to neglect the role, especially in peacetime, of the service departments and specialist military supply departments which have differed markedly from most other state agencies. The 1986 Westland crisis, when there was a conflict at the very heart of the British state between the dirigiste Procurement Executive of the MOD and the less interventionist DTI over the future ownership and control of Britain's sole helicopter manufacturer is only a recent example of a much longer division of intention and intervention between the civil and military departments of the British state. A brief analysis of postwar industrial policy in Britain not only demonstrates the important differences in the support given by successive governments to the defence and civil sectors of the economy (Lee, 1996) but also undermines the argument advanced by technocratic pragmatism that Britain has never possessed a coherent industrial strategy.

Defence industrial policy has received a disproportionate share of Britain's national financial, scientific and technical resources because it has been perceived as an entirely necessary and legitimate form of state intervention. In sharp contrast, civil industrial policy has been shaped by a series of intermittent and frequently ineffectual interventions. This pattern for postwar industrial policy in Britain was established by the Attlee Government in 1945. Although it embarked upon a major programme of domestic social and economic reform, it did not develop a comprehensive planning machinery for industrial recovery of the sort that was taking shape in postwar France under the direction of Jean Monnet. The Government's commitment to nationalization did not deliver a more proactive industrial policy for civil manufacturing but instead built upon its wartime plans to extend nationalization to a relatively small number of industries. The Board of Trade inherited the principal responsibility for civil industrial policy but, as Middlemas has suggested, its plans to revive the prewar trade associations meant placing responsibility for industrial modernization in the hands of organizations which lacked the resources necessary to develop an effective supply-side strategy (Middlemas, 1986, p. 51). Whilst France under Monnet was regarded as possessing an effective civil industrial policy, Britain was seen as having developed 'at best only a collection of unrelated expedients' (*The Economist*, 14 December 1946).

This 'collection of unrelated expedients' in the civil sector contrasted sharply with the development of industrial policy towards the defence sector where a Joint War Production Staff was created to work for a Ministerial Production Committee in the newly formed MOD At the same time, a Committee on Defence Research Policy was created to oversee military research, and to each of these committees was appointed a permanent chairman who, along with the Chief Staff Officer and Permanent Secretary at the MOD, acted as the four principal ministerial advisers. Broadbent has noted that these same four pillars could be identified some four decades later in the figures of the Chief of Defence Procurement, the Chief Scientific Adviser, the Chief of the Defence Staff, and the Permanent Under-Secretary of State (Broadbent, 1988, p. 17). Moreover, Edgerton contends that the postwar Ministry of Supply may rightly be called 'the British Ministry of Industry and Technology, dwarfing the efforts of the Board of Trade and the Department of Scientific and Industrial Research in this respect'. The Ministry of Supply, which shaped postwar defence industrial policy until 1959, when it was renamed the Ministry of Aviation and lost its Army supply functions to the War Office, was itself the direct descendant of the wartime industrial ministries, that is, the Admiralty, the Ministry of Supply and the Ministry of Aircraft Production. Whilst historians have tended to focus on the 'bonfire of controls' that Harold Wilson conducted during his tenure at the Board of Trade in the late 1940s, from where he also established the National Research and Development Corporation, Edgerton asserts that Wilson increasingly regarded the Board of Trade's industrial policies as ineffective, and wanted to extend the example of the military industrial style of provision of guaranteed markets and state competition to civil sectors of the economy (Edgerton, 1991b, pp. 161–2).

Wilson was unable to put his ideas of the late 1940s about civil industrial policy fully into effect until after his election initially to the leadership of the Labour Party, following the sudden death in January 1963 of Hugh Gaitskell, and latterly as Prime Minister in October 1964. However, it should not be thought that the period of Conservative Government from 1951–64, which has often been portrayed as an era preoccupied with 'Butskellism' and 'Stop Go' macroeconomic management to the exclusion of microeconomic, supply-side issues, was one during which the British state's pursuit of a technology-oriented defence policy was in any sense diminished. On the contrary, throughout the 1950s and early 1960s, Conservative Governments under the leadership of four different Prime Ministers not only continued to devote more than half total national R & D expenditure to military R & D, but also extended state support to civil industries, most notably nuclear power and civil aerospace. Believing that nuclear power offered both a more cost-effective basis for defence policy through deterrence and a major competitive advantage to industry and commerce through the supply of almost limitless amounts of cheap energy, in 1955 Britain launched the world's most ambitious nuclear programme. By 1959 more than half of state spending on civil science was being devoted to nuclear R & D State spending on civil science alone increased by an average of 13 per cent between 1951 and 1959 (Vig, 1968, pp. 19–20).

In the case of the British aircraft manufacturers, the state financed no less than 70 per cent of the industry's output between 1950 and 1964. As Edgerton has noted, 'In 1954 defence expenditure was £1.5 billion in current prices, and £300 million of this was spent in the aircraft industry. Ministry of Supply expenditure on aircraft, engines and spares increased from about £80m in the late 1940s to £210m in 1954–55. Research and development expenditure increased from £23m in 1949 to £60m in 1954'

(Edgerton, 1993b, p. 11). State assistance was not confined to an increase in financial support. In order to overcome the problem of too many domestic aircraft manufacturers lacking the resources to privately finance the escalating costs of R & D, a wholesale rationalisation of the British aircraft industry was undertaken in 1959. However, rather than entrust this responsibility to the firms themselves, the Minister of Aviation, Duncan Sandys, used the leverage provided by his department's control of state funding for future projects to lead the process himself. The Ministry of Aviation possessed its own very detailed blueprint for the future of the British aircraft industry under which there would be a reduction from seventeen to five manufacturers. Of these five chosen firms, two would manufacture airframes, two would manufacture aero-engines, and the other (Westland) would manufacture helicopters. The rationalisation was completed within two months of the first public knowledge of Sandys' ultimatum to the aircraft manufacturers.

The Conservatives' enthusiasm for such centrally-directed state intervention becomes easier to comprehend when it is remembered that in his *The Middle Way*, originally published in 1938, Macmillan had advocated the abandonment of piecemeal industrial planning in favour of 'conscious regulation' or 'national planning' to modernise private industry upon the basis of technical and economic efficiency (Macmillan, 1966, pp. 7–18). In the immediate aftermath of the Conservative Party's crushing defeat by Labour in the 1945 General Election, Macmillan had been instrumental in the drawing up of his party's Industrial Charter, which had cast aside laissez-faire economics in favour of a system of 'humanised capitalism' under which 'modern Conservatism would maintain strong central guidance over the operation of the economy' (Butler, 1971, p. 145). Furthermore, during the late 1950s, Macmillan was adamant that his twenty-year-old agenda for state-led modernization was as equally valid for the Britain that he was by now governing as Prime Minister as for the Britain of the interwar period. Thus, although before the publication of the Industrial Charter, he had contended that new growth industries were ripe for 'free initiative and speculation' in the private sector, the Conservative Government during Macmillan's premiership developed new industries such as nuclear power and aerospace in the public sector under state control and direction (Harris, 1972, p. 87).

Even this degree of state intervention under Macmillan was insufficient for some Conservatives. In 1957, Aubrey Jones, the Minister of Supply, feared that a decline in aircraft procurement might lead to redundancy amongst teams of state-funded scientists. To surmount this problem, Jones suggested to Macmillan that the Ministry of Supply should be transformed into a Ministry of Technology which would 'facilitate the transfer of knowledge from the military to the civil field' and 'utilise the expertise developed in the placing of military research and development contracts to put it also at the disposal of civil industry' (Jones, 1985, p. 85). In the event, Macmillan dismissed Jones' proposals for a strengthening of civil industrial policy in favour of an administrative reorganization in 1959 which strengthened the authority of the Minister of Defence (Dockrill, 1988, pp. 66–7). Macmillan's alternative strategy for modernizing civil industry in the early 1960s was based upon the twin pillars of British membership of the European Economic Community, to provide a larger market for domestic industry and commerce, and the introduction from July 1961 of indicative planning, to provide a longer term alternative to the 'Stop Go' policies of the previous ten years. Indicative planning entailed the calculation and promulgation of a national growth target of four per cent per annum in the hope that this might increase confidence amongst private sector manufacturers sufficiently to persuade them to increase investment to a level that would deliver the government's growth target. However, in the absence of any effective agency for bringing about this transformation in Britain's economic prospects, aside from the newly created tripartite National Economic Development Council, National Economic Development Office, and Economic Development Councils, indicative planning merely served to avoid the necessity for the sort of centrally directed state intervention that Sandys had implemented in the aircraft industry barely two years before. Aubrey Jones was once more in the vanguard of Conservative critics who regarded this approach as inadequate given his perception of the need for both the state and industry to become 'scientifically and technically conscious' (Vig, 1968, p. 75).

The sort of institutional innovation in the field of civil industrial policy which Aubrey Jones had demanded of the Conservative Governments of the late 1950s and early 1960s was only realised after the election of the first Wilson Government in October 1964. Wilson had spoken of his plan to 'harness Socialism to science, and science to Socialism' in his speech to the 1963 Labour Party Conference at Scarborough and the 1964 Labour Party manifesto duly promised to implement an agenda for industrial modernization which would 'go beyond research and development and establish new industries, either by public enterprise or in partnership with private industry' (Vig, 1968, p. 34). This agenda was implemented through three principal institutional and policy innovations. The first was the drawing up of a National Plan by the newly created Department of Economic Affairs (DEA) under the leadership of George Brown. Brown believed that industry required a clear picture of the potential growth of the British economy in the five years ahead if it was to have the confidence to increase its investment for the future. When the National Plan was presented in September 1965, it envisaged a target for economic growth of 25 per cent between 1964 and 1970, the equivalent of an average annual growth rate of 3.8 per cent which was less than the 4 per cent per annum target sought by the Conservatives' previous policy of indicative planning. In the event, the National Plan was wound up within a year. It was, as Opie has suggested, 'conceived October 1964, born September 1965, died (possibly murdered) July 1966' (Opie, 1972, p. 170. The primacy accorded by Wilson to the defence of the pound, which ensured that the Treasury's preoccupation with short-term macroeconomic policy would enjoy primacy over the DEA's longer-term planning objectives, eliminated the prospect of an immediate devaluation as a mechanism for stimulating Britain's exports. This, coupled with the National Plan's failure to clearly identify the policy instruments by which its growth targets were to be achieved, guaranteed its premature demise.

The Wilson Government's second institutional innovation was the creation of the Ministry of Technology (Mintech) which the 1964 General Election manifesto portrayed as a means 'to guide and stimulate a major national effort to bring advanced technology and new processes into industry' (Vig, 1968, p. 102). In practice, as Edgerton has suggested, Mintech was to acquire so many industrial policy responsibilities, especially after its merger with the much larger Ministry of Aviation in February 1967, that 'it gave England an Industry Ministry of much greater scope than any other in the capitalist world; Japan's much-vaunted MITI is a minnow by comparison' (Edgerton, 1991a, p. 105). Indeed, this British industrial superministry assumed responsibility for so many aspects of civil and defence industrial policy that it had to be structured into three groups – Aviation, Engineering, and Research. With the exception of food and drink, pharmaceuticals, building materials, and printing and publishing, by October 1969 Mintech had become responsible for industrial policy for virtually the whole both of civil manufacturing and military R & D and procurement. As both Edgerton and Gummett have asserted, Mintech had become a bespoke Ministry of Industry and certainly disproves the technocratic pragmatists' argument that Britain has never possessed either a coherent industrial strategy or a ministry within Whitehall with sufficient power to implement such a policy (Edgerton, 1991a, p. 104; Gummett, 1980, p. 46). The only way to sustain the idea that industrial policy is the missing element in British economic policy is to ignore the postwar historiography of the British state in general and Mintech in particular. That, in essence, is what technocratic pragmatists have done (for example, Cowling and Sugden, 1993).

The third of the Wilson Government's institutional innovations in the field of industrial policy was the establishment of the Industrial

Reorganization Corporation (IRC) in December 1966. As with Duncan Sandys' earlier reorganization of the British aircraft industry, the rationale underlying the creation of the IRC was the fear that too few British manufacturers were of a size sufficient to finance the R & D required to maintain their competitiveness in world markets. The objective of the IRC was therefore to promote industrial profitability by encouraging and assisting the reorganization or development of any industry in which it felt that its intervention would be beneficial. To achieve this objective, the IRC was provided with the facility to draw up to £150 million in order to be able either to accelerate the concentration of manufacturing industry or to 'establish or develop, or promote or assist the establishment or development of any industrial enterprise' (Young and Lowe, 1974, p. 40). Despite its resources, the IRC did not become involved in more than fifty mergers or takeovers, constituting no more than two per cent of the total merger activity in the period 1967–70 (Newton and Porter, 1988, p. 156).

The respective interventions of the DEA, Mintech and the IRC could not prevent the UK's share of world exports of manufactures falling by an annual average of 4.5 per cent between 1964 and 1970 (Walker, 1987, p. 203). Furthermore, despite the fact both that its Conservative predecessors had cancelled no fewer than 26 major aircraft projects between 1951–64 at a cost of £300 million, and that it had cancelled major defence projects, such as the TSR2 aircraft, the supersonic version of the Harrier jump-jet, the replacement for the Hunter, and the HS-681 tactical transport aircraft, the Wilson Government's greater interest in supporting civil industries had not prevented it from continuing the postwar British state tradition of providing massive financial assistance to the military aerospace industry. For example, in 1967, against the background of increasing industrial unrest and economic austerity, the Government had given the go-ahead for Britain's participation in the production stage of the Tornado multi-role combat aircraft, a collaborative venture between the British, Italian and Germans, which was projected to cost the taxpayer around £4 billion (Dockrill, 1988, pp. 91–3). The incoming Heath Government in June 1970 therefore found itself with an industrial policy inheritance where the priorities established by the state's historic commitment to a policy of liberal militarism had not been seriously challenged. It soon became apparent that, irrespective of its early rhetoric, the Heath Government would not mount a challenge to this industrial policy orthodoxy either. Although the extent of state intervention in civil industry did increase throughout the 1970s under both the Heath Government and its successor, this trend did not amount to a movement away from state support for military industries. It instead reflected the extent to which civil manufacturing businesses in both the private and public sectors in Britain during the 1970s were to experience difficulties in the increasingly demanding global trading conditions which arose from the collapse of the Bretton Woods international economic order in 1971 and the Arab Oil Crisis in 1973–74 which demanded a response from government because of the serious domestic political dividend that the collapse of any of these companies would have delivered.

Prior to the 1970 General Election, Harold Wilson had labelled Edward Heath 'Selsdon Man' after the Selsdon Park Hotel in London where a key Conservative strategy meeting had been held. Wilson was seeking to conjure up an image of a return to nineteenth century laissez-faire economics under a future Heath Government. However, as Holmes has indicated, if 'Selsdon Man' ever existed, he was a 'technological, managerial man looking to a European commitment to aid the regeneration of competition in industry and personal initiative in the wealth creating process rather than the wealth distributing process' (Holmes, 1982, p. 11). Heath's agenda for modernizing Britain would be accomplished within the post-war framework of the mixed economy and welfare state, but would be conducted through 'a new style of government' based on a 'fresh', in essence technocratic, approach to decision-making that promised to be 'deliberate and thorough', and use the 'best advice' and 'up-to-date techniques' (Conservative Party, 1970, p. 13). To facilitate this 'new style of government', Heath launched an immediate administrative reorganization of Whitehall which resulted in the creation of two new 'superministries', the Department of the Environment and the Department of Trade and Industry (DTI). The DTI was created from the Board of Trade and those elements of Mintech which were responsible for civil manufacturing. This reorganization of responsibility for civil industrial policy raised the question of where responsibility for defence industrial policy would reside. The Ministry of Aviation Supply was created as a temporary holding operation, but it was abolished in May 1971 when the newly-created Procurement Executive of the MOD had assumed responsibility for the whole of defence procurement. As with its predecessors, the Heath Government thereby ensured that the state traditon of liberal militarism would be reflected in its reorganization of administrative structures.

These institutional innovations were intended to signify the introduction of modern, efficient, technocratic management techniques to the public sector rather than a renewed enthusiasm for further intervention. In his speech to the 1970 Conservative Party Conference, John Davies, the Secretary of State for Trade and Industry, indicated that the Heath Government would not bail out or bolster 'lame duck' industries. The state was however prepared to provide a 'helping hand' but not an 'open-ended liability' to certain major industries, notably shipbuilding and aerospace. This initial commitment to qualified disengagement was demonstrated by the 1971 Industry Act which not only abolished the IRC, but also repealed key sections of the 1968 Industrial Expansion Act which had provided the state with general powers to intervene selectively in industry without the constraint of having to enact separate legislation on each occasion (Fleming, 1980, p. 143). However, the mantle of disengagement was soon cast aside to reveal Heath's essentially technocratic and managerialist instincts when the Government intervened to save the floundering aero-engine manufacturer, Rolls-Royce at an estimated cost of £170m. The company was engaged in a series of politically sensitive collaborative ventures in both the civil and defence sectors, and so those Rolls-Royce assets deployed in defence and collaborative ventures were nationalised (Hayward, 1983, pp. 109–20). The departure from disengagement that was signalled by the Heath Government's rescue of Rolls-Royce and the floundering Upper Clyde Shipbuilders was institutionalized in the 1972 Industry Act which provided ministers with very wide-ranging powers to intervene. Section 7 of the Act enabled ministers to provide discretionary assistance to projects that would create or safeguard employment in assisted areas or regions. Section 8 of the Act allowed ministers to provide aid for individual companies or projects, in the form of grants, guarantees, loans or equity (Grant, 1982, p. 50).

The powers to intervene provided by the 1972 Industry Act were so extensive that the Wilson and Callaghan Governments were able to use the Act as a basis for their own industrial policies. Whilst the Wilson Government divided the DTI into the separate Department of Trade and Department of Industry (DOI), its principal institutional innovation in the civil industrial policy sphere was the creation of the National Enterprise Board (NEB). The Labour Party's October 1974 General Election manifesto had envisaged that the NEB would be established to 'extend public ownership into profitable manufacturing industry by acquisitions, partly or wholly, of individual firms; to sitmulate investment; to create employment in areas of high unemployment; to encourage industrial democracy; to promote industrial efficiency' (Budd, 1978, p. 133). Wilson, however, was determined from the outset that the NEB would not play such 'a marauding role' and in practice it soon became preoccupied with rescuing a new generation of 'lame ducks', most notably British Leyland (BL) into which it poured no less than £569 million of the £777 million that it received during the tenure of the Wilson and Callaghan Governments' (Wilson, 1979, p. 33). Indeed, Fleming has concluded that the NEB played little more than a peripheral role in the development of civil manufacturing in the period 1974–79 despite the fact that it accounted for almost one-third of the state's total spending on general aid to industry from 1975–76 to 1978–79 (£608 million out of £2.06 billion at 1978 prices) (Fleming, 1980, p. 149). Rather than promoting innovation, around 95 per cent of the NEB's expenditure was allocated to the rescuing of struggling manufacturers such as BL, Rolls-Royce, Alfred Herbert and Cambridge Instruments.

The other elements of the Wilson and Callaghan Governments' civil industrial policies, namely the establishment of planning agreements and the support schemes emanating from the November 1975 White Paper, *An Approach to Industrial Strategy*, were equally ineffective. Only one planning agreement was signed with an employer in the private sector (Chrysler UK) and the public sector (the National Coal Board). Neither was of any great significance to Britain's industrial performance because the agreements delivered neither an increase in governmental control over corporate strategy nor a marked improvement in industrial relations. At the same time, whilst no fewer than fifteen sectoral schemes were established to support civil manufacturing between 1974 and 1979, overall state expenditure on industrial and regional support fell around 25 per cent below the planned level in 1978–79 largely because of a lack of demand from firms reluctant to innovate. Indeed, the support schemes were so ineffective that in February 1979, Sir Douglas Wass, the Permanent Secretary at the Treasury, was able to record that no less than seven of the schemes to subsidize employment in manufacturing were not only unlikely to break even but actually expected to incur losses at a pace more rapid than the rate of economic growth.

Despite the recurrent economic crises experienced during the 1970s, military industrial policy and spending on military equipment remained buoyant. One of the impetuses behind new procurement programmes was the creation by the European members of NATO of a European Defence Improvement Programme. Britain's contribution included the announcement in the February 1972 Defence White Paper of an accelerated procurement programme of Type 42 destroyers and Type 21 frigates for the Navy, and extra Buccaneer and Nimrod aircraft for the RAF. In April 1973 the authorization was also given for the construction of three through-deck cruisers. Having originally been conceived as a 12 579 ton ship with only a helicopter carrying capacity, the design of the through-deck cruiser was soon transformed into a 19 000 ton aircraft carrier with the capacity to carry the Harrier vertical take-off and landing aircraft. Only months after an attempt to cut costs, in May 1975 the Wilson Government ordered Sea Harriers for these ships raising the total cost of the carrier programme to £2.36 billion over 20 years (Chalmers, 1985, p. 102). Indeed, between 1974–75 and 1978–79, spending on defence equipment increased by 29.5

per cent in real terms whereas spending on personnel in the same period declined by 8 per cent (Chalmers, 1985, p. 98). Dennis Healey, as Chancellor of the Exchequer, had proposed an annual cut in defence spending of £500 million in 1975 because he thought that the defence industry was too large and that scarce skilled labour should be released to civil manufacturing for when there was an upturn in economic growth. To achieve this cut would have meant the cancellation of three major defence equipment programmes – the Tornado fighter, the through-deck cruiser and the secret £1 billion Chevaline project to modernize the warheads on Britain's submarine-borne Polaris missiles. The Cabinet refused to agree to these cancellations but, as Chalmers has suggested, the justification for cancellation of these projects was no different from that which had led the first Wilson Government in 1965 to cancel the TSR2 and the CVA-01 aircraft carrier programme (Chalmers, 1985, p. 101). Admittedly, the Defence Review of December 1974, which aimed to reduce defence spending from 5.5 per cent of GNP in 1975 to 4.4 per cent by 1985, had seen the navy lose one-seventh of its surface fleet (Dockrill, 1988, pp. 103). Despite these cuts, new procurement projects continued to be funded, for example, the decision in September 1978 to order a new Main Battle Tank for the British Army at a cost of £1 million each, three times the cost of its predecessor the Chieftain (Dockrill, 1988, p. 109).

Limited but ineffective initiatives were undertaken to increase international collaboration in equipment procurement and to persuade defence manufacturers to diversify into civil markets. In 1975, the Defence Secretary, Roy Mason, in his capacity as chairman of Eurogroup, the European members of NATO, became a strong advocate of the notion of a 'Two-Way Street' in defence procurement, whereby European armed forces would purchase US equipment and US forces European equipment in an attempt to standardize equipment across NATO (Carver, 1992, p. 115). Unfortunately, the initiatives of both Eurogroup and the Independent Programme Group, an organization consisting of the Eurogroup plus France, were unable to escape the constraints of the exercise of national interests characteristic of defence industries and procurement. Confronted by the prospect of rationalization and redundancy at their company because of cuts in defence procurement, trades unionists at Lucas Aerospace campaigned for the 'right to work on socially useful technologies' and drew up a proposal, the Corporate Plan of January 1976, detailing a series of new civil products that their company could develop which would both save jobs and address social needs (Elliott, 1977, p. 2). The unions' proposals included the manufacture of medical equipment, like kidney machines, transport systems, such as electric vehicles, and alternative energy technology such as solar collectors. The company published its official response in April 1976 which concluded that it intended to continue to focus on its traditional manufacturing businesses in the aerospace and defence industries. It argued that its existing civil and military products were all of use to the community and that it constantly reviewed the possibility of diversifying into other non-aerospace markets where there was an equivalent level of technology (Elliott, 1977, p. 11). Whilst the Corporate Plan received widespread support from the labour movement, Wainwright and Elliott have contended that the Government did little to support it (Wainwright and Elliott, 1982, p. 1). As a consequence of these failed initiatives, defence manufacturing remained both a prominent source of employment and a major drain on the Exchequer and performance of the civil economy at the end of the 1970s. In 1979–80, it was estimated that around 400 000 jobs in manufacturing were sustained by the military procurement programme, whilst a further 140 000 jobs were derived from export contracts for British military equipment (Smith, 1980, p. 113).

LIBERAL MILITARISM IN THE 1980s AND 1990s

The election of the first Thatcher Government in May 1979 marked something of a watershed in the development of civil industrial policy in Britain. For the first time in the postwar period, a government was elected whose Prime Minister believed that individual entrepreneurial initiative rather than state intervention provided the solution to British decline. To wean civil manufacturers from their dependency upon state intervention, the Thatcher Government would seek to restore an enterprise culture in Britain where once more individual entrepreneurs and their companies, as they had done at the height of Britain's industrial prowess in the period from 1770 to 1870, would focus their entrepreneurship on the opportunities for profit provided by open and competitive markets rather than state subsidies. The problem for the Thatcher Government in general, and for Sir Keith Joseph at the Department of Industry (DOI) in particular, was that the promised land of the enterprise culture could only be restored once the state had disengaged itself from the institutional and policy legacy of postwar civil industrial policy. In the short term, this meant rolling forward rather than rolling back the frontiers of state intervention in the nationalized industries.

Unlike their policies towards civil manufacturing, which marked a major departure from what had gone before, the Thatcher Governments' policy towards defence manufacturers during the 1980s was largely shaped by the legacy of the Callaghan Government and its commitment to meet in full NATO's Long-Term Defence Programme which demanded a 3 per cent annual increase in real terms in defence spending. This commitment accorded with the Thatcher Governments' desire to restore the authority of the British state overseas as well as domestically by identifying defence as the first charge on national resources. Between 1978–79 and 1984–85, defence spending increased by 29 per cent in real terms and procurement spending by 47 per cent in real terms in a period when many other areas of public spending were contracting in real terms (Chalmers, 1992, p. 37). However, in the latter half of the 1980s, with the collapse of communism and the end of the Cold War, British defence spending began to decline quite markedly especially after the 'Options for Change' review of defence policy in July 1990. Despite the impetus given to defence procurement by the honouring of Callaghan's NATO spending commitment, the 1980s continued the postwar pattern of a disparity between the armed forces' constant demands for new and better equipment and substantial but nevertheless limited resources for procurement. In 1980, the Secretary of State for Defence, John Nott, recognised that nothwithstanding the 3 per cent annual real increase in the defence budget, the MOD's ten-year programme was unrealistic due to the escalating cost of defence equipment. For example, the cost of a Type 42 destroyer had risen to £85 million whilst the Sting Ray lightweight torpedo programme alone would be £920 million. No less than 41 per cent of the defence budget in 1980 was being spent on equipment, so during the following year Nott attempted to control future defence spending by proposing substantial cuts in the Royal Navy's surface fleet. The fleet would be reduced to 'about 50' vessels, not least by not ordering any more Type 42 destroyers and by selling one of the Navy's aircraft carriers to Australia. The intervention of the Falklands War, and the lessons that the MOD chose to learn from it, ensured that many of Nott's intended cuts were reversed. Thus, in 1983–84, the share of the total defence budget taken by equipment had risen to 46 per cent.

Defence industrial policy did not escape the rigours of the Thatcher Governments' drive to instill greater effiency and value for money in the public sector. An end was sought to over-pricing, 'cost-plus' contracting and escalating project costs through the introduction of competition for defence contracts, the transfer of financial risk from the customer to the supplier, and the maintenance of closer control of costs at each stage of production. Organizational changes within the MOD in 1981, designed to give greater ministerial control over the procurement process, were followed in 1983 by the introduction of Michael Heseltine's Management Information System for Ministers and Top Management (MINIS). This entailed the devolution of managerial responsibility to lower level officials, and an emphasis upon increasing international collaboration in weapons procurement. Drawing upon his commercial experience, Heseltine also created an Office of Management and Budget to secure stronger control over the MOD's corporate planning. In December 1984, Heseltine divided the post of Chief of Defence Procurement between it and a new Chief of Defence Equipment Collaboration (Broadbent, 1988, pp. 74, 79). Peter Levene, an industrialist, was appointed as Chief of Defence Procurement with a remit to make the Procurement Executive 'more commercially minded' and to promote competition for contracts (Taylor and Hayward, 1989, p. 79). This would be achieved in part by abolishing the right of the contractor which had undertaken development work to automatically receive the first production order. At the same time, it was hoped that there would be cost savings from greater international collaboration, not least at the development stage of the European Fighter Aircraft (EFA) and the EH101 helicopter projects.

To facilitate the transfer of technology from the defence to the civil sector, Heseltine also created Defence Technology Enterprises (DTE) in 1984 to identify commercially applicable innovations that could be transferred from military R & D programmes to civil industry. Although the MOD stood to benefit from a share in DTE's profits, in its first three years of operating DTE identified only about 25 innovations that attracted limited financial backing from civil industry (Taylor and Hayward, 1989, p. 81). The 1987 Defence White Paper announced that the MOD would participate in the Goverment's 'Next Steps' civil service reforms to delegate executive functions of government to agencies by examining the feasibility of uniting the main Defence Research establishments into one agency (Carver, 1992, pp. 150, 153). The Defence Research Agency was duly established, albeit not until April 1991. In the interim in 1989, the Cabinet's Advisory Council on Science and Technology (ACOST) had proposed that the Agency should exploit the expertise at its disposal by developing a much wider role in industrial policy as a national centre of excellence in technology. However the Cabinet soon put a stop to any possibility of a revival of proactive intervention by the backdoor by rejecting ACOST's proposal.

Whilst there was a rapid decline in output and employment in civil manufacturing during the early 1980s, rising defence spending ensured that defence manufacturing increased as a percentage of manufacturing GDP from 8.1 per cent in 1978 to 12.2 per cent in 1983. Between 1986 and 1990, Britain became the world's fourth largest arms exporter of major conventional weapons, a total of $7.8 billion at 1985 prices. However, this total amounted to only 0.8 per cent of total national exports during this period, so the opportunity cost of devoting such a large share of national spending on R & D in manufacturing to defence industries appeared very high for civil manufacturers. Admittedly, in 1992 alone, British defence contractors won orders worth more than £5 billion, about 20 per cent of the world market for defence exports, but this was but a small share of Britain's total manufactured exports of £97 billion and could not compensate for a trade deficit in manufactures of about £14 billion. The 100 000 jobs supported directly or indirectly by arms exports appeared a poor dividend from having devoted more than half the state's total spending on R & D for so many years. Furthermore, the privatization of some of Britain's largest defence manufacturers during the 1980s, through the sale of BAe, Rolls-Royce, Shorts, British Shipbuilders' warship yards, the Royal Ordnance Factories, Ferranti, and the management of the Royal Dockyards, has neither weakened the dependence of these companies upon domestic defence contracts, nor diminished the status of the MOD as the most important provider of direct state assistance to industry in Whitehall. For example, the 1993 Defence Estimates projected that the MOD's procurement budget for 1993–94 would total £9.915 billion, providing £636 million for research, £2.134 billion for development, and £7.145 billion for production (HMSO, 1993, p. 61). UK industry had won contracts for 75 per cent of the value of the equipment procured during the previous five years, whilst in 1991 alone, the MOD had placed 37 000 new contracts with 6 400 contractors, thereby taking its total of active contracts in 1992 to 127 000 placed with over 10 000 contractors. In 1993, the defence sector accounted for about 9 per cent of manufacturing GDP and employed about 400 000 people, bringing new export orders worth about £6 billion, second only to the US and approximately 20 per cent of the world market for armaments.

Since Britain 'entered the 1990s with the largest and strongest military–industrial–scientific complex in Western Europe', the prospect has arisen that for defence manufacturers the 'peace dividend' brought about by the end of the Cold War may prove to be decidedly unpalatable (Edgerton, 1991b, p. 165). Spending on military equipment peaked in 1985 and was set to fall by 18 per cent in real terms between 1986–87 and 1990–91. The 1987 White Paper (DTI, 1987), which constituted the Government's response to a House of Lords Select Committee report on *Civil Research and Development* (House of Lords, 1986), disclosed that the Government envisaged a gradual decline in the real level of defence R & D over the following decade. Soon after, the January 1988 White Paper, *DTI – The Department for Enterprise* (DTI, 1988) indicated that the Government did not intend to compensate for this decline in support for military manufacturers by a corresponding increase in state assistance to civil R & D Indeed, state spending on civil R&D would also decline in real terms as DTI support for single company projects was withdrawn. The increased profitability of manufacturers at that time was held to demonstrate not only that the market was the best judge of which innovations to develop but also that the private sector was now able to afford the finance for product development. The more recent White Paper, *Realising our Potential: A Strategy for Science, Engineering and Technology*, has merely affirmed the Major Government's commitment to a further reduction in state spending on R & D which will leave it one-fifth lower in real terms in 1995–96 than in 1987–88 (HMSO, 1993, p. 39).

The fear of Opposition politicians, some Conservative backbenchers, and representatives of major manufacturers has been that Britain's 'peace dividend' will take the form of a decline in manufacturing output, profitability, and competitiveness unless measures are taken to stimulate the civil sectors of manufacturing. One of the most frequently touted solutions to the threat posed by defence-cut driven deindustrialization has been the creation of a Defence Diversification Agency to encourage defence manufacturers to convert their technologies and production lines to civil uses (Smith, 1993; HMSO, 1993, p. 45). This argument, as Edgerton has contended, is founded on 'the unproven assumption that defence firms are better at doing any sort of R & D than civil firms, that there are sunk costs in equipment and in learning/skills which should be exploited, and that there is a shortage of skilled R & D personnel for civil firms' (Edgerton, 1993b, p. 52). However, whilst both Harold Wilson in the late 1940s, and Aubrey Jones in the late 1950s, had recognized the potential for applying the expertise of the warfare state to the civil sectors of both the state machinery and its policies towards manufacturing, since 1979 the Thatcher and Major Governments have steadfastly rejected the need for a new state agency to encourage diversification.

Largely as a consequence of Britain's relative success in the arms trade, aerospace remains one of the few manufacturing industries employing advanced technologies in which Britain remains a major global player. Indeed, in 1991, Britain captured an 11.7 per cent share of world markets for aerospace products, against an 8.7 per cent share of world markets for manufactures in general. Whilst the wisdom of providing additional state assistance to an industry in which the sales of the largest player, the US aerospace industry, exceeded those of Britain's by nine times in 1990 (House of Commons, 1993, pp. 9, 11), might appear dubious, it seems inevitable that British governments will continue to come under heavy pressure to continue with major projects, not least because the future of both BAe's and GEC's defence businesses are now inextricably linked to the question of whether, when, in what form and at what cost, the European Fighter Aircraft (EFA) project will proceed. The EFA constitutes the latest and most ambitious of a series of multinational collaborative ventures in the European aerospace industry intended to produce standardized equipment for national airforces across Europe at a cheaper cost than would be possible if such a venture were undertaken by a single nation. However, as with the earlier precedent set by the Multi-Role Combat Aircraft project, which delivered the Tornado aircraft behind schedule and at considerable cost, the EFA's development and production costs have escalated whilst its estimated date for entry to service has rapidly retreated.

When the Cabinet gave the go-ahead for British participation in the EFA project in 1988, the original cost of the entire programme had been £21 billion, with Britain contributing 33 per cent of the costs and procuring 250 aircraft. In June 1994, the head of Defence Procurement at the MOD informed the House of Commons Public Accounts Committee that the total cost of the project had risen to £42 billion, twice the original estimate, with Britain contributing £3.5 billion to the development phase and £10.5 billion to the production costs of the aircraft. In March 1995 the MOD disclosed that the project's costs to the UK had risen by almost £100 million a month since the previous June to reach a new total of £14.9 billion (*The Sunday Times*, 12 March, 1995). Although an estimated 40 000 jobs in the British aerospace industry are held to depend on the EFA programme, the dramatic escalation in costs is reported to have caused the MOD to conduct an appraisal of the whole project, including an evaluation of alternative aircraft that might be procured from US manufacturers (*The Sunday Times*, 10 July, 1994). However, the principal threat to the future of EFA emanates from Germany where there have been disputes over who should meet the spiralling costs of development, and where doubts have arisen over the wisdom of German participation in the production stage – an issue that has only recently been resolved following the provision by the German parliament of an additional DM571m (£260m) to complete the German part of development work.

During 1992, the German Defence minister, Volke Ruhe, had repeatedly raised doubts about the need to proceed with a fighter that had been conceived to combat the threat from the now defunct Soviet Union. It was only after its partners had managed to convince Germany that the project's costs could be cut by up to 30 per cent through better organization and less ambitious technical specifications that Germany decided to remain a partner in the EFA, although it announced its intention to cut its planned order from 250 to 140 aircraft whilst insisting on maintaining a 33 per cent share of the development work. Britain continues to insist that the original agreement to develop the EFA tied production work directly to the number of aircraft purchased by the consortium's member governments. Therefore, Germany's order for 140 aircraft should be reflected in a cut in its share of production work from 33 per cent to 23 per cent. Given widespread hostility towards the EFA project in Germany, a cut in Germany's share of production below 30 per cent might make it difficult to secure parliamentary agreement. German withdrawal from the project at such an advanced stage would push the cost of each fighter well beyond £50 million unless further design modifications were to be agreed by the remaining EFA partners – Britain, Italy and Spain. The market for the EFA was once optimistically forecast as up to 2,000 aircraft but the four partners are unlikely to order even a third of this total. If Germany, as one of the world's richest national economies, has doubts over its capacity to afford the EFA, the prospects of export sales to countries outside the oil-rich states of the Gulf would appear remote, especially given the increased competition from the much cheaper fighter aircraft being marketed by the Russian aerospace industry.

The German government's hesitation over the wisdom of proceeding with the EFA has coincided with a major drive by Germany's largest aerospace company, Deutsche Aerospace (DASA) to become a leading player in global aerospace markets through a major investment strategy financed from a successful DM3 billion (£1.25 billion) rights issue by its parent company, Daimler-Benz, Germany's largest corporation. The efforts by the private sector in Germany to expand its output by an investment-led strategy have been complemented by the decision of the German government to finance a DM1.2 billion (£500 million) programme of state subsidies to research and technology, which has been initiated to counteract the estimated £3 billion ($2 billion) of subsidies that the giant US aerospace is receiving annually from the US government. DASA and the German government have also resolved a longstanding dispute concerning the development costs of the EFA which has resulted in DASA receiving approximately DM500 million. The seemingly bright future for the German aerospace industry in the medium- to long-term, bolstered by the prospect of ever closer Franco German strategic political, military and industrial links, contrast vividly with the current condition of the aerospace industry in Britain.

In 1991 BAe had found it difficult to raise £432 million from investors in a rights issue to help it to address its short-term costs of restructuring. More recently, its failure to secure a Taiwanese partner for its struggling regional jets business, led to the announcement of further job losses and raised the question of how it could hope to finance the costs of new products in the civil aerospace sector. BAe has been in the vanguard of those companies supporting the DTI's own Aviation Committee's National Strategic Technology Acquisition Plan (NSTAP) which had called for a £1 billion state investment over ten years. This recommendation, which has been endorsed by a report from the House of Commons Trade and Industry Committee (House of Commons, 1993), would demand an almost five-fold increase in the existing level of state support for R & D in the aerospace industry. Ironically, on the very eve of the announcement by the German government of their own version of NSTAP, the Secretary of State for Trade and Industry, Michael Heseltine, was informing the Trade and Industry Committee that the Government would not sanction further state support for civil aerospace. In fact, under existing expenditure plans, state support for aerospace R & D is projected to decline from £26 million to £22 million per annum over the next five years. Heseltine's Industry Minister, Tim Sainsbury, has suggested to British aerospace companies that rather than look to the British government for additional assistance, they should look overseas for industrial partnerships in order to defray the costs of R & D (*The Guardian*, 29 May, 1994).

The continuing bias in state support for domestic manufacturing towards producers of high-technology weaponry has meant that the most important industrial policy decisions confronting the Major Governments have concerned the procurement of three new aircraft. The first decision concerned the choice of aircraft to replace the RAF's fleet of Hercules transport aircraft. The choice lay between the next generation of C-130J Hercules II aircraft produced by the US company Lockheed and the Future Large Aircraft (FLA) project, a five-nation European collaborative venture. Whilst the C-130J would be available almost immediately to the RAF, would involve about 36 UK companies in its manufacture, and would entail Lockheed undertaking to place £1 billion of contracts with UK companies, the FLA would not be available until 2002 at the earliest. In addition, the UK had withdrawn from full membership of the FLA project in 1989, but failure to order the FLA would risk the UK losing its design leadership in wing technology to the German aerospace company DASA and thereby compromise the UK's future participation in the Airbus programme, because the newly-formed military subsidiary of Airbus would be responsible for the management of the FLA project (*Financial Times*, 6 September, 18 December, 1994).

The FLA revived memories of the Westland helicopter crisis, because once again the MOD, backing the C-130J on the grounds of its cost-effectiveness in an era of sharply-reduced defence spending, had found itself confronting the DTI, backing full U.K. participation in the FLA project because of the implications for the future of the UK aerospace industry. The RAF was known to want the C-130J because of its being the next generation of a combat-proven aircraft, and because of its availability at a time when funds were available to buy it. The FLA will only be available when the EFA is taking a large part of the RAF's budget. In the event, the Major Government's procurement decision was a compromise; a £1 billion contract for 25 C-130J aircraft. It was placed with Lockheed, but at the same time the UK announced its return to full membership of the FLA project with a view to purchasing 40 to 50 FLA at a much later date. However, the decision to split procurement between the C-130J and the FLA has not pleased the UK's European partners who suspect the UK's less than wholehearted commitment to the FLA. The head of the French military procurement agency objected to the UK's rather tentative commitment to purchase the FLA, whilst DASA has indicated that it intends to compete against BAe for contracts on the FLA's wing manufacture.

The second controversial procurement decision confronting the Major Government concerned the procurement of new transport helicopters for the Army. As with the RAF's replacement transport aircraft, the choice facing the Government was between a proven product from a US manufacturer, the Boeing Chinook, and the Anglo—Italian EH101, a project in which the MOD had already invested £1 billion and which is vital to the future of Westland, the UK's sole helicopter manufacturer and prime UK contractor for the EH101. The preference of the RAF, who operate the transport helicopters for the Army, was for the Chinook because the EH101 would involve a one-off cost of £300 million in new servicing facilities at a time of shrinking defence budgets. The Government once again has settled for a compromise, purchasing an additional 6 Chinooks but spending the bulk of its £1.2 billion order on 22 EH101s. However, although the EH101 order secured the future of part of its workforce for the next decade, Westland almost immediately suffered the blow from losing a $235 million contract to Eurocopter for the supply of 14 anti-submarine helicopters to the United Arab Emirates. This has inevitably placed even greater pressure on the Government to support UK manufacturers when making its third major procurement decision concerning the choice of new attack helicopter for the Army. The problem it faces is that UK manufacturers have aligned themselves with three rival consortia for the £2 billion order. The Army's preference, the AH-64A Apache from the US firm McDonnell-Douglas, if ordered would be manufactured under licence by Westland, but the AH-1W Cobra Venom, produced by the US firm Bell incorporates GEC avionics, whilst an order for the Franco—German Tiger would yield a 20 per cent share of production work to BAe.

THE POLITICAL DIVIDEND FROM LIBERAL MILITARISM

In a recent report for the World Development Movement, a pressure group which campaigns for political action to defeat global poverty, Ben Jackson has identified the degree to which defence manufacturers in the UK have been subsidized by the British taxpayer. In contrast to the relative absence of support for exporters from civil manufacturing firms, Jackson points to the fact that the MOD's Defence Export Services Organisation (DESO) employs more than 700 people and had a budget of £44.1 million in 1994 to promote exports of arms from the UK (Jackson, 1995, p. 12). Since 1990, during a period of cuts both in expenditure and personnel in most sectors of the civil service, DESO has grown by a quarter. Jackson asserts that this means that 'In proportion to their share of Britain's total exports, arms are given ten times as much government promotion as civil exports' (Jackson, 1995, p. 12). In addition to DESO's activities, there are 126 British military attaches based in 70 different countries who devote an officially estimated one-third of their time promoting arms exports. Despite their efforts, Jackson suggests that the scale of Britain's arms exports are often exaggerated, because the figures most commonly quoted are for new orders or agreements to purchase weapons rather than actual deliveries. Thus, Roger Freeman, the Minister of State for Defence Procurement, was able to claim in December 1994 that the UK had won new export orders worth about £7 billion in 1993 when it had actually exported only £1.9 billion of arms that year. Indeed, 'Weapons have made up only 1.7 per cent of Britain's total yearly average exports since 1985 – though they represent 8.4 per cent of exports to developing countries' (Jackson, 1995, p. 13). Given that the World Development Movement estimates that the British government is spending at least £384 million per annum on the promotion of arms exports, this means in effect that the taxpayer rather than foreign governments is financing around one-fifth of Britain's arms exports.

Setting aside the important moral questions raised by the manufacture and export of arms from Britain to non-democratic regimes where weapons may be used for the suppression of domestic populations, there is a direct commercial cost to the much larger volume of exports of civil manufactures caused by the subsidies that the state provides to British defence manufacturers. Jackson illustrates this cost by reference to the Export Credits Guarantee Department (ECGD), accountable to the Secretary of State for Trade and Industry, which guarantees the loans that commercial banks provide to foreign governments to enable them to purchase British exports. These guarantees act as an effective subsidy to exporters because they reduce both the commercial risk of exporting to foreign markets and the cost of financing export deals which would be higher without the security provided by the ECGD's support. Jackson has noted how in 1988, Alan Clark, the then Trade Minister, announced a new £1 billion ECGD package of credits for arms exports, the first and only time that a credit facility had been extended to a specific sector rather than a country. This fund was effectively withdrawn in August 1991 through its incorporation into the ECGD's overall budget. But this was not before £834 million had been spent offering generous subsidies to arms exports. Furthermore, in 1992–93, the budget for the cover provided by the ECGD was increased by almost one-third, with arms exports almost doubling their share of ECGD support (Jackson, 1995, pp. 20, 28). The generosity of state support for defence exporters contrasts vividly with the support available to civil businesses. Jackson notes that 'While export credits for arms sales rose 86 per cent between 1991–92 and 1993–94, those for all civil businesses rose just 14 per cent' (Jackson, 1995, p. 30). The effect has been that many civil exporters have been 'crowded out' of lucrative export markets by the disproportionate allocation of ECGD subsidies to arms exporters. For example, Malaysia's decision to purchase BAe Hawks in 1991 was facilitated by £272 million of export credits which, when combined with the £417 million supporting the now infamous Pergau Dam contract, meant that 99 per cent of Malaysia's total export credit allocation for 1991 was being absorbed by just two projects. Indeed, the £500 million sale of Hawks to Indonesia in the following year absorbed no less than 98 per cent of the cover for all British exports to this particular market in 1992–93 (Jackson, 1995, pp. 29, 33).

If the commercial dividend from basing Britain's industrial policy on the principle of liberal militarism has been questionable, the political dividends have also been potentially damaging. The Westland helicopter crisis in 1986 has proven to be the first of a series of major political scandals and embarassments for the Thatcher and Major Governments resulting directly from Britain's trade in and support for the manufacturing and export of arms. For example, in November 1994, as a consequence of a legal action brought by the World Development Movement against the British Government's spending on foreign aid, the High Court ruled that Douglas Hurd, the Foreign Secretary, had acted illegally when providing £234 million of foreign aid for the Pergau Dam project in Malaysia. Hurd had overridden the advice from his most senior aid official that the Pergau Dam was both 'uneconomic' and 'a very bad buy' on the grounds that there were 'wider considerations' to be taken into account, not least the 'interests of British industry' (Jackson, 1995, p. 45). The High Court ruled that Hurd had acted unlawfully but the more important political and commercial subtext concerned the link between official aid and arms exports. Britain's bilateral aid to Malaysia had risen by 139 per cent during the 1980s, an increase coinciding with negotiations between the British and Malaysian governments over major arms contracts. Although the link between official aid and arms exports was repeatedly the subject of official denials, in March 1988, for example, the then Defence Secretary, George Younger, had 'signed an agreement with the Malysian Government promising aid worth one-fifth of the arms deal' that had been negotiated (Jackson, 1995, p. 46).

After a month's consideration, Douglas Hurd decided not to appeal against the High Court's ruling, but the Pergau Dam affair was nevertheless deeply embarassing to the Major Government, not least because it was far from an isolated example of the poisoned legacy bequeathed to it by the penchant of the Thatcher Governments for seeking arms exports from politically suspect regimes. The promotion of the export of arms to the Middle East during the 1980s, which saw more than £5 billion of ECGD cover being made available during this period, has left the legacy of a trio of political intrigues. The first concerned the 1985 British £20 billion Al-Yamamah arms contract with the Saudi Arabian government which was brokered by a team of middle-men who earned a commission of £240m. One member of that team was the Prime Minister's son, Mark Thatcher, was was reported to have received £12m for his part in arranging the deal (*The Sunday Times*, 2 April, 1995). The second intrigue involved the sale of equipment to Iraq which was the recipient of more than £3 billion of export credits during the 1980s. In January 1989 the British machine tool manufacturer Matrix Churchill sought ECGD cover to export machine tools to Iraq via Chile. The company had recently received £6.5 million of export credits for exports to Chile and was at the time the fastest growing machine tool manufacturer in Britain. In March 1989, Matrix Churchill was permitted a further £4 million of E.C.G.D. cover for its exports to Iraq via Chile. However, two years later, Paul Henderson, the former managing director of Matrix Churchill was charged, together with two company executives, of breaking the Government's ban upon the export of lethal equipment to Iraq by selling machine tools capable of being used for manufacturing munitions. During their trial, Henderson and his fellow defendants insisted that the Government and security services had not only known all along about the use to which the machine tools would be put in Iraq but also actively encouraged Matrix Churchill to export its products to Iraq. The problem for the lawyers was that they could only prove the Government's knowledge and encouragement of the deal by reference to key government documents. Several ministers, notably Malcolm Rifkind, the Secretary of State for Defence, and Kenneth Clarke, the Chancellor of the Exchequer, attempted to prevent the court from examining the documents by signing Public Interest Immunity Certificates to indicate that the documents could not be made public without endangering the national interest. The trial judge demanded to see the documents in order to establish whether there was indeed a genuine threat to the national interest. He decided that there was none but what the documents did disclose was that Matrix Churchill's exports to Iraq had received official support via ECGD credits even though they contravened the Government's own ban on arms exports to Iraq (Jackson, 1995, p. 62).

In the aftermath of the collapse of the Matrix Churchill trial, and amidst accusations that ministers had not only misled Parliament but also been prepared to tolerate prison sentences for British exporters even though they had been cooperating with the security services, John Major established an official inquiry into the arms-to-Iraq affair led by Lord Justice Scott. During its proceedings, the Scott Inquiry has raised a number of important issues, not least that of the use of official secrecy to mask important changes in government policy over arms-to-Iraq. However, before it could publish its findings, the proceedings of the Scott Inquiry have been overtaken by a third major political intrigue concerning the involvement of Jonathan Aitken, the Chief Secretary to the Treasury, with a company that breached the arms embargo on Iran during its war with Iraq. In September 1988, Aitken, then only a backbench MP, had joined the board of BMARC, a manufacturer of guns and ammunition. In 1986, BMARC had won a contract to supply Iran with 140 naval guns. Under pressure from journalists and Opposition MPs, Aitken had indicated that he had attended three BMARC board meetings before resigning from the board in March 1990 but had known nothing about the contract to supply arms to Iran. A former BMARC chairman, Gerald James, has subsequently revealed that minutes of board meetings, which were seized by the MOD in 1991 and not disclosed to the Scott Inquiry, show that Aitken attended five rather than three board meetings. James is adamant that Aitken would have to have been 'blind and deaf' not to have known about the deal with Iran (*The Guardian*, 14 June, 1995). The Scott Inquiry declined Aitken's request to investigate the allegations against him but these were rekindled when Michael Heseltine made an unexpected statement to the House of Commons on the 13th June 1995 in which he admitted that a DTI investigation had found that its own controls over exports of weapons and military technology in the 1980s had been inadequate. A sample survey of all military list licence applications for exports in the period 1986 and 1989 had shown that no fewer than 74 per cent of applications had not included all the full supporting documentation because the DTI staff concerned had been overstretched by a doubling in the number of applications between

1984 and the end of 1985. The DTI had approved BMARC's final shipment in December 1988, three months after Aitken had become a BMARC director (*Financial Times*, 14 June, 1995). It may be more than coincidental that both Matrix Churchill and Astra, BMARC's parent company, both went into receivership shortly after their involvement with arms sales in breach of the official embargo.

CONCLUSION

Industrial policy has not been the missing link in British economic policy during the twentieth century. It is merely that the pattern of Britain's industrialization, and more recent deindustrialization, has taken a peculiar form. Technocratic intervention has been implemented through the institutions of the warfare state rather than through the agency of a long term civil industrial policy. This strategy of liberal militarism was highly effective during the construction of the British Empire when Britain possessed the wealth to underpin its military power. The danger now for Britain, as Paul Kennedy has suggested in his *The Rise and Fall of the Great Powers*, is that it is diverting too large a proportion of its resources away from wealth creation towards military purposes, which is likely to further weaken national power over the longer term (Kennedy, 1988, p. xvi). Despite the postwar dissolution of the Empire, and the defence cuts that have accompanied the end of the Cold War, Britain continues to maintain armed forces whose scale and sophistication take account neither of Britain's relative economic decline nor their contribution to it. As long as an industrial policy is maintained that develops new generations of expensive weaponry, the temptation will arise for politicians, especially those troubled by the domestic political and social consequences of Britain's economic decline, to rekindle populist sentiments of nationalism and xenophobia by deploying British armed forces in wars such as those recently in the Gulf and Bosnia, if only to justify the weapons existence and to maintain the pretence of Britain punching above her weight in world politics.

Although the World Bank has recently suggested that technocratic and pragmatic administration provide the keys to understanding the relationship between economic growth and public policy in the high–performing Asian economies, it has equally asserted that the developmental strategies pursued by countries such as Japan and Korea have depended on sets of factors which are 'almost unique' to these economies (World Bank, 1994, p. 102). There is little to be gained from exhorting governments to recreate these 'almost unique' institutional structures in Britain. The policy failures of previous British government demonstrate the shortcomings of looking abroad for foreign industrial policy models to provide a panacea for relative industrial decline at home. At the same time, the fact that no fewer than 373 UK civil servants and senior military personnel moved from the public to the private sector to join rival defence contractors during 1993 and 1994 indicates that, recent defence cuts notwithstanding, Britain's military industrial complex is still a potent force (*The Guardian*, 25 January, 1995). However, given that the House of Commons' Public Accounts Committee has found not only that about 80 per cent of major defence equipment projects in the UK are running behind schedule by an average of 32 months but also that there are 'large cost over-runs' on a significant number of projects (*Financial Times*, 15 December, 1994), the benefits to the competitiveness of UK manufacturing of continuing to devote such a large proportion of state support to defence manufacturers will remain at least highly questionable for the foreseeable future.

REFERENCES

Addison, P. (1986), 'Warfare and Welfare', *London Review of Books*, 24 July, pp. 7–8.

Anderson, P. (1987), 'The Figures of Descent', *New Left Review*, 161, pp. 20–77.

Barnett, C. (1986), *The Audit of War: The Illusion and Reality of Britain as a Great Nation* (London: Macmillan).

Broadbent, E. (1988), *The Military and Government: From Macmillan to Heseltine* (London: Macmillan).

Budd, A. (1978), *The Politics of Economic Planning* (Manchester: Manchester University Press).

Butler, R.A. (1971), *The Art of the Possible* (London: Hamish Hamilton).

Carver, M. (1992), *Tightrope Walking: British Defence Policy since 1945* (London: Hutchinson).

CBI (1991), *Competing with the World's Best: The Report of the CBI Manufacturing Advisory Group* (London: Confederation of British Industry).

CBI (1992), 'Making it in Britain: Partnership for World Class Manufacturing',*The Report of the CBI National Manufacturing Council,* (London: Confederation of British Industry).

Chalmers, M. (1985), *Paying for Defence: Military Spending and British Decline* (London: Pluto).

Chalmers, M. (1992), 'British economic decline: the contribution of military spending', *The Royal Bank of Scotland Review*, 173, pp. 35–46.

Conservative Party (1970), *A Better Tomorrow: The Conservative Programme for the Next Five Years* (London: Conservative Central Office).

Cowling, K. (1990), 'The Strategic Approach to Economic and Industrial Policy', in Cowling, K. and R. Sugden (eds.), *A New Economic Policy for Britain: Essays on the Development of Industry* (Manchester: Manchester University Press).

Cowling, K. and R. Sugden (1993), 'Industrial strategy: the missing link in British economic policy', *Oxford Review of Economic Policy*, pp. 83–100.

Dockrill, M. (1988), *British Defence since 1945* (Oxford: Blackwell).

DTI (1987), *Civil Research and Development,* Government Response to the First Report of the House of Lords Select Committee on Science and Technology, Cmnd 185 (London: HMSO).

DTI (1988), *DTI – The Department for Enterprise* (London: HMSO).

Edgerton, D. (1991a), *England and the Aeroplane: An Essay on a Militant and Technological Nation* (London: Macmillan).

Edgerton, D. (1991b), 'Liberal militarism and the British state', *New Left Review*, 185, pp. 138–70.

Edgerton, D. (1991c), 'The prophet militant and industrial: the peculiarities of Correlli Barnett', *Twentieth Century British History*, 2, 3, pp. 360–79.

Edgerton, D. (1993a), 'Research, Development and Competitiveness', in Hughes, K. (ed.), *The Future of UK Competitiveness and the Role of Industrial Policy* (London: Policy Studies Institute).

Edgerton, D. (1993b), 'British research and development after 1945: A re-interpretation', *Science and Technology Policy*, April, pp. 10–16.

EEF (1992), *Industrial Strategy: Proposals for Recovery and Sustained Growth* (London: Engineering Employers Federation).

Elliott, D. (1977), *The Lucas Aerospace Workers' Campaign* (London: The Fabian Society).

Fischer, F. (1990), *Technocracy and the Politics of Expertise* (London: Sage).

Fleming, M. (1980), 'Industrial Policy', in Maunder, P. (ed.), *The British Economy in the 1970s* (London: Heinemann).

Freeman, C. (1980), 'Government Policy', in Pavitt, K. (ed.), *Technical Innovation and British Economic Performance* (London: Macmillan).

Freeman, C. (1987), *Technology Policy and Economic Performance: Lessons from Japan* (London: Pinter).

Friedman, D. (1988), *The Misunderstood Miracle: Industrial Development and Political Change in Japan* (Ithaca: Cornell University Press).

Gerschenkron, A. (1966), *Economic Backwardness in Historical Perspective: A Book of Essays* (Cambridge, Mass.: Belknap Press).

Godley, W. (1988), 'Manufacturing and the Future of the British Economy', in Barker, T. and P. Dunne (eds.), *The British Economy after Oil: Manufacturing or Services?* (London: Croom Helm).

Gould, B. (1989), *A Future for Socialism* (London: Jonathan Cape).

Grant, W. (1982), *The Political Economy of Industrial Policy* (London: Butterworth).

Gummett, P. (1980), *Scientists in Whitehall* (Manchester: Manchester University Press).

Harris, J. (1990), 'Enterprise and welfare states: a comparative perspective', *Transactions of the Royal Historical Society*, 40, pp. 175–95.

Harris, N. (1972), *Competition and Corporate Society: British Conservatives, the State and Industry 1945–1964* (London: Methuen).

Hayward, K. (1983), *Government and British Civil Aerospace: A Case Study in Post-war Technology Policy* (Manchester: Manchester University Press).

Henderson, P. (1986), 'Innocence and Design: The Influence of Economic Ideas on Policy', *The 1985 Reith Lectures* (Oxford: Basil Blackwell).

Hennessy, P. (1989), *Whitehall* (London: Fontana Press).

Hennessy, P and C. Anstey (1991), *From Clogs to Clogs? Britain's Relative Economic Decline since 1851* (Glasgow: Strathclyde Papers on Government and Politics in association with 'Analysis', BBC News and Current Affairs).

HMSO (1993), *Realising our Potential: A Strategy for Science, Engineering and Technology*, Cmnd 2250 (London: HMSO).

Holmes, M. (1982), *Political Pressure and Economic Policy: British Government 1970–1974* (London: Butterworth Scientific).

House of Commons (1993), *British Aerospace Industry*, Third Report of the House of Commons Select Committee on Trade and Industry (London: HMSO).

House of Lords (1985), *Overseas Trade*, Report of the House of Lords Select Committee, 1984–85 Session, HL238-1, (London: HMSO).

House of Lords (1986), *Civil Research and Development*, Report of the House of Lords Select Committee on Science and Technology, 1986–87 Session, HL20-1 (London: HMSO).

House of Lords (1991), *Innovation in Manufacturing Industry*, Report of the House of Lords Select Committee on Science and Technology, 1990–91 Session, HL18-1 (London: HMSO).

Hughes, K. and I. Christie (1993), 'Internationalisation and Industrial Policy' in Hughes, K. (ed.), *The Future of UK Competitiveness and the Role of Industrial Policy* (London: Policy Studies Institute).

Jackson, B. (1995), *Gunrunners Gold: How the Public's Money Finances Arms Sales* (London: World Development Movement).

Johnson, C. (1982), *MITI and the Japanese Miracle: The Growth of Industrial Policy, 1925–1975* (Stanford, California: Stanford University Press).

Jones, A. (1985), *Britain's Economy: The Roots of Stagnation* (Cambridge: Cambridge University Press).

Kagarlitsky, B. (1990), *The Dialectic of Change* (London: Verso).

Kennedy, P. (1988), *The Rise and Fall of the Great Powers: Economic Change and Military Conflict from 1500 to 2000* (London: Unwin Hyman).

Keynes, J.M. (1936), *The General Theory of Employment, Interest and Money: The Collected Writings of John Maynard Keynes* (London: Macmillan).

Labour Party (1991), *Modern Manufacturing Strength* (London: The Labour Party).

Labour Party (1993), *Making Britain's Future* (London: The Labour Party).

Leadbeater, C. (1991), 'Britain's days of judgement', *Marxism Today*, June, pp. 14–20

Lee, S.D. (1996), 'Manufacturing 1945–1994' in D. Coates (ed.), *Industrial Policy in the U.K.* (London: Macmillan).

List, F. (1928), *The National System of Political Economy* (translated by Sampson Lloyd) (London: Longmans).

Macmillan, H. (1966), *The Middle Way: A Study of the Problems of Economic and Social Progress in a Free and Democratic Society* (London: St. Martin's Press).

Middlemas, K. (1986), *Power, Competition and the State, Volume 1: Britain in Search of Balance 1940–61* (London: Macmillan).

MSF (1992), *Manufacturing Matters: The Need for a National Industrial Strategy* (London: Manufacturing, Science, Finance Union).

Nelson, R. (1993), 'A Retrospective', in Nelson, R. (ed.), *National Innovation Systems: A Comparative Analysis* (Oxford: Oxford University Press).

Nelson, R. and N. Rosenberg (1993), 'Technical Innovation and National Systems', in Nelson, R. (ed.), *National Innovation Systems: A Comparative Analysis* (Oxford: Oxford University Press).

Newton, S. and D. Porter (1988), *Modernization Frustrated: The Politics of Industrial Decline in Britain since 1900* (London: Unwin Hyman).

Onis, Z. (1991), 'The logic of the developmental state', *Comparative Politics*, October, pp. 109–26.

Opie, R. (1972), 'Economic Planning and Growth', in Beckerman, W. (ed.), *The Labour Government's Economic Record 1964–1970* (London: Duckworth).

Pavitt, K. (ed.) (1980), *Technical Innovation and British Economic Performance* (London: Macmillan).

Playfair, L. (1852), *Industrial Instruction on the Continent* (London: Royal School of Mines).

Pollard, S. (1982), *The Wasting of the British Economy: British Economic Policy 1945 to the Present* (London: Croom Helm).

Rothwell, R. and W. Zegveld (1985), *Reindustrialization and Technology* (Harlow: Longman).

Smith, D. (1980), *The Defence of the Realm in the 1980s* (London: Croom Helm).

Smith, J. (1993), *Speech delivered to the Manufacturing Matters Conference*, Queen Elizabeth II Conference Centre, London, 20th October.

Smith, K. (1984), *The British Economic Crisis: Its Past and Future* (Harmondsworth: Penguin).

Taylor, T. and K. Hayward (1989), *The UK Defence Industrial Base: Development and Future Policy Options* (London: Brassey's).

Vig, N. (1968), *Science and Technology in British Politics* (Oxford: Pergamon).

Wade, R. (1990), *Governing the Market Economy: Economic Theory and the Role of Government in East Asian Industrialization* (Princeton: Princeton University Press).

Wainwright, H. and D. Elliott (1982), *The Lucas Plan: A New Trade Unionism in the Making?* (London: Allison & Busby).

Walker, D. (1987), 'The First Wilson Governments, 1964–1970', in Hennessy, P. and A. Seldon (eds.), *Ruling Performance: British Governments from Attlee to Thatcher* (Oxford: Blackwell).

Williams, E.E. (1896), *Made in Germany* (London: Heinemann).

Wilson, H. (1979), *Final Term: The Labour Government 1974–1976* (London: Weidenfeld & Nicolson).

World Bank (1994), *The East Asian Miracle: Economic Growth and Public Policy*, A World Bank Policy Research Report (Oxford: Oxford University Press).

Young, S. and A. Lowe (1974), *Intervention in the Mixed Economy* (London: Croom Helm).

5. Manufacturing British Decline

Simon Lee

INTRODUCTION

Although there are many measures of Britain's relative economic decline, by far the most important is the decline of manufacturing. In its report, *Competitiveness of UK Manufacturing* (House of Commons, 1994), the House of Commons Trade and Industry Committee has identified three reasons why manufacturing is critical to the performance of the national economy. Firstly, manufacturing accounts for by far the largest share of exports. For example, in 1992, 62.6 per cent of total UK exports were manufactured goods. Service industries accounted for only 23.4 per cent of exports. Secondly, because only about 20 per cent of the output of Britain's service industries can be exported, manufactures are vital because it is their greater tradeability in overseas markets which offers Britain the means by which to finance her imports of food, raw materials and foreign manufactures. Indeed, the Committee found that for every 1 per cent decline in UK exports of manufactures, its exports of services would have to increase by 2.5 per cent merely to compensate for such a loss. Thirdly, the presence of a competitive manufacturing sector in Britain is vital because a substantial and increasing proportion of service industries is dependent on manufacturing for its business. Indeed, the Committee found the distinction between manufacturing and services is becoming harder to identify (House of Commons, 1994, pp. 21–2). Domestic manufacturing is therefore vital to Britain's trade performance, the prosperity of her population, and the competitiveness of the non-manufacturing sectors of her economy.

Singh has suggested that an efficient manufacturing sector is 'one which (currently and potentially) not only satisfies the demands of consumers at home, but is also able to sell enough of its products abroad to pay for the nation's import requirements', provided that these objectives are achieved at 'socially acceptable levels of output, employment and the exchange rate' (Singh, 1983, p. 242). By any of Singh's criteria, Britain now possesses, and is likely to possess for the foreseeable future, an 'ineffficient' manufacturing sector. The most immediate and intractable problem for Britain is that its manufacturing sector has now contracted to such an extent that the size of the tradeable sector of the national economy is too small for it to be able to pay for the nation's import requirements. From 1963, when the value of the UK's trade in manufactures was 275 per cent greater than that of her manufactured imports, to 1983 the UK sustained an annual balance of payments surplus on her trade in manufactures of between £1.5 billion and £6.0 billion (House of Lords, 1985, p. 7). But from 1984 to the present day, through periods of both economic boom and recession, the UK has sustained a substantial deficit on her trade in manufactures for the first time since the Industrial Revolution. In 1989, Britain's visible trade deficit reached almost £25 billion or nearly five per cent of GDP. Between 1979 and 1989, whilst UK exports rose by 18.7 per cent, imports rose by 56.5 per cent (Hutton, 1995, pp. 74, 78). Indeed, the recession of 1990–93 was the first in the UK during which manufactured imports have risen.

Table 5.1: The UK balance of payments

Current Account	Visible trade (balance)	Invisible trade (balance)	Current Balance
1983	-1 537	5 066	3 529
1985	-3 345	5 583	2 238
1987	-11 582	6 599	-4 983
1989	-24 683	2 171	-22 512
1990	-18 809	541	-18 268
1991	-10 284	2 632	-7 652
1992	-13 406	2 867	-10 539
1993	-13 680	2 799	-10 881

Source: Central Statistical Office, 1994

To denote the process of manufacturing decline, frequent reference has been made by economists, historians and political scientists to the concept of deindustrialization, which Thirlwall has defined as 'the absolute loss of jobs in industrial activities and particularly in manufacturing industry' (Thirlwall, 1982, p. 22). Total employment in industry and manufacturing in Britain reached a peak in 1966 and has been declining ever since. Britain lost 47 per cent of its employment in manufacturing between 1971 and 1993. A 30 per cent decline alone was registered between 1979 and 1990 compared with a decline during the same period of 17 per cent in France, 11 per cent in Italy, and 5 per cent in the US, no change in Germany and an expansion of 13 per cent in Japan (House of Commons, 1994, p. 20). Even Nigel Lawson, the Thatcherite who above all other Cabinet ministers during the 1980s refused to accept the particular importance of manufacturing to national economic performance, has acknowledged that between 1979 and 1981 employment in manufacturing declined by 2 million or 14 per cent of the total employed (Lawson, 1992, p. 55). However, when analysing the relative decline of manufacturing in Britain, our definition of deindustrialization must broaden from a narrow focus on manufacturing employment to the equally important matter of manufacturing output and investment, for it is only when these factors are taken into account that the true extent and significance of deindustrialization for Britain becomes apparent.

Whilst the share of GDP in constant prices accounted for by manufacturing has declined in all the major industrial countries, the UK is unique amongst them in experiencing almost stagnant manufacturing output in the past two decades. In 1992, UK manufacturing output was less than 1 per cent above its 1973 peak, whereas, during the same period, output in Germany rose by 25 per cent, in France by 27 per cent, in Italy by 85 per cent, and in Japan by 119 per cent (House of Commons, 1994, p. 16). In the first quarter of 1993, the index of UK manufacturing output stood at 133.5, compared to 103.9 in the first three months of 1979, the last full quarter of manufacturing activity under the Callaghan Government. During the first fourteen years of Conservative Government, manufacturing output had grown on average by only 0.8 per cent per annum. Even in 1989, at the peak of an economic boom, 'manufacturing output had grown at no more than 1.2 per cent per year from the peak of the previous cycle' (Hutton, 1995, p. 77). Having accounted for 32 per cent of Britain's GDP in 1972, and 28 per cent in 1980, manufacturing contracted so rapidly in the following decade that by 1992 it was responsible for generating only 20 per cent of GDP (Davis, Flanders and Star, 1992, p. 46). The pattern of investment in manufacturing in Britain is equally disconcerting. From 1979 to 1989, investment in manufacturing grew by a mere 12.8 per cent, compared with a 108 per cent increase in investment in the UK services sector as a whole, and a 320.2 per cent increase in investment in financial services (Glyn, 1992, p. 84). Bank lending to manufacturing in the UK increased in constant price terms by only 49 per cent between 1980 and 1991 and declined, as a percentage of total bank lending, from 27.7 per cent in 1980 to 10.8 per cent in 1991. This 49 per cent increase in bank lending to manufacturing is put into perspective by the 801 per cent and 648 per cent increases respectively in lending to the property and personal sectors (CBI, 1992, p. 22).

These disturbing industrial trends have not passed unnoticed. In 1985, a House of Lords Select Committee report on *Overseas Trade* asserted that a poor performance in manufacturing undoubtedly contained 'the seeds of a major political and economic crisis in the foreseeable future' (House of Lords, 1985, p. 56). In 1991, the House of Lords' Select Committee on Science and Technology warned that Britain's manufacturing base was in decline, that its home markets were increasingly penetrated by imports, and that its share of world markets in manufactures was too small. The Committee concluded that 'The implications for our future prosperity are grave' (House of Lords, 1991, p. 29). This chapter explores the process of deindustrialization and its implications for the future of Britain. It commences with an analysis of the competing explanations of deindustrialization, including the thesis of the 'hollowing out' of manufacturing in Britain. This process is then illustrated by reference to two of Britain's major manufacturers, British Aerospace (BAe) and the General Electric Company (GEC). The policies of the Thatcher Governments towards manufacturing are then analysed together with the reaction that these policies drew from select committee inquiries and the more recent counterblast against deindustrialization that has been advanced by both politicians and economists. The chapter concludes by considering the Major Governments' policies towards manufacturing.

THE DEINDUSTRIALIZATION OF BRITAIN

Whilst there is widespread agreement about the fact of deindustrialization in Britain, consensus does not extend to its causes. Rowthorn and Wells have contended that the deterioration in the trade balance in manufacturing has been 'to a large degree, unavoidable, and would have occurred on much the same scale even if postwar British industrial development had been crowned with success' (Rowthorn and Wells, 1987, p. 3). Indeed, industrial success in the form of higher productivity and more rapid labour shedding might have brought an even steeper decline in manufacturing's share of total employment. Britain's poor postwar performance in manufacturing should not therefore be measured in terms of a deteriorating trade balance or a declining share of total employment, or indeed of there being 'too few producers' in the British economy as Bacon and Eltis have suggested (Bacon and Eltis, 1976), but rather by the fact that those continuing to work in manufacturing have been working at too low a level of productivity (Rowthorn and Wells, 1987, pp. 3–4). Rather than being an example of 'positive' deindustrialization, which occurs as a consequence of sustained economic growth in a fully employed, highly developed economy, where rapid productivity growth in manufacturing does not lead to unemployment because labour displaced from manufacturing by automation or other labour-saving methods, is absorbed by a dynamic services sector, Britain in the 1980s should be seen as an example of 'negative' deindustrialization. Rowthorn and Wells contend that this constitutes a symptom of economic failure rather than economic success, the product of stagnating real incomes and industrial output, where displaced labour has not been absorbed by the services sector and has resulted in rising unemployment (Rowthorn and Wells, 1987, p. 25).

Although negative deindustrialization might account for Britain's more recent economic performance, Rowthorn and Wells suggest that relative economic decline in the longer term may be attributable to another form of deindustrialization. This has been caused by changes in the structure of Britain's foreign trade and has occurred 'when, for some reason, the pattern of net exports shifts away from manufactures towards other goods and services', resulting in a transfer of resources and labour from manufacturing to other sectors of the British economy. As a consequence, Britain has experienced 'a radical shift in its pattern of trade specialization during the postwar period' which has in turn had a major impact on the structure of the national economy, especially its structure of employment. Indeed, it is the peculiar size and magnitude of this shift in trade specialization which helps to account for the particularly large decline in manufacturing employment in Britain, in terms both of relative shares of those employed and of absolute numbers (Rowthorn and Wells, 1987, pp. 6–7). To account for these trends in trade specialization, Rowthorn and Wells explore three possible explanations, the first of which is the 'Maturity thesis'. This thesis locates Britain's relative decline within a more general theory of economic development and structural change that traces the contraction over time of employment in agriculture and industry and the concomitant expansion of employment in the services sector. It is this decline in the share of industry in total employment that the Maturity thesis seeks to explain. Given that Britain was one of the most affluent national economies in the 1950s, and that industry's share of total employment fell from 47.9 per cent in 1955 to 35.7 per cent in 1981, whilst the services sector's share expanded from 46.7 per cent to 61.7 per cent over the same period, Rowthorn and Wells suggest that the Maturity thesis appears 'quite convincing' as an explanation of Britain's postwar deindustrialization (Rowthorn and Wells, 1987, p. 218).

A second potential explanation lies with what Rowthorn and Wells term the 'Specialization thesis', which seeks to account for deindustrialization in terms of a stream of autonomous developments that have had an enormous cumulative impact on the national trade structure and pattern of specialization. These autonomous developments include the discovery of North Sea Oil, a reduction in real terms in the cost of imports of food and raw materials, an increase in domestic food production that has reduced the need to import, a reduction in the demand for imported raw materials as a consequence of changing production methods and composition of output, and increased exports from the services sector in areas such as finance, consultancy and civil aviation. Rowthorn and Wells suggest that these developments may explain both the dramatic improvement in the UK's trade balance in non-manufactures and the dramatic deterioration in its trade balance in manufactures. When Britain was 'the workshop of the world' in the nineteenth century, it had to be a massive net exporter of manufactures in order to pay for its imported food and raw materials, but in the postwar period the need to export manufactures has diminished because of autonomous developments in the UK's trade in non-manufactures. Thus the evaporation of the UK's historic trade surplus in manufactures should not be seen as a testimony to industrial failure but predominantly a response to developments in other non-manufacturing sectors of the economy. The problem with this explanation is that it does not pay sufficient attention to the way in which the interventions of postwar British governments protected the interests of non-manufacturing sectors of the economy, not least those of finance and commerce in the City of London, at the expense of manufacturing interests. Furthermore, the UK's trade surplus on services is no longer sufficient to be able to cover the much larger deficit on its trade in manufactures.

The third potential explanation for deindustrialization identified by Rowthorn and Wells is what they term the 'Failure thesis'. This thesis portrays the decline of manufacturing as a symptom of wider economic failure, with the weakness of manufacturing providing not only the main reason why the UK has become a relatively poor country, with the lowest per capita incomes in Northern Europe, but also the explanation for its high rate of unemployment nationally (Rowthorn and Wells, 1987, pp. 223–4). Rowthorn and Wells conclude that the Failure thesis actually explains very little of the UK's decline in manufacturing employment and that most of this decline may be accounted for by the two other theses. The Maturity thesis emphasizes that Britain had reached the point of economic maturity in the 1950s, whilst the Specialization thesis attributes significance to the major changes in the UK's pattern of trade specialization since 1950. Rowthorn and Wells' own conclusion is that the loss of manufacturing employment was inevitable irrespective of that sector's postwar performance. Had the manufacturing sector been more dynamic, just as many jobs would have been lost through higher productivity. However, the authors appear to discount the possibility that expanding manufactured output might have generated additional employment. At the same time, Rowthorn and Wells contend that of the 2.9 million manufacturing jobs that were lost from the UK economy between 1966 and 1983, approximately 60 per cent were bound to disappear simply because the economy had reached maturity by 1966. Another 30 per cent were lost simply because of the changes in the U.K.'s trade specialization, for example, North Sea Oil and greater food self-sufficiency, but only 10 per cent of manufacturing jobs were lost as a consequence of poor economic performance (Rowthorn and Wells, 1987, pp. 247–8).

For Rowthorn and Wells the explanation of deindustrialization in Britain lies more with economic maturity and trade specialization than with industrial failure. However, the particular severity of Britain's industrial decline has raised the question of whether deindustrialization might be attributed to some peculiar quality possessed by the British people and expressed through their institutions. For Williams, the key to understanding deindustrialization lies with a recognition of 'the conditioning influence of a coherent set of specifically national institutional conditions' (Williams, 1983, p. ix). His contention is that economic theory necessarily disregards the considerable variations in the specific institutional conditions that influence manufacturing enterprises in different advanced capitalist economies. Economists have therefore failed to identify a problem for British manufacturers which is, in several important respects, peculiar to Britain, and which may be explained in terms of 'four national conditions of enterprise calculation'. These conditions are management control over the labour process, market limitations, the relationship of manufacturing industry to financial institutions, and the inter-relationship between manufacturing industry and government.

In the case of management control over the labour process, Williams contends that the problem for manufacturing does not lie with lazy or strike-prone workers, but with the way in which production has been overmanned and poorly organized. Further constraints have been placed on British manufacturers by the structure of their domestic market and its particular composition of demand. With two-thirds or more of manufacturing output sold on the domestic market in the past, firms were conditioned against paying proper attention to marketing problems overseas. For example, in the car industry, until recently British firms failed to maintain and expand European dealer networks that were essential for volume sales, whilst the ranges of cars that they developed were not designed with the much larger European car market in mind. A third obstacle to manufacturing success has arisen from the relationship between industry and financial institutions in Britain. The latter have failed to provide sufficient funds on favourable terms for investment in businesses' organic growth but have instead conditioned large companies to engage in the pursuit of short-term financial advantage by facilitating takeovers and mergers. The final constraint on manufacturers in Britain identified by Williams is that brought about by the policies of successive postwar governments which have not only concentrated upon but also grossly mismanaged macroeconomic policy when there was no good reason to imagine that demand management rather than supply-side policies was the most effective means to encourage business expansion.

From his analysis of deindustrialization, Williams generates two theses which seek to challenge the assumption that government policy towards manufacturing is coherent in addition to being diverse. The first thesis is that 'National governments have a plurality of economic policies and these policies are not necessarily mutually consistent and compatible' (Williams, 1983, p. 92). This thesis is important because it moves away from the widely held contention, discussed in the previous chapter, that merely by replacing the existing Whitehall and Westminster governing elites with an alternative technocratic elite, industrial decline could be reversed by the pursuit of a coherent national industrial strategy. Williams points to the plurality, incoherence and uncertainty that surround government policies towards manufacturing and which consequently preclude technocratic visions of perfectly coordinated and administered industrial strategies. His second thesis, that 'National economic policies are practices which have specific preconditions in the material and institutional conditions of government calculations', is also important because it acknowledges not only that there may be a disjuncture between government policies and the conditions of enterprise calculation, but also that there are not simple, straightforward interests in manufacturing which can and should be served and promoted by government policy (Williams, 1983, p. 94). The problems encountered by manufacturers may vary enormously between different industries and companies. An emphasis on a single policy prescription, e.g. the frequent demands from the CBI for higher state spending on R & D, may be highly inappropriate and completely miss the causes of competitive disadvantage in specific industries and firms. There is not therefore a single, linear path for developing either manufacturing success at the sectoral or company level or indeed the public policies intended to promote it.

THE 'HOLLOWING OUT' OF GEC AND BAe

Because he was writing in mid-1982, Williams felt that it was premature to evaluate the impact of Thatcherite policies on manufacturing. However, by the end of the decade, in company with Williams and Haslam, Williams had developed the thesis of 'hollowing out' to depict how the pace of deindustrialization in Britain had accelerated during the 1980s. 'Hollowing out' had occurred as a consequence of the actions of large British firms which had been reducing their interest in domestic manufacturing whilst increasing their interest both in manufacturing overseas and in the services sector of the global economy. Williams, Williams and Haslam developed their thesis from an analysis of 25 large British firms (with annual sales of more than £2 billion) about whom data was obtained for the period from 1979 to 1989. Overseas employment had always been of importance to these firms but whereas in 1979 it had accounted for 38 per cent of total employment, by 1989 it accounted for 53 per cent or some 200 000 jobs. In sharp contrast, during the same period, domestic employment in manufacturing businesses owned by these firms had fallen by 29.1 per cent or 330 000 jobs. Further investigation revealed that these jobs had actually all disappeared in the period from 1979 to 1983 and that there had not been a recovery in employment in manufacturing despite the more general economic recovery in Britain during the mid- to late-1980s. Moreover, no less than 33 per cent of the increase in overseas employment since 1979 was accounted for by the activities of just two large companies, Hanson and BTR, both of which had made major investments in North America. These figures illustrate the capacity of just a few major firms to act in a manner which could deprive Britain of 'national champions' in sectors of strategic importance for the national trade balance in manufacturing. (Williams, Williams and Haslam, 1990, pp. 466–8). Indeed, this process had become so far advanced by 1990 as to place constraints on the future effectiveness of any attempts to develop a national industrial policy. Therefore, if Britain's deindustrialization was to be stemmed, let alone reversed, the authors' contention was that 'hollowing out' must be identified and addressed as part of a wider European problem because of the likely dominance of German production in EU manufacturing (Williams, Williams and Haslam, 1990, p. 456).

To illustrate the process of hollowing out at the level of the individual company, Williams, Williams and Haslam focused amongst others on two of Britain's largest manufacturers, the General Electric Company (GEC) and British Aerospace (BAe). These companies are of particular interest because both are heavily dependent on defence markets and have, as a consequence of the end of the Cold War, faced important choices about their future business strategies which in many ways mirror the wider problems confronting government and industry alike in Britain, one of the most defence dependent economies in the OECD In his earlier analysis of GEC, John Williams had sought to challenge what he claimed was the widespread belief that GEC had been possibly the most consistently successful major British manufacturer since the early 1960s. Williams characterized the performance of GEC under the stewardship of its managing director since 1963, Lord Weinstock, as one of 'soaring financial success and more leaden productive attainment' (Williams, 1983, p. 153). For example, the modern GEC had itself been fashioned by the Industrial Reorganization Corporation (IRC) in 1967 from a merger of two other major British electrical engineering companies, English Electric (EE) and Associated Electrical Industries (AEI) with the old GEC. The acquisition of these two companies had cost GEC less than £16 million and yet it had managed to gain control of businesses with net assets of around £460 million (Williams, 1983, p. 138). The acquisition of EE and AEI was the first of a number of expert financial transactions masterminded by Lord Weinstock, which were facilitated by the state assistance of government intervention. GEC has subsequently continued to generate a substantial financial dividend for its shareholders, not least from the 'cash mountain' of earnings which the company has preferred to bank rather than invest in new ventures or expand the output of its existing businesses. During the 1970s, GEC's undoubted financial dividend for its shareholders was not accompanied by any significant growth in its real output, especially in the rapidly expanding markets for consumer electronics and semiconductors. GEC's output rose by only 13 per cent between 1970 and 1981, with output virtually stagnant between 1970 and 1978. The company's strategy of growth through acquisition has not led to any expansion in employment. On the contrary, since 1970 GEC has disposed of more firms than it has acquired. If the supposedly most successful manufacturing company in Britain had been unable to expand its employment or output, then Williams concluded that the future for manufacturing in Britain must appear bleak (Williams, 1983, pp. 153–5).

In their more recent analysis of GEC's performance, Williams, Williams and Haslam have asserted that the company's corporate strategy has been characterized both by a retreat from manufacturing in general and manufacturing in contested markets in particular, and by consolidation in the more protected markets of defence contracting. Williams had previously pointed to the conversion of a factory intended for the production of microchips to the manufacture of torpedoes (Williams, 1983, p. 159). For Williams, Williams and Haslam, GEC has become 'a rentier capitalist firm whose profits increasingly come from short-term investment and shareholdings in electrical businesses which somebody else manages' (Williams, Williams and Haslam, 1990, p. 169). The company has indeed entered joint ventures with Alcatel-Alsthom of France to form GEC-Alsthom, the world's second-largest power engineering business, and has allowed Siemens of Germany to acquire a 40 per cent share in GPT, its telecommunications business. As a consequence, GEC's core manufacturing businesses are now all in sectors which, at least until recently, have been heavily subsidized by large scale procurement of equipment by governments. Lord Weinstock has stated that 'Any expansion must involve either new technology or new markets' (*The Sunday Times*, 10 July, 1994), but there is a danger that its existing joint ventures have if anything accentuated GEC's tendency to hoard resources in its cash mountain and narrowed the scope for further acquisitions. At the end of financial year 1993–94, GEC possessed cash reserves of £2.82 billion within the company, equivalent then to around one third of GEC's Stock Market valuation, and of which £1.47 billion was held by its joint venture companies. GEC technology, in its telecommunications and power engineering businesses, has now become so enmeshed with that of its partners that it is unlikely to be able to contemplate any independent acquisitions in either of these markets without the prior consent of its partners (*Financial Times*, 7 July, 1994). At the level of the individual company, for GEC the hollowing out of British manufacturing has appeared to make sense over the past quarter century because the profitable financial management of its cash reserves has afforded it a degree of protection from the need to undertake more risky investments in new manufacturing businesses. For Britain, at the level of the national economy, the hollowing out of electronics businesses by GEC and other large British companies such as Thorn EMI has meant the absence of a large-scale British presence in many of the most dynamic industrial markets of the last two decades, with a concomitant impact both on the balance of payments and Britain's dependence on foreign inward investment and technological innovation.

In many respects, the corporate history of British Aerospace (BAe) has parelleled that of GEC in that, since BAe's creation through the nationalization in 1977 of Scottish Aviation, the British Aircraft Corporation, and the aviation division of Hawker Siddeley, its profitability has largely depended on state largesse, principally in the form of massive defence contracts but also through its acquisition from the state, at a substantial initial discount, of privatized companies, that is, the Rover Group and Royal Ordnance. However, after its own phased privatization in 1981 and 1984, BAe did make a much more concerted effort than GEC at the time to dilute its dependence on defence contracting. Diversification into civil markets was principally achieved through the £150 million purchase of the Rover Group in 1988 (a subsequent National Audit Office report suggested that it should have paid £206.5 million), and the purchase of the construction company Ballast Needham and the property company, Arlington. In the case of the latter company, the purchase was not undertaken until after the collapse of the domestic property boom had left Arlington with substantial liabilities. It should also be remembered that BAe's limited diversification into civil markets took place after its £190 million purchase in 1987 of Royal Ordnance from the taxpayer, an acquisition intended to strengthen its core defence manufacturing business.

BAe's diversification appeared to reap an instant dividend when its profits increased from £293 million in 1989 to £400 million in 1990. Most of this increase, however, was generated by BAe's defence businesses rather than its civil aircraft manufacturing activities or its recent acquisitions in the motor vehicle and property sectors. Indeed, whilst Rover contributed profits of £52 million in 1990, it then proceeded to accumulate losses of £170 million, £151 million and £9 million in the following three years. Indeed, such was the dowturn in BAe's financial performance that on one day in 1992, the company's share price fell by 44 per cent. BAe's reaction to the failure of its diversification to deliver higher profitability, at least in the short term, was to undertake a renewed hollowing out of its civil manufacturing businesses in order to be able to concentrate its resources on its more profitable defence interests. The company's executive jet manufacturing business was sold to an overseas purchaser, Raytheon, whilst BAe entered protracted and unsuccessful negotiations with the Taiwan Aerospace Corporation in the hope of forming a joint venture partnership for BAe's loss-making regional jet airline manufacturing business. These deals would enable BAe to concentrate its civil aircraft manufacturing interests on its 20 per cent interest in the European Airbus consortium. Further negotiations have occurred to incorporate BAe's satellite manufacturing interests in Matra Marconi Space, an Anglo French joint venture in which GEC has a 49 per cent share, and to merge BAe's missile manufacturing business with that of Matra. BAe's data processing operations have also been sold to an overseas company, Computer Sciences Corporation of the US, whilst Ballast Needham has been another notable disposal.

Despite these attempts to refocus BAe's corporate strategy towards its core defence interests, the key to whether BAe would make a more decisive contribution to the hollowing out of British manufacturing surrounded its future policy towards the Rover car manufacturing business. In August 1993, just five years after its purchase of Rover, BAe was freed from restrictions imposed by the British government on the disposal of Rover to another manufacturer. At that time, BAe announced that it did not intend to sell Rover because it regarded motor vehicles, along with defence, commercial aircraft and aerostructures, as one of its core businesses. Although BAe enjoyed access to the industrial support of Honda, which held a 20 per cent stake in Rover, and had clearly made a vital contribution to the quality, engineering and composition of Rover's products and production lines, BAe's chairman, John Cahill, made it clear that the company's ultimate strategy was to support and protect its main defence business by cash generation and cost reduction, not least through the further disposal of non-core businesses. To make a major impact on its balance sheet, one of the few major options open to BAe was to rid itself of the financial drain imposed by Rover. Although Rover had produced pre-tax profits of £52 million in 1990, the onset of recession in the European car market meant that it was no longer trading profitably, accumulating losses of £170 million in 1991, £151 million in 1992, and £9 million in 1993. It was not then althogether unexpected when BAe announced in January 1994 that Rover would be sold to the German car manufacturer, BMW for £800 million. Given the contemporary British scepticism towards matters European and the customary popular suspicion concerning German motives, a wave of industrial nationalism similar to that which had surrounded Jaguar's sale to Ford in 1989 might have been anticipated. In the event, the sentiment that accompanied the sale of Rover was more one of regret than rancour coupled with a widespread opinion that Rover might ultimately benefit from having access to the greater financial resources and engineering expertise of BMW. In his subsequent evidence to the House of Commons Trade and Industry Committee, the Secretary of State for Trade and Industry, Michael Heseltine, expressed his personal regret that ownership of Rover had been transferred to a German company but that there had not been any 'serious British option' of a takeover or management buy-out at the time (*The Times*, 7 July, 1994). Perhaps the greatest long-term damage to manufacturing in Britain that Rover's sale to BMW might inflict is the danger that Japanese companies will be dissuaded from future industrial partnerships with British firms. Japanese inward investment and its associated working practices had been instrumental during the 1980s in changing popular perceptions of the benefits of overseas as opposed to domestic ownership and control of manufacturing plants in Britain. Paradoxically, throughout the sale of Rover, both the interests of and the vital role that Honda had played in the transformation of Rover's performance were largely ignored. If Britain wishes to remain competitive in or even re-enter world markets for many engineering products, it cannot afford to risk alienating existing and potential Japanese investors.

Under its new German ownership, Rover is expected to invest almost £2 billion in the UK before the millenium, an increase of nearly £700 million over the investment planned under BAe's ownership, which will see production rise from 478 600 in 1994, up 16 per cent from 1993 and the highest level since 1989, to around 750 000 in 2000. The benefits to BMW of the acquisition of Rover have already become apparent. For example, following on from the signing in October 1994 of a memorandum of understanding with Proton, the Malaysian car manufacturer, to produce Rover engines under licence in Malaysia, in December 1994, Rover announced that it had signed a joint venture agreement with the Indonesian government to make 25 000 cars a year in Indonesia from 1997 (*The Guardian*, 23 December, 1994). This coincided with Rover's plans to recruit an additional 1450 workers to cope with increased production and Land Rover's disclosure that it had produced 39 per cent more vehicles in 1994 than in the previous year. Furthermore, the chairman of BMW has stated that Rover-produced cars will return to the North American market in the near future, as well as spearheading BMW's drive into the rapidly growing Asian markets. Although it has sold its 20 per cent stake in Rover, and has indicated that it intends no further large collaborative projects with Rover, Honda has announced that it will buy a new range of diesel engines designed and developed by Rover (*Financial Times*, 7 October, 1994; 31 January, 1995). Rover will also be investing £25 million in a new design and engineering centre as part of its five year, £1.5 billion car development programme (*The Guardian*, 1 December, 1994). The financial return to BMW from Rover is likely to be in the medium to long term since in 1994 Rover contributed only £4.8 million to BMW profits, albeit that Rover's profits before tax and interest charges were thought to be £80 million (*The Guardian*, 17 March, 1995). However, unlike its former UK competitors in the vehicle manufacturing industry, BMW is not constrained in its corporate development by the dictates of short-termism imposed from the City of London and is therefore able to entertain and undertake such strategic investments.

It should not be thought that the hollowing out of BAe's major civil manufacturing business has necessarily secured the company's industrial and financial future. Within a month of Rover's sale to BMW, it was disclosed that Rover's accounts had included a hidden £271 million cash reserve which meant that BAe had in effect raised only £439 million, little more than half the anticipated proceeds. Whilst its defence aerospace manufacturing business has remained profitable (making profits of £412 million on total sales of £4.5 billion in 1994, and with a record order book worth £9.7 billion), BAe has consistently lost money from its regional aircraft manufacturing business. In the period 1992–94, the company has made provisions totalling £1.5 billion to cover restructuring costs. The demand for this type of aircraft is set to grow but the problem has been that 17 manufacturers have been seeking to compete in the same market. To alleviate these losses, BAe has launched a joint marketing venture with ATR, jointly owned by Aerospatiale of France and Alenia of Italy. The model that the European manufacturers hope to replicate for regional aircraft is that of the Airbus consortium. Hollowing out at BAe has not been confined to its regional aircraft business. B.Ae. has also cut 750 jobs from its Airbus division and has lost a further 850 jobs as a consequence of having sold its corporate jets business to the US manufacturer, Raytheon, which has subsequently transferred production to the other side of the Atlantic. BAe has also seen employment in its missile division decline from 16 500 in 1989 to 3 800 in 1995. It has been seeking to merge its missile interests with those of Matra of France and has agreed to pay Matra £50 million to secure a 50 per cent share in the venture, with up to £100 million being paid at a later date depending on the extent of sales from Matra's existing, pre-merger order book. However, a potential obstacle to the venture remains the French government's last-minute demands for assurances that the UK will purchase European rather than US missiles in future (*Financial Times*, 1 April, 1995).

It was perhaps inevitable, given BAe's need for industrial partners to share spiralling development costs and GEC's proclivity for absorbing ailing British manufacturers at minimal financial cost to itself, that the prospect of a merger between the defence businesses of the two companies should have been contemplated in July 1993. Such a deal would have created what at that time would have been the world's largest defence contractor, with annual sales of around £7.5 billion (*The Sunday Times*, 11 July, 1993). The leaking of the companies' discussions to the national press was sufficient to bring them to a premature conclusion with an agreement that there would be a moratorium on hostile bids to take over each other for a period of two years. More recently, GEC and BAe have been engaged in a takeover battle to control VSEL, the manufacturer of Trident and

Trafalgar-class nuclear submarines for the Royal Navy. In October 1994, BAe offered £478 million for VSEL. A fortnight later, GEC replied with a £532 million counter-bid to which BAe duly responded with a £559 million revised offer. The auctioning of VSEL was then interrupted for nearly four months by the Secretary of State for Trade and Industry, Michael Heseltine, who referred both bids to the Monopolies and Mergers' Commission (MMC). The MMC would look into the public interest implications of BAe's bid, and the public interest and competition implications of GEC's bid. When the MMC reported, Heseltine decided to overrule its findings and side with a minority report from two MMC panellists which recommended that there were no competition grounds that warranted blocking either bid and that therefore the market should be left to decide the fate of VSEL. Heseltine's decision encouraged BAe to raise its offer for VSEL to £648 million but this merely inspired GEC to land the knockout punch with a bid of £835 million. As a consequence of its successful bid, GEC now enjoys a virtual monopoly of UK warship manufacturing capacity and is in pole position for a number of major orders, most notably a £2.5 billion contract for up to 5 Trafalgar-class submarines and a £500 million order for two new Royal Navy assault ships. The value to GEC of its takeover of VSEL will be undermined if either or both of these orders are cancelled or reduced in scale by future defence cuts.

The battle to control VSEL reflects the fight between GEC and BAe to establish themselves as the prime UK defence contractor. GEC, under Lord Weinstock's stewardship, appears to be seeking to develop a UK defence manufacturing national champion, whereas BAe has been seeking to consolidate its interests through a series of cross-European joint ventures. Had BAe won control of VSEL, it would have been able to become a prime contractor for warships, as well as military aircraft and missiles, in a market which despite the peace dividend is projected to be worth £112 billion in the period to 2010. However, the value to the trade performance of UK manufacturing as a whole, of two of its major companies being involved in an expensive auction for a manufacturer whose future prospects are dependent upon the largesse of government and the progress of arms control negotiations rather than the purchasing power of consumers in competitive but growing markets, remains dubious GEC's victory over BAe for control of VSEL cannot disguise the long-term impact of the hollowing out caused by its cumulative withdrawal from many civil manufacturing businesses. GEC had a turnover of £6.3 billion in 1993 but this is miniscule compared with the German electronics multinational Siemens whose turnover was £33.6 billion during the same period. Indeed, Siemens' R & D spending alone is equivalent to around 60 per cent of

GEC's total sales whilst its workforce of 391 000 employees dwarves GEC's 93 000 (*The Independent on Sunday*, 18 June, 1995).

For BAe, the longer term dividends of the hollowing out resulting in particular from its sale of Rover remain uncertain. On the one hand, the cash generated by Rover's sale together with the £170 million raised from a rights issue as part of its efforts to fund a VSEL takeover have strengthened BAe's finances markedly. On the other hand, as the previous chapter demonstrated, BAe's future now depends entirely on its ability to compete in the aerospace industry where both the civil and military sectors are fiercely competitive. In the civil sector, BAe's marketing agreement with ATR, has given BAe a means of stemming the losses from its commercial aircraft division which had lost £1.79 billion in the three years to 1994. BAe also possesses a 20 per cent share of the Airbus consortium which is becoming more profitable. In the military sector, BAe has recently reached agreement on a joint marketing venture with Saab of Sweden for the latter's Gripen fighter. BAe has also been offered a 20 per cent share of the Eurocopter Tiger attack helicopter programme, a similar share of the NH90 medium-sized military transport helicopter project, and may soon complete the merger of its missile business with Matra of France. On the other hand, BAe's failure to diversify into profitable civil manufacturing businesses leaves it particularly dependent on future defence procurement decisions, especially those surrounding the EFA. Furthermore, BAe's ability to compete in both civil and military aerospace markets in the future will be contingent upon its capacity to finance its share of the development costs of new products. With less than £1 billion of shareholders funds, despite its annual turnover of more than £6 billion, BAe may eventually find itself unable to meet these costs especially given the increasing reluctance of the British government to regard launch aid as anything other than an unnecessary subsidy and distortion of the aerospace market. In that eventuality, the hollowing out of domestically-owned manufacturing may take a major step forward with the takeover of all or part of BAe's aerospace businesses by GEC or a foreign multinational such as DASA.

THE THATCHER GOVERNMENTS AND MANUFACTURING

The hollowing out of British manufacturing gained momentum during the 1980s. Whilst the Thatcher Governments' policies accorded favourable treatment to the City of London and the property sector, through changes to the taxation system that in effect delivered huge subsidies to these sectors of the British economy, their industrial policies did not accord any privileged status to manufacturing (with the notable exception of defence manufacturers as documented in the previous chapter). For Thatcherism, a principal cause of deindustrialization was previous state intervention. Manufacturers had become accustomed to acting as entrepreneurs in the realm of politics, concentrating their efforts on lobbying ministers for subsidies as successive governments engaged in the ultimately futile exercise of attempting to pick industrial winners (Burton, 1979). By recreating an enterprise culture in Britain, where entrepreneurs would once again be inspired by the freedom of the open market to innovate and create wealth because of the possibility of generating profits which would not be taxed at a punitive rate, the Thatcher Governments hoped to cure domestic manufacturers of what they saw as their addiction to state subsidies. Two of the most important policy mechanisms by which this transformation was to be attempted were privatization and the promotion of inward investment in Britain by foreign manufacturers.

Privatization offered a remedy to one of the most intractable industrial policy problems confronting the first Thatcher Government in 1979, namely the future of those manufacturers in the public sector, most notably British Steel and British Leyland (BL), the sole remaining British-owned volume car manufacturer. As Thatcher herself has acknowledged, she knew that her Government's policy towards BL would have 'an impact on the psychology and morale of British managers as a whole, and I was determined to send the right signals' (Thatcher, 1993, p. 114). However, the possibility of a wholesale liquidation or break up of BL to signal to manufacturing industry that it would have to survive in future without state subsidies was thought to be neither politically feasible, given that 150 000 people were employed by the company (many of them in marginal seats in the Midlands), nor economically feasible, given that the closure of the company would cost the balance of trade in manufactures an estimated £2.2 billion and the Government up to £1 billion.

Given that the economic costs of closure to the Government were almost identical to the £990 million cost of funding BL's corporate plan, whilst the political costs were infinitely higher in a period of recession and growing social unrest, Thatcher concluded that 'the political realities had to be faced' (Thatcher, 1993, p. 121). BL was duly rescued but not before Sir Keith Joseph had argued in Cabinet against the recommendation of his own DOI officials that the company be saved by further state subsidies. In the case of British Steel, the cost of facing up to 'the political realities' was even higher. When BL had announced losses of £535 million in March 1981, its losses had been exceeded only by those of British Steel which reported a deficit of £660 million. Sir Keith Joseph's response to this parlous predicament in the 1981 Iron and Steel Bill was to face up to the financial consequences of past mistakes by immediately writing off £3.5 billion of British Steel's capital and allowing the company to borrow an additional £1.5 billion without parliamentary approval. This followed his announcement only three days earlier that the DOI would guarantee loans of £200 million to ICL, the troubled state-owned computer manufacturer.

Once the political advantage of its magic formula of simultaneously cutting state borrowing (at least in the short term), generating resources for tax-cutting budgets (at least in the short term), and promoting the Government's wider agenda of a property-owning democracy, popular capitalism had been discovered, privatization was to become one of the principal elements of Conservative industrial policy, especially during the latter half of the 1980s. However, advocates of privatization have too readily overlooked the huge competitive advantage given to many state-owned manufacturers by the large cash injections and/or government contracts that they received in the early 1980s. This oversight has enabled such advocates to argue it was the act of transfer itself, from the inescapably inefficient public sector to the inherently more efficient private sector, which has been the most important factor in these companies' performance since their privatization. In reality, the act of privatization did not necessarily guarantee former state-owned manufacturers commercial success or continuing British ownership and control in the private sector. For example, after the telecommunications multinational STC had acquired ICL from the Government in August 1984, equity in STC soon became the second worst performing share on the London Stock Exchange between December 1984 and July 1985 (Kelly, 1987, p. 79). STC eventually sold ICL to the Japanese computer manufacturer Fujitsu in 1990. In a similar vein, when Thorn EMI paid £95 million in July 1984 for INMOS, the innovative silicon chip designer and manufacturer that had been built up by the NEB, it appeared to have paid a relatively small price for entering the market for semi-custom chips with a potentially world-beating product, INMOS' transputer or 'computer on a chip' (McClean and Rowland, 1985). Unfortunately, because it lacked the industrial and financial resources that rival semiconductor manufacturers had found essential for financing costly innovation and weathering severe and sudden fluctuations in the demand for their products, Thorn EMI spent several fruitless years and several hundred million pounds in an ultimately futile attempt to make INMOS an industrial world-beater. In the end, Thorn E.M.I. admitted defeat and not only sold INMOS to Thomson, the French state-owned electronics manufacturer, but also divested itself of its other civil electronics manufacturing businesses as it moved away from manufacturing towards the musical publishing and retailing business. Thomson has subsequently sold 70 per cent of INMOS to QPL, a Hong Kong-based manufacturer.

One of the most important economic policies implemented by the first Thatcher Government was the abolition of exchange controls. By enabling capital to flow more freely to and from Britain, this and later deregulatory measures contributed to the promotion of Britain as the optimal location for foreign direct investment by multinationals wishing to benefit from the creation of the Single European Market. During the 1980s, Britain attracted more than 40 per cent of total US and Japanese investment in Europe. In 1990 foreign-owned companies accounted for 22 per cent of manufactured output, 27 per cent of capital investment and 16 per cent of manufacturing employment in Britain (CBI, 1992, p. 12). Indeed, in 1990, foreign direct investment into the UK accounted for 3.8 per cent of GDP, which was more than twice the EC average of 1.7 per cent (Davis, Flanders and Star, 1992, p. 62). Given their hostility towards the idea of state intervention in civil manufacturing, for the Thatcher Governments inward investment offered a primarily market-led solution to the problem of how to re-enter lost export markets so as to improve the UK's trade performance. Japanese investment, for example, has transformed the U.K.'s trade performance in the manufacture of colour televisions. In 1977, no less than 48 per cent of the UK market for colour televisions was taken by imports and only 2 per cent of the 2 million sets manufactured in Britain were being exported. With virtually all British-owned and based colour television manufacturing ending by 1988, the prospects for the balance of trade in this particular sector appeared dire. However, quite the contrary proved to be the case because by 1987 the retreat of indigenously owned companies from the consumer electronics market had been more than compensated for by the establishment in the UK of no fewer than 18 of the 32 Japanese plants manufacturing televisions and other consumer electronics products located in the EC. As a consequence, the UK's balance of trade has been transformed to the extent that in 1991, UK trade in colour televisions registered an export surplus of more than one million sets and a trade surplus of £446 million (Eltis and Fraser, 1992, p. 8).

By exposing domestic manufacturers to greater competition from foreign companies operating in Britain with more efficient management techniques and working practices, the Thatcher Governments hoped that inward investment would also act as a catalyst to promote more rapid growth of productivity, output and investment across the whole of UK manufacturing. Furthermore, the very presence of so much foreign investment would serve as one of the clearest vindications of the Governments' own investment of a large amount of political capital and taxpayers' money in the reform of both the trades unions and personal and corporate taxation so as to deliver a disciplined workforce and incentives for higher productivity and profitability. It is the British car industry which is held to have been the principal beneficiary of this particular aspect of Thatcherite industrial policy. During the 1980s, Britain was chosen by the three major Japanese car manufacturers – Nissan, Toyota and Honda – as the location for their principal manufacturing base within the EC. Nissan was the first to begin production in 1986, but with the opening of the Toyota and Honda plants in the early 1990s the prospect has arisen of the transformation of the UK into a large net car exporter by the late 1990s. The volume of UK car imports had already fallen by 10 per cent in 1990 and by an additional 31 per cent in 1991, whilst car exports had increased in volume by 20 per cent in 1990 and 28 per cent in 1991 (Eltis and Fraser, 1992, p. 9).

It should not be thought that the arrival of the Japanese plants in the UK was greeted with universal acclaim, or that their impact upon UK manufacturing performance would be entirely benign. In 1991, an announcement by Nissan of a £100 million expansion programme and the creation of an additional 1000 new jobs virtually coincided with the disclosure by Ford of a loss of £590 million and 2 100 redundancies (Eltis and Fraser, 1992, p. 10). Whilst some of these losses might be accounted for as much by the depth of the recession in both the domestic and the European car markets as by the competitive challenge posed by the Japanese, the extent and timescale of the nett gains for the UK car industry from Japanese investment remain uncertain. An intensive investigation of manufacturing performance and management practices in automotive component companies in the UK and Japan revealed that it was only in Japan that world class performance could be identified (Andersen Consulting, 1993, p. 19). Whilst some UK component suppliers could achieve impressive levels of productivity or quality, none were achieving both simultaneously. Indeed, the world class Japanese suppliers were outperforming their UK competitors by margins of 2:1 in productivity and 100:1 in quality. The investigation concluded that UK firms would have to make very significant changes but that there was also a 'unique window of opportunity to learn from lean producers such as Toyota, Nissan and Honda' (Andersen Consulting, 1993, p. 5). Whether the presence of these Japanese companies manufacturing plants in the UK will necessarily lead to automation rather than liquidation for other UK-based manufacturers is one of the key questions for industrial policy in the late 1990s. For the present, inward investment in general, and Japanese investment in particular, should not be regarded as a panacea for transforming the performance of civil manufacturing in the UK. By 1990, Japanese investment accounted for only 4 per cent of total foreign direct investment in Britain (Eltis and Fraser, 1992, p. 5). Indeed, whilst a third of all Japanese direct investment in Europe since 1951 had been in Britain, US-owned firms provided a UK presence some 16.5 times greater than their Japanese competitors. Furthermore, in recent years, only about one third of foreign direct investment has been in the manufacturing sector, with a much larger proportion of investment focused on financial services (Davis, Flanders and Star, 1992, pp. 64–5). At the same time, any benefits in terms of increases in manufacturing output and employment that may have arisen from inward investment have been more than offset by the 'hollowing out' of indigenous British manufacturers.

DOCUMENTING DEINDUSTRIALIZATION

The acceleration in the deindustrialization of Britain during the 1980s did not pass without comment. In the mid-1980s, the then Leader of the Opposition, Neil Kinnock, based his book about the future of Britain on the question of manufacturing revival (Kinnock, 1986). At the same time, having resigned from the Cabinet over the question of the future of Westland, Britain's sole helicopter manufacturer, Michael Heseltine placed the need for an industrial strategy at the heart of his alternative, non-Thatcherite Conservative manifesto (Heseltine, 1987). However, it has been from the Select Committees of both Houses of Parliament that some of the most comprehensive and damning analyses of Britain's performance in manufacturing have emanated. In July 1984, a Select Committee of the House of Lords was appointed under the chairmanship of the Conservative peer, Lord Aldington, 'to consider the causes and implications of the deficit in the United Kingdom's balance of trade in manufactures; and to make recommendations' (House of Lords, 1985, p. 5). Given that select committees of the Upper Chamber are not renowned for the radicalism of their recommendations, few commentators could have anticipated that when its report was published in October 1985, the Aldington Committee would conclude that there was the possibility of 'a major social and economic crisis in our nation's affairs in the foreseeable future' if national attitudes in Britain towards trade and manufacturing did not change, and change radically (House of Lords, 1985, p. 6).

In its analysis of the causes of Britain's trade imbalance in manufactures which had emerged in 1983, the Aldington Committee criticized the economic policies implemented by the first Thatcher Government because its reliance on exchange rate adjustment had not solved the underlying problems causing lack of industrial competitiveness, but had rather contributed to sustaining them. In the Committee's opinion, the rapid appreciation in the value of sterling in the period 1979–80, which had contributed to the loss of nearly 20 per cent of manufacturing output in Britain, was not attributable solely to the effects of North Sea Oil but was also a direct product of 'government policy which not only did little to accommodate the effect of oil but also pushed up interest rates and altered expectations through the Medium Term Financial Strategy' (House of Lords, 1985, p. 37). In its analysis of whether there was a problem for the British economy, the Committee took particular issue with 'fundamental assumptions on which the Treasury's response to this question was predicated' (House of Lords, 1985, p. 42). Above all, the Committee could accept neither the then Chancellor of the Exchequer Nigel Lawson's argument that the trade deficit in manufactures was less important as a measure of economic performance than total output, nor his contention that the decline both in manufacturing as a percentage of GDP and in the balance of trade was an inevitable consequence of the surplus on the North Sea Oil account. The Treasury view was that there would be a spontaneous, automatic and compensatory recovery in manufacturing output as oil production declined but the Committee thought that this complacent and automaticist analysis was 'unrealistic and dangerously short-sighted' (House of Lords, 1985, pp. 42–4).

In its report, the Aldington Committee duly proceeded to challenge four key assumptions underpinning Government policy. Firstly, it suggested that it would be wrong for the Government to base its future strategy on a depreciating currency, assuming depreciation to be the inevitable consequence of a decline in oil production. The Committee cited evidence challenging the size of the effect of North Sea Oil on sterling's value. Moreover, this depreciation, even if it occurred, would be likely to be gradual and therefore too gentle to have the short, sharp shock which would stimulate manufacturing recovery. Secondly, the assumption that tomorrow's manufacturing industries would be different from today's should not be exaggerated. Existing industries should not be written off as incapable of innovation. New industries would take many years to develop. For example, by the time of the Committee's investigations Britain was already running a huge trade deficit in information technology, an industry whose future importance to Britain's prosperity had been acknowledged with the appointment of a Minister for Industry and Information Technology at the DOI. Thirdly, the Committee was sceptical as to the capacity of British industry to gain overseas market share without a change in policies and attitudes. Fourthly, the Committee questioned whether the manufacturing capacity now existed or would exist in the future for Britain to be capable of meeting an upturn in its domestic or export markets. The costs of sudden re-entry into manufacturing would be prohibitive. In any case, such innovation would take a long time to develop – the long-term factor not being given 'proper attention in Treasury thinking'. Britain would not find economic salvation in its invisible earnings because its share of world invisible trade had fallen more rapidly since 1969 than its share of world visible trade. Nor could the trade deficit be eliminated by overseas or inward investment because in neither case would the flows be of sufficient magnitude to eliminate the imbalance (House of Lords, 1985, pp. 44–7).

The Aldington Committee concluded that, without action to expand the manufacturing base and to address import penetration of domestic markets, there would be a number of adverse and worsening effects for British society. Manufacturing would contract 'to the point where the successful continuation of much of manufacturing is put at risk'. There would be 'an irreplaceable loss of GDP' and 'an adverse balance of payments of such proportions that severely deflationary measures will be needed'. The Government would be the recipient of 'lower tax revenue for public spending on welfare, defence and other areas' whilst society would suffer from 'higher unemployment, with little prospect of reducing it' with 'the economy stagnating and inflation rising, driven up by a falling exchange rate' (House of Lords, 1985, pp. 47–8). To surmount this 'grave threat to the standard of living of the British people', the Committee identified some major factors which had contributed to manufacturing strength in other economies from which Britain might usefully learn some important lessons. More successful manufacturing economies had developed a sense of national purpose, uniting 'all the main economic agents – government, employers, unions and banks', promoted by agencies such as MITI in Japan and the Commissariat du Plan in France. These economies had also adhered to a long-term view of economic development which transcended their institutional structures, and possessed national education and training systems to help to nurture a longer-term perspective. The implementation of an industrial policy had also been a characteristic of more successful manufacturing economies with financial institutions enjoying a direct relationship with industry which enabled them to play an active role in the successful development of manufacturing. Governments in such economies had displayed a rhetorical commitment to free trade, whilst implementing both tariff and non-tariff barriers to trade. Companies for their part had displayed 'attention to quality, good marketing, paying attention to consumer requirements, labour-force motivation and cooperation, effective training, sufficient investment in R & D and up-to-date technology such as flexible manufacturing systems, etc.' (House of Lords, 1985, pp. 49–54).

The Committee asserted that many of these factors were transferable to Britain, although they would clearly be an anathema to the incumbent Thatcher Government.

Since House of Lords' Select Committees are not renowned for the radicalism of either their analysis of or prescriptions for government policies, the Aldington Report threatened to be a major political embarassment for a government which already had more than its fair share of political and economic problems. To limit the political fallout from its publication, the Government obtained a copy of the embargoed Report prior to its official launch and proceeded to deliver a pre-emptive strike of its own against Aldington's findings. In the vanguard of this premeditated assault was Nigel Lawson, who dismissed the Aldington Report as 'special pleading dressed up as analysis, and assertion masquerading as evidence' (*Official Record*, 3 December 1985, c. 1253). In a previous parliamentary exchange, Lawson had refused to concede that any sector of the British economy, including manufacturing, was uniquely important (*Official Record*, 9 February 1984, c. 1009). Lawson's memoirs reveal that he has remained wedded to the assumption that there would inevitably be some 'crowding out' of manufacturing exports and investment in Britain by the diversion of resources into North Sea Oil production but that there would be a compensatory 'crowding back into the manufacturing sector' as oil production declined (Lawson, 1992, p. 196). In the event, the further deindustrialization of Britain that has occurred since Lawson's departure from office is demonstrative of a failure of crowding back into manufacturing to occur because, despite the Treasury's assumptions to the contrary, competitiveness in manufacturing which produces higher investment, productivity and output, and ultimately higher living standards, cannot be turned on instantaneously especially when previous government policies have helped to liquidate a substantial part of manufacturing activity in Britain.

The Aldington Report was by no means an isolated example of a House of Lords' Select Committee report taking issue with the Government's policies towards manufacturing. In 1991, the House of Lords' Select Committee on Science and Technology, in its report *Innovation in Manufacturing Industry* (the Caldecote Report), picked up the analysis of deindustrialization in Britain where the Aldington Report had left it in 1985. The Caldecote Report warned of the 'grave' implications for Britain's future prosperity of the failure of manufacturing industry to remain competitive, and the increasing penetration of domestic markets by imported manufactures (House of Lords, 1991, p. 29). Like its predecessor, the Caldecote Report identified the most urgent need for Britain as a radical change in national attitudes since it believed that antipathy towards manufacturing continued to run deep in British society. To remedy this antipathy, Government must take the lead, with the Report citing the evidence of some of its witnesses which had pointed to 'the absence in the United Kingdom of any body charged with the remit of formulating a "long-term technical policy in key areas" as is done by MITI in Japan' (House of Lords, 1991, p. 25). In keeping with its response to the Aldington Report, the Government was not persuaded of the necessity for a more proactive policy towards manufacturing. In his evidence to the Caldecote Committee, Peter Lilley, the then Secretary of State for Trade and Industry had repeated Lawson's contention that the balance of payments was not an indication of the competitiveness or otherwise of British industry but was rather 'a reflection of the excess demand and inflationary pressures in an economy' (Lilley, 1991, p. 359). If this had indeed been the case during the consumer and property-led boom of the late 1980s, Lilley was attributing Britain's poor performance in manufacturing to the mismanagement of the macroeconomy by Nigel Lawson.

However, the problem with this argument is that in the period since the end of the boom, which has been marked by the longest and most severe recession in Britain since the 1930s, there has been a singular absence of excess demand and inflationary pressures. Nevertheless, Britain's balance of payments' deficit has remained in substantial deficit throughout this period, a fact which appears not only to undermine Lilley's analysis but also the assertion in the official response to the Caldecote Report orchestrated by Lilley's department that a transformation had taken place in the performance of UK manufacturing during the 1980s through the creation of 'a framework in which enterprise and initiative have been able to flourish, not by intervention and subsidy' (DTI, 1991, p. 3).

THE COUNTERBLAST AGAINST DEINDUSTRIALIZATION

Both the literature and the debates about the performance of manufacturing in Britain during the 1980s have tended to be dominated, at least in numerical terms, by analyses that have asserted that the pace of deindustrialization has accelerated and that this will have a detrimental impact on British society. However, the intellectual tide has not been all in one direction. Several important challenges to the orthodoxy have been published in recent years. For example, Crafts' analysis of deindustrialization seeks to dispel the notion propagated by so many commentators and interested parties that the UK's substantial trade deficit in manufactures can and should be remedied by the implementation of a 'high-profile industrial policy'. He readily acknowledges the long-term implications of deindustrialization, not least the fact that the smaller manufacturing base will 'probably mean losses to real income growth from terms-of-trade effects in the 1990s'. Indeed, when coupled with the effect of inappropriate macroeconomic policies, the effect might be that the UK would suffer the balance of payments' constraint on its economic growth identified by other commentators (Crafts, 1993, p. 63). But for Crafts, the solution to this problem does not lie in a return to a high-profile industrial policy. On the contrary, it lies in the elimination of the policy errors of the past, and if the Aldington and Caldecote Committees had advocated just that then Crafts would be in wholehearted agreement with them. Where he departs from their analysis of and prescriptions for policy is in his assertion that the Lords have gone considerably further than this limited measure and 'veered off down the path of interventionism and protectionism'. Crafts does not see the need for intervention to nurture 'infant industries' because if the gains from innovation can be captured by the firm, then he contends that 'well-functioning capital markets will finance worthwhile infant industries' (Crafts, 1993, pp. 64–6). What Crafts appears to overlook is that capital markets in Britain have not functioned well in the past in the provision of capital to new firms and industries, a fact borne testament to by the series of schemes that successive Labour and Conservative governments have contemplated and initiated in an attempt to surmount this key market failure.

More controversially, Crafts suggests that industrial policies are 'inherently protectionist' which seems to overlook the fact that assistance has been given to manufacturing companies in Britain, regardless of the nationality of their ownership, and whilst maintaining an open market in the ownership and control of such businesses. Where Crafts does make a vital contribution to the debate about manufacturing and industrial policy is in citing the work of those who have documented the disastrous consequences of pouring billions of pounds of taxpayers' money into loss-making projects such as Concorde and nuclear power (Hayward, 1983; Stoneman, 1991). The multitude of past errors in British industrial policy have almost universally been ignored by those who have advocated further attempts at proactive state intervention. By passing over this inglorious history, and by not even attempting to provide an explanation as to why industrial policy failed in the past, such advocates have left the way clear for proponents of market-led solutions to discard the principle of industrial policy wholesale as when, for example, Crafts refers to the fact that the Thatcher Governments 'sensibly' gave up trying to pick winners (Crafts, 1993, p. 71). He points to British Steel as the exemplar of the benefits to competitiveness of the reduction of costs and overmanning. What he fails to acknowledge is that in the case of British Steel, British Airways and other privatized industries, much of this cost reduction occurred because of major investment undertaken by the government in these industries before their transfer to the private sector. It was this investment, at least as much as the act of transfer itself, which has accounted for any improvement in their trading performance in the years immediately following privatization. Moreover, such largesse by the taxpayer which enabled the financing of rapid programmes of redundancy and restructuring, has not been an option for many manufacturing firms in the private sector because of the prohibitive costs of restructuring to their shareholders. The tradition of massive restructuring and large productivity gains in the public sector prior to privatization has been continued in the case of the Post Office, British Coal and British Rail. The example of the Post Office in particular has demonstrated that it is possible for a business to be run successfully under state ownership, and that the principal obstacle to further expansion and greater profitability has not been the absence of private ownership and control, but the inability of management to be able to secure access to finance from private sector institutions because of antiquated Treasury rules.

It is not, therefore, the principle of state intervention in manufacturing firms which needs to be discarded when evaluating present and future options for industrial policy, but rather the way in which the public and private sectors interact to promote the competitiveness of manufacturing. However, for Crafts, any future industrial policy should be 'targeted on specific market failures, tightly cash-limited and subject to independent public scrutiny and audit'. At the same time, he does concede that the UK remains 'relatively weak in long-term investments, including human capital and R & D, the factors emphasized by new growth theory as engines of long-term success'. As a consequence, benefits might arise from government intervention to 'reduce short-termism and to strengthen human capital formation' provided that such intervention preserves 'the disciplines of competition' (Crafts, 1993, pp. 74–7). The problem with this analysis is that Crafts has already recognized that short-termism in investment has been encouraged by 'the unique exposure of British companies to hostile takeover', and by 'the relative absence of long-term consensual relationships between British firms and their workers', which has led to high levels of job turnover and poaching of trained employees which in turn has produced a persistent low level of skills' (Crafts, 1993, p. 74). When the disciplines of competition have led to insufficient long-term investment in the British economy, especially in the training of its workforce, it seems somewhat paradoxical to base future industrial policy on those very same disciplines. Crafts' conclusion, that manufacturing's present problems have arisen largely from errors in macroeconomic policy which should be remedied rather than added to by the pursuit of misguided supply-side interventions at the microeconomic level, places him firmly in the same corner as Thatcherites such as Peter Lilley and the late Lord Ridley, Lilley's predecessor at the DTI (Ridley, 1991).

Whilst Crafts has sought to challenge the thesis of deindustrialization in general, and the prescription of a proactive government-led industrial policy in particular, the Conservative Research Department (CRD) has attempted to challenge the conventional wisdom about the performance of manufacturing in Britain during the 1980s. In his Foreword to the CRD's analysis, Norman Lamont claimed that the belief that manufacturing industry is in decline is one of a number of 'self-denigrating myths' about the British economy. Lamont concedes that manufacturing was in decline until 'the early 1980s', but since then he contends it has been on 'a strengthening long-term trend'. To support this analysis, he points to a 66 per cent increase in British exports of manufactures between 1981 and 1991, a faster rate of increase than any of the other Group of Seven (G7) industrial economies (CRD, 1993, p. 2). Lamont also notes that between 1982 and the start of the most recent recession, manufacturing output had grown by an 'impressive' 30 per cent. That Lamont should be able to put forward such an upbeat assessment of British manufacturing during the worst domestic recession since the 1930s, and that the CRD itself should feel able to regard the idea of a declining manufacturing base as 'a myth', is testament to a highly selective use of statistics.

Lamont's reference to manufacturing decline until 'the early 1980s' points to the way in which he wishes to ignore the fact that industrial output fell by 17.4 per cent in the recession of 1979–82 during the tenure of the first Thatcher Government. For its part, the CRD draws comfort from the fact that output in the recession of the early 1990s has fallen by a mere 7.5 per cent, claims that 'the recession was caused by a lack of demand, not incapacity to supply', and suggests that Britain's manufacturing base is now 'as it were, "deeper but narrower"' as a consequence of the growing trend towards specialization in international trade (CRD, 1993, p. 10). If Britain does now 'specialize' in particular industries, it is largely because its presence in other sectors has been destroyed, not by some inevitable international division of labour, but by two recessions in which the role of the government in which Lamont served has been culpable. Despite Lamont's assertions to the contrary, Britain's manufacturing problems do lie primarily on the supply side. This has been demonstrated during both the unsustainable economic boom of the late 1980s, when the trade deficit in manufactures mushroomed at a time of record demand, and during the recent recession, when the demand for imported manufactures has remained buoyant. There has been no shortage of demand in the British economy in recent years, but merely a shortage of demand for British manufactures because of their inability to supply products which combine reliability and good design with a competitive price and efficient after-sales service.

The claims about British manufacturing advanced by the CRD and Norman Lamont have been analysed in turn and largely refuted by Ian Shepherdson, a leading economist in the City of London. His analysis begins by noting how the CRD's measurement of the growth of manufactured output at an annual average of 3.7 per cent between 1982 and 1989 is only possible by ignoring the recession of 1979–82 (Shepherdson, 1993, p. 2), a recession so severe as to be surpassed in its length and its depth only by that suffered by Britain less than a decade later. When the CRD's unfortunate statistical myopia is corrected, it is evident that Britain's manufacturing output fell by no less than 17 per cent between the second quarter of 1979 and the fourth quarter of 1982. Indeed, in the first quarter of 1993, the index of UK manufacturing output stood at 133.5, compared to 103.9 in the first three months of 1979, the last full quarter of manufacturing activity under the Callaghan Government. This means that during fourteen years of Conservative government, manufacturing output had risen by an average of only 0.8 per cent per annum. Even if the 1979–82 recession is ignored, the fact remains that in the period 1982–92, the increase in British manufacturing output of 22.0 per cent was only about half of the 43.2 per cent increase achieved in the US, and only around two-thirds of the West German increase of 31.5 per cent (Shepherdson, 1993, p. 2).

The CRD's analysis attempts to dilute the impact of deindustrialization in Britain by identifying a parallel decline in manufacturing in other OECD economies. However, Shepherdson suggests that whilst such decline may be an aspect of economic development, it cannot be permitted to proceed too far too quickly or it may be a sign of weakness rather than strength. After all, Germany and Japan, the national economies that have maintained the largest manufacturing sectors, have also been the two most successful post-war economies in sustaining non-inflationary, export-led growth. More importantly for Britain, given her dependence on exports to pay for imports of food, raw materials and, increasingly, foreign manufactures, manufactures constituted no less than 70 per cent of total UK exports in 1992, with each unit of UK manufacturing production generating on average more than 10 times as much foreign currency income as each unit of service sector output. Most disturbingly of all, since 1984 Britain has been running a large trade deficit on manufactures, equivalent, for example, to 1.9 per cent of GDP in the latter half of 1992. Even in the unlikely event of the value of Britain's imports remaining static, Shepherdson estimates that the value of Britain's manufacturing exports would have to increase by 14 per cent just to achieve equilibrium in its trade in manufactures. In practice, Britain's exports of manufactures by volume grew by an average of only 8.8 per cent between 1982 and 1992, a period during which values of imported manufactures rose by an average of 10.3 per cent (Shepherdson, 1993, p. 4).

The question arises as to how this disturbing picture of manufacturing in Britain can be reconciled with the CRD's assertion that a productivity miracle occurred during the 1980s. Shepherdson duly concedes that not only did the supply-side revolution presided over by the Thatcher Governments transform the capacity of British manufacturers to use resources more efficiently, but also the improvement in British productivity outstripped the performance of its principal competitors. Hourly labour productivity in manufacturing did grow by an average of 4.7 per cent per annum between 1979 and 1989, compared with only 1.7 per cent annual growth between 1973 and 1979 (Glyn, 1992, p. 77). Before the election of the first Thatcher Government, Britain had been bottom of the international productivity league table (CRD, 1993, p. 18). But the CRD's claims appear to carry less conviction when it is remembered that hourly labour productivity in UK manufacturing averaged a growth rate of 4.2 per cent in the period 1960–73, and that the improved productivity performance in Britain during the 1980s did not extend from manufacturing and mining to other sectors of the economy such as distribution, finance and business services where there was a marked growth in employment (Glyn, 1992, p. 79). It is also unfortunate that, because domestic manufacturers began their improvement from such a low base, the level of productivity in UK manufacturing still remains well below that of its competitors. Indeed, the CBI has noted that in 1990, UK manufacturing productivity was still around 30 per cent lower than that in Germany, 35 per cent lower than in Japan and about 45 per cent lower than in the US (CBI, 1991, p. 5). More importantly, Shepherdson notes that the productivity gains in British manufacturing were the product of a decline in employment rather than an expansion in output (Shepherdson, 1993, p. 5). Indeed, 51.6 per cent of the growth in UK manufacturing productivity in the period 1979–89 was the product of reduced employment, which fell by 26 per cent in total, whilst total manufacturing output during this period increased by only 12.2 per cent (Glyn, 1992, p. 79). Therefore, manufacturers may have been the beneficiaries of a dramatic, but one-off boost to their productivity which is unlikely to recur during the 1990s without a dramatic and as yet non-existent upsurge in investment.

THE MAJOR GOVERNMENTS AND MANUFACTURING

When John Major became Prime Minister in November 1990, he inherited a national economy whose performance during the tenure of his immediate predecessor, in terms of manufacturing investment, output, productivity and trade had been little more than disastrous. During the 1980s investment in manufacturing in the UK had risen on average by only 2 per cent per annum. This investment record would have been even worse had it not been for the fact that the level of direct inward investment more than doubled during the decade to 12 per cent of total domestic capital formation (Hutton, 1995, pp. 8, 57). Following his narrow General Election victory in April 1992, and against the backdrop of a severe domestic recession, John Major sought in a series of interviews and speeches to emphasize the importance that he personally attached to the performance of UK manufacturing. In March 1993, he proclaimed not only that he 'passionately believed' in the necessity of a widening and expanding industrial base but also that during the 1980s he had in fact held to a minority view against the Thatcherite orthodoxy that service industries would not be enough to sustain national prosperity (*The Independent*, 4 March, 1993). Just over a week later, Major asserted that his ambition was to help industry to fight its battles. However, in setting out his six own point strategy for assisting industry (see below), he was quick to qualify his emphasis on manufacturing, in case anyone should be given the mistaken impression that his government was moving towards support for the type of proactive national industrial strategy advocated by some trade associations (EEF, 1992; UKIG, 1993). Not only did Major acknowledge the importance of recovery in every sector of the economy, with no special priority or significance being attached to any recovery in manufacturing, but he also identified the importance of the services sector of the UK economy in general and the City of London in particular as a huge generator of export earnings. Furthermore, any increase in the DTI's budget or salience within Whitehall was ruled out by Major's affirmation of his refusal to return 'to a failed past of subsidies and state intervention.'

John Major's Policy for Assisting Manufacturing in Britain

(1)   Ensuring that 'the fundamentals are right', meaning above all else, low inflation, but also a 'highly competitive' exchange rate, and 'industrial peace just in time to take advantage of the huge opportunity presented by the European Single market'.

(2)   The Government's 'European policy' of securing a 'unique version' of the Maastricht Treaty that achieved 'the best of both worlds for

inward investors: a Britain inside Europe and outside the Social Charter' which after the ratification of the Treaty would make Britain 'the best launch pad for manufacturing success in Europe'.

(3)   The rolling back of regulation at local government, national government and European Community level (the manner of the latter's implementation to be analysed by Heseltine's Deregulation Initiative) because 'red tape costs jobs'.

(4)   The construction of 'new bridges between British research and its industrial application', through the appointment of William Waldegrave as the minister responsible at Cabinet level for science, research and development, and his imminent publication of a White Paper on the links between research and wealth creation.

(5)   Perhaps the most important strand, the Government's policies for education, specifically the locking of maths, science and technology into the national curriculum for every child, ministerial review of education and training for 16-19 year-olds by John Patten and Gillian Shepherd, especially craft and practical training.

(6)   Opening the door to more exports through completion of GATT, the provision of extra export credits and allowing top businessmen to accompany the Prime Minister on foreign visits.

Source: The Daily Telegraph, 12 March, 1993.

The key test for the second Major Government's policies towards manufacturing had come with Michael Heseltine's appointment as Secretary of State for Trade and Industry in a Cabinet reshuffle following the 1992 General Election. Following his resignation from the Cabinet in 1986 over the Westland helicopter crisis (Linklater and Leigh, 1986), Heseltine had published two volumes of non-Thatcherite conservatism in which he had identified a leading role for the state in a national industrial strategy (Heseltine, 1987; 1989). Heseltine's analysis was simple. Britain's relative industrial decline could be stemmed if the Government possessed the appropriate political will – his! If ever became installed at the DTI, he would 'dispel the false belief which has misled too many in my party, that there is a heresy called "intervention" to which unsound Conservative administrations eschew' (Heseltine, 1987, p. 82). As for manufacturing, Heseltine had pointed to the 'initial brusque reaction' of the Government (of which he was then a part) to the Aldington Report. The decline of manufacturing should not be accepted as inevitable, not least because it remained the key wealth creator for the present. It would therefore be 'complacent to assume that manufacturing can be allowed to decline further without undermining economic recovery' (Heseltine, 1987, p. 90).

However, since his appointment at the DTI, careful steps have been taken by his Thatcherite Cabinet colleagues to deny Heseltine the opportunity to fulfil either his previous promises to pursue a proactive state policy towards manufacturing or his subsequent pledge at the 1992 Conservative Party Conference to intervene 'before breakfast, before lunch, before tea, and before dinner'.

Heseltine's arrival at the DTI was soon greeted by a Commons statement on the 16th June 1992 from Norman Lamont, the then Chancellor of the Exchequer, that the work of the National Economic Development Council (NEDC) was to be wound up. The significance of this statement for future industrial policy was that the NEDC was the institution whose framework the Aldington Report had thought 'should be developed as a source of advice' on a medium-term industrial strategy (House of Lords, 1985, p. 64), and whose chairmanship Heseltine had envisaged seizing for himself from the Chancellor of the Exchequer once he was installed at the DTI (Heseltine, 1987, p. 119).The prospects of a proactive industrial strategy were further diminished when Major, in pursuing the fourth element of his own industrial policy, that is, the building of new bridges between British science and industry, had appointed William Waldegrave (and not Heseltine) as the minister with the responsibility at Cabinet level for science, research and development and for the drawing up of the White Paper on the links between research and wealth creation (HMSO, 1993). In the subsequent period, the prospects for intervention have waned still further with Heseltine's initially less than impressive stewardship of the pit closures programme, his department's passive stance towards the collapse of the Leyland DAF commercial vehicle manufacturing business and the BMW takeover of Rover, and the reports of rows with Cabinet colleagues over his proposal for an English Development Agency. The reaction of one of the Cabinet to this proposal was reported as 'Michael doesn't realise that state intervention and planning went out of fashion in the 1980s. He never gives up, but I don't think he will win' (*The Sunday Times*, 14 March, 1993). Heseltine got his development agency, operating under the chairmanship of his political mentor (Lord) Peter Walker, but along with his initiatives for improving the performance of UK manufacturing, Heseltine's desire and capacity for intervention have been curtailed by the Government's attempts to cut public expenditure.

The broad parameters of the Major Government's policies towards manufacturing have been most clearly set out recently in its White Paper, *Competitiveness: Helping Business to Win* (HMSO, 1994a), and in its response to the House of Commons' Trade and Industry Committee's report, *Competitiveness of UK Manufacturing* (House of Commons, 1994).

In its White Paper, the Government neither accorded special priority to manufacturing nor contended that any additional industrial policy measures specific to manufacturing should be implemented. Despite the UK's large trade deficit in manufactures, this was a White Paper which conceptualised the economic performance of the UK in terms of the competitiveness of all sectors rather than the strategic importance of an industrial policy to enhance the performance of UK manufacturing. In its inquiry, like other major select committee inquiries into the performance of UK manufacturing (House of Lords, 1985; 1991), the Trade and Industry Committee concluded that 'A strong manufacturing sector is of fundamental importance to the UK, and poor performance in manufacturing would have an impact far beyond the manufacturing sector'. Although it acknowledged that the primary responsibility for competitiveness and growth lay with manufacturers themselves, the Committee's report also contended that 'some problems, especially short-termism, cannot be dealt with by individual companies and require government action'. Apart from effective macroeconomic management, the Committee suggested that the Government's priorities should be 'education and training, finance for industry and the relationship between financial institutions and companies' (House of Commons, 1994, p. 124). In its observations on the Trade and Industry Committee's report, whilst it accepted that the relative decline of UK manufacturing is 'long-standing and deep-seated', the Government argued that it is tackling 'the fundamental weaknesses in the UK economy through its market-based reforms' (HMSO,1994b, p. vi). Rather than accept the evidence submitted to the Committees concerning the dependence of a signficant proportion of the UK service sector on manufacturing, the Government defined the relationship between manufacturing and services in terms of the former's dependence on the efficiency of the latter, drawing attention to the service sector's employment of 16 million people and contribution of two-thirds of total output to illustrate the vital nature of its performance. Indeed, the Government identified the US economy as the world's most successful despite its having the smallest share of manufacturing, as a percentage of GDP, of all the Group of Seven (G7) countries. As its policies have demonstrated, for the Major Government manufacturing does not merit any particular priority over other sectors of the economy unless related to the procurement of weapons.

In many respects therefore, the Major Governments have pursued more Thatcherite policies towards UK manufacturing than the Thatcher Governments themselves. Firstly, like Margaret Thatcher, John Major began his premiership with counter-inflationary monetary policies which accentuated the impact upon UK manufacturers of a sluggish international economy to create the longest and severest post-war domestic recession. The pressure on UK manufacturers would not have been relaxed but for the Government's involuntary decision to withdraw from the Exchange Rate Mechanism of the European Monetary System in September 1992. Withdrawal resulted in a 15 per cent devaluation of sterling against other major currencies and immediately enhanced the price competitiveness of UK manufactured exports. However, many manufacturers chose to use the devaluation to enhance their profit margins rather than increase their share of overseas markets. Secondly, the Major Governments have steadfastly refused to provide state assistance to struggling manufacturers, notably the commercial vehicles manufacturer, Leyland DAF and the shipbuilders, Swan Hunter. Thirdly, the importance of inward investment to the performance of UK manufacturing has also remained as a central theme of government policy. Foreign-owned companies account for around 17 per cent of all UK manufacturing jobs, 23 per cent of net output and 33 per cent of net capital expenditure. However, the danger to the performance of the UK economy of this growing dependence on inward investment has been illustrated by the fact that net investment in the UK by overseas companies grew by only 5 per cent between 1992 and 1993 to reach £9.3 billion, well short of the £17.4 billion invested in 1989. Furthermore, the UK's share of inward investment has fallen from 28 per cent of total inward investment in the OECD in 1990 to 13.8 per cent in 1993. Having attracted more than 40 per cent of inward investment in the European Union throughout the 1980s, the DTI has also disclosed that the UK is now attracting only 35 per cent of such investment

Under the Major Governments, the UK car industry has remained the flagship for the benefits for UK manufacturing of inward investment. At the time that John Major became Prime Minister, the UK was only the fifth largest car manufacturer in Europe. However, by 1993 it was making more cars than Italy, and is projected to overtake Spain by 1997 to become Europe's third largest car manufacturer behind Germany and France. Indeed, car production is forecast to increase from 1.47 million in 1994, a 6.6 per cent increase from 1993 and the highest UK output since the era of peak production of 1.92 million in 1972, to around 2.2 million in 2000. This expansion in manufacturing is entirely the product of investment decisions taken by foreign-owned companies, all of which are intending to increase their manufacturing capacity in the UK. For example, Toyota has announced that it will invest a further £200 million in its UK plant to double capacity to 200 000 vehicles a year by 1998. This decision will take Toyota's overall investment in the UK to around £1.2 billion, and will mean that it will be spending about £400 million per year with its more than 100 UK-based component suppliers. Doubts, however, remain as to the ability of inward investment to transform the competitiveness of UK manufacturing. For example, a recent study by Andersen Consulting has analysed the manufacturing performance and management practices of 71 components manufacturing plants, including 12 in the UK, to discover how many are 'world-class' in terms of their productivity and quality. The study found that UK productivity is amongst the worst in Europe to the extent that, despite possessing some of the lowest labour costs in Europe, the UK's unit labour costs were exceeded only by those of Germany. None of the UK plants was able to meet the benchmarks for 'world-class' performance, and typical UK plants would have to double their output with the same labour force to achieve 'world-class' productivity. Moreover, despite their adoption of many Japanese manufacturing techniques, the study found that the productivity gap between UK and Japanese plants was widening. The picture is not entirely downbeat, since Alan Marsh, the vice-chairman of Toyota Motor Europe, has stated that his company has seen '500 per cent increases in supplier efficiency since we started operating in Britain five years ago' (*The Independent on Sunday*, 19 March, 1995). What such improvements demonstrate is just how inefficient many UK manufacturers had become before the stimulus provided by inward investment offered them a route towards competitiveness and survival. Nevertheless, the UK trade performance in cars, trucks and components demonstrates how far the industry has to go to match its overseas competitors. In 1993, the UK recorded its second worst trade deficit in this sector of £5.1 billion, compared to £2.8 billion in 1992 and £1 billion in 1991. Whilst this amounts to a marked improvement on the record £6.6 billion deficit in 1989, it shows that inward investment and the dependence that it has created in the UK motor industry on the investment decisions of foreign manufacturers will not necessarily guarantee an improved trade performance.

CONCLUSION

In recent years, the deficit which has featured most in debates about British economic policy has been that arising from financing the public sector rather than that from Britain's trade in manufactures. Whilst eliminating or reducing the public sector deficit may involve some difficult and politically unpalatable choices, especially with regard to the future of the welfare state in Britain, it is at least a process over which governmental determination of both the levels of government spending and taxation ensures a degree of control. It is not clear, however, whether government possesses the requisite policy instruments to be able to reduce the trade deficit in manufactures, even if it was to be made a top political priority. For the trade deficit to be reduced, the volume and value of UK exports of manufactures needs to increase dramatically whilst the volume and value of UK imports of manufactures needs to simultaneously and sharply decrease. The former appears to require an increase in business investment, the latter a decrease in individual consumption. Unfortunately, one of the consequences of the bias in the Thatcher Governments' policies towards investment in sectors other than civil manufacturing, most notably retailing and the domestic property market, is that these sectors have now assumed the status of the engines of both economic and political recovery for the Major Government.

During the 1980s, the expansion in retailing and home ownership tended to increase the propensity for consumers to purchase foreign imports. Since voters have not experienced the so-called 'feel good factor' from the export-led economic growth that has occurred since Britain's ignominious departure from the Exchange Rate Mechanism of the European Monetary System in September 1992, it appears that economic recovery in Britain and a reduction in the trade deficit in manufactures are now mutually incompatible policy goals. Given a choice between, on the one hand, attempting to reduce the trade deficit in manufactures through measures to boost investment in both the public and the private sectors and, on the other hand, cutting personal taxation and government spending in a belated and possibly mistaken attempt to increase the likelihood of its own political survival (since there is little recent electoral or opinion poll evidence that voters would prefer tax cuts at the expense of reduced spending on public services, especially health and education), the Major Goverment is unlikely to choose the former option.

REFERENCES

Andersen Consulting (1993), *The Lean Enterprise Benchmarking Project* (London: Andersen Consulting).

Bacon, R. and W. Eltis (1976), *Britain's Economic Problem: Too Few Producers* (London: Macmillan).

Burton, J. (1979), *The Job Support Machine: A Critique of the Subsidy Morass* (London: Centre for Policy Studies).

CBI (1991), *Competing with the World's Best*, The Report of the CBI Manufacturing Group (London: Confederation of British Industry).

CBI (1992), *Making it in Britain: Partnership for World Class Manufacturing*, The Report of the CBI National Manufacturing Council (London: Confederation of British Industry).

Crafts, N. (1993), *Can Deindustrialization Seriously Damage Your Wealth?: A Review of Why Growth Rates Differ and How to Improve Economic Performance* (London: Institute of Economic Affairs).

CRD (1993), *The Performance of British Manufacturing* (London: Conservative Research Department).

Davis E., S. Flanders and J. Star (1992), 'British industry in the 1980s', *Business Strategy Review*, Spring, pp. 45–69.

DTI (1991), *Innovation in Manufacturing Industry*, Government Response to the First Report of the House of Lords Select Committee on Science and Technology (London: HMSO).

EEF (1992), *Industrial Strategy: Proposals for Recovery and Sustained Growth* (London: Engineering Employers Federation).

Eltis, W. and D. Fraser (1992), 'The contribution of Japanese industrial success to Britain and to Europe', *National Westminster Bank Quarterly Review*, November, pp. 2–19.

Glyn, A. (1992), 'The "Productivity Miracle", Profits and Investment', in Michie, J. (ed.), *The Economic Legacy 1979–1992* (London: Academic Press).

Hayward, K. (1983), *Government and British Civil Aerospace: A Case Study in Post-war Technology Policy* (Manchester: Manchester University Press).

Heseltine, M. (1987), *Where There's a Will* (London: Hutchinson).

Heseltine, M. (1989), *The Challenge of Europe: Can Britain Win?* (London: Weidenfeld & Nicolson).

HMSO (1993), *Realising our Potential: A Strategy for Science, Engineering and Technology*, Cmnd 2250 (London: HMSO).

HMSO (1994a), *Competitiveness: Helping Business to Win*, Cmnd 2563 (London: HMSO).

House of Commons (1994), *Competitiveness of UK Manufacturing Industry*, Second Report from the House of Commons Trade and Industry Committee, 1993–94 Session, HC41-I (London: HMSO).

House of Lords (1985), *Overseas Trade*, Report of the House of Lords Select Committee, 1984–85 Session, HL238-1 (London: HMSO).

House of Lords (1991), *Innovation in Manufacturing Industry*, Report of the House of Lords Select Committee on Science and Technology, 1990–91 Session, HL18-1 (London: HMSO).

Hutton, W. (1995), *The State We're In* (London: Jonathan Cape).

Kelly, T. (1987), *The British Computer Industry: Crisis and Development* (London: Croom Helm).

Kinnock, N. (1986), *Making our Way: Investing in Britain's Future* (Oxford: Basil Blackwell).

Lawson, N. (1992), *The View from No.11: Memoirs of a Tory Radical* (London: Bantam Press).

Lilley, P. (1991), *Innovation, Competition and Culture: speech delivered by the Secretary of State for Trade and Industry at the University of Warwick*, 21 May (London: Department of Trade and Industry).

Linklater, M. and D. Leigh (1986), *Not with Honour: The Inside Story of the Westland Scandal* (London: Sphere Books).

McClean, M. and T. Rowland (1985), *The INMOS Saga: A Triumph of National Enterprise?* (London: Frances Pinter).

Ridley, N. (1991), *My Style of Government: The Thatcher Years* (London: Hutchinson).

Rowthorn, B. and J. Wells (1987), *Deindustrialization and Foreign Trade* (Cambridge: Cambridge University Press).

Shepherdson, I. (1993), 'Myth, legend, and fact: manufacturing under the Tories', *Greenwell Gilt Weekly*, 455, 19 July, pp. 2–7.

Singh, A. (1983), 'UK Industry and the World Economy. A Case of Deindustrialization?', in Feinstein, C. (ed.), *The Managed Economy: Essays in British Economic Policy and Performance since 1929* (Oxford: Oxford University Press).

Stoneman, P. (1991), *The Promotion of Technical Progress in UK Industry: A Consideration of Alternative Policy Instruments* (Warwick: Warwick University Business School Research Papers, No.11).

Thatcher, M. (1993), *The Downing Street Years* (London: Harper Collins).

Thirlwall, A. (1982), 'Deindustrialization in the United Kingdom', *Lloyds Bank Review*, April, pp. 22–37.

UKIG (1993), *Manufacture or Die: A Policy Statement and Recommendations on the Future of the UK's Economy by the UK Industrial Group* (Aldershot: United Kingdom Industrial Group).

Williams, J. (1983), 'G.E.C. – an Outstanding Success?' in Williams, K., D. Thomas and J. Williams, *Why are the British Bad at Manufacturing?* (London: Routledge and Kegan Paul).

Williams, K. (1983), 'Introduction: Why are the British bad at Manufacturing?', in Williams, K., D. Thomas and J. Williams, *Why are the British Bad at Manufacturing?* (London: Routledge and Kegan Paul).

Williams, K., J. Williams and C. Haslam (1990), 'The hollowing out of British manufacturing', *Economy and Society*, 19, 4, pp. 456–90.

6. The City and British Decline

Simon Lee

INTRODUCTION

The three previous chapters have sought to demonstrate the degree to which explanations of Britain's relative economic decline have focused on the failure of the British state to play the leading, strategic role in the development of industry that has been widely identified as one of the prerequisites of long term economic success in other national economies. This chapter seeks to analyse another widely identified prerequisite for economic and industrial success, namely the presence in a national economy of financial institutions committed to and organized for the purposes of providing long term investment capital to domestic businesses in general and manufacturing industry in particular. In this regard, financial institutions in Britain, above all those located in the City of London, have been almost universally criticized because of their alleged preoccupation with the provision of financial services for international commerce and concomitant neglect of the provision of long-term investment capital for domestic industry. The issue of whether there is a fundamental disjuncture between the interests and priorities of international commerce and those of domestic industry is one of the central themes of the whole debate about the contribution of the City of London to British decline.

It is important to recognize at the outset that the phrase 'City of London' is often used as if it is synonymous with the entire financial services sector of the British economy. Whilst this is indeed a convenient shorthand, two qualifications to its use should be made. Firstly, whilst the City has tended to generate the larger part of Britain's total net invisible earnings, for example, £6 billion out of a total of £11.7 billion in 1989, many major financial institutions are located beyond the precincts of the Square Mile (Durham, 1992, p. 38). McRae has identified Edinburgh as the thirteenth largest financial centre in the world, and there are major centres in Birmingham and Manchester too (*The Independent*, 30 January, 1992). Secondly, the use of the shorthand 'the City', or indeed 'finance', as a collective noun implies a homogeneity and clear identity of interests amongst the constituent parts of the financial services sector in Britain. This somewhat distorts and oversimplifies what is in practice a highly complex and diverse pattern of institutions and markets. It is this very complexity and diversity which has made the City such an intractable problem both for those responsible for its regulation and for those seeking to understand the nature of its power and influence upon the development of the British economy. At the very least, the City presents the student of British decline with a crucially important dilemma. On the one hand, the City's invisible earnings have long had the benefit of helping Britain to finance its traditional deficit on its visible trade in food and raw materials. On the other hand, the order of priorities in economic policy that has been sustained by successive governments to maintain international investors' confidence about the future profitability of their financial operations in London has arguably been one of the key factors in the deterioration in Britain's trade performance in manufacturing. Despite its undoubted commercial success, the City's present and future earnings are unlikely to be sufficient to finance Britain's much larger visible trade deficit.

BANKS VERSUS EQUITY MARKETS

The contribution that the financial system has made to relative economic decline in general, and deindustrialization in Britain in particular, has been emphasized by recent contributions to the literature of international political economy. Zysman has suggested that the role of the financial system in any national economy is to 'transform savings into investment and to allocate those funds among competing users' (Zysman, 1983, p. 57). In the literature that has focused specifically upon the allocation of finance for industrial development, a central distinction has been drawn between those national economies such as Japan and Germany, where industry has been financed primarily by loans from banks, and those national economies such as Britain's where industry has had to raise capital on equity markets. Although it remains a matter of contention amongst economic historians and politicians alike, the majority of commentators have concluded that bank-financed industrial development has been more successful in the longer term not least because equity markets tend to possess much shorter time horizons in relation to when they expect to receive dividends from their investments. In the aftermath of the collapse of communism, Albert has suggested that the rivalry between bank-financed and equity market-financed industrial development has taken the form of a global rivalry between two distinctive forms of capitalism. These are the 'Rhine model' of capitalism as practised in Germany and Japan and the 'neo-American model' of capitalism which is to be found in the US and Britain (Albert, 1993).

For Albert, 'the combat between the two major forms of capitalism is fundamentally that of the short term vs. the long term, the present vs. the future' (Albert, 1993, p. 65). Built upon core values of security, solidarity and redistribution, Rhine capitalism possesses an overriding concern for the longer term and regards the company as an expression of the partnership between capital and labour. With its operating principle of 'the profitable management, through speculation, of individual risk', neo-American capitalism emphasizes short-term profitability and individual financial success (Albert, 1993, p. 86). Albert therefore contends that the Rhine model of capitalism is both economically and socially superior to the neo-American model, because it encompasses an interpenetration, rather than a separation, of finance and industry which has three benefits for industrial development in the longer term. Firstly, the banks that operate within the financial system of Rhine capitalism tend to be interested in the long-term interests of businesses because they regard their investment as an enduring commitment which may involve risks in the short term in order to secure the long-term dividend of corporate success. Secondly, their concern for the long term makes Rhine capitalism's banks stable shareholders which in turn gives their industrial clients the freedom to concentrate on business development and not to be concerned with the counter-takeover strategies that tend to characterize businesses operating in the hostile markets of neo-American capitalism. Thirdly, because banks and their industrial partners have developed such a dense web of mutual interests and the practise of business development through consensus, Rhine capitalism is not so easily destabilized as its neo-American rival (Albert, 1993, p. 109).

The clear implication of Albert's assertion of the superiority of Rhine capitalism is the economic and social inferiority of the British financial system for industrial development. Indeed, Hutton has contended that 'The story of British capitalism is at heart the peculiar history of the destructive relationship between British finance and industry' (Hutton, 1995, p. 112). Hutton's *The State We're In* constitutes one of the most important contributions to the debate about Britain's relative economic decline to have been published in the past two decades. Its importance stems from the challenge that it has laid down to the political economy of the New Right which has dominated intellectual debates in Britain, if not the actual conduct of government policy, since the late 1970s. Unashamedly locating his analysis within the discipline of political economy, Hutton links economics and economic performance to the wider operation of British society and its political system. He recognizes that markets are 'embedded in a country's social system and values' and that therefore Britain's market economy and the relationship that it has created between finance and industry is not a spontaneous act of nature, as the New Right has suggested, but 'socially produced and politically governed' (Hutton, 1995, pp. 16–17). As a consequence, any transformation of the relationship between finance and industry in Britain that might be deemed necessary to improve national economic performance cannot be detached from a much broader agenda of political and social change.

Hutton's central economic argument is that the private sector in Britain has sought too high a rate of return on its investments largely because finance for industry has been generated from an equity market-based financial system and clearing banks which have lacked the commitment to industrial innovation and investment of their continental European and Japanese rivals. This lack of commitment has emanated from the London Stock Market's desire for liquidity, that is, 'the ability to be able to reverse a lending or investment decision and return to the status quo ante of holding cash' (Hutton, 1995, p. 132). Because British banks have had themselves to borrow large amounts of money from short-term money markets, it has not been very attractive financially for them to lend on a long-term basis to industry. A more attractive alternative for Britain's capital markets has been the development of a financial culture that has delivered innovative financial instruments and a willingness to trade in them. However, Britain's financial system has not developed in a political and social vacuum and therefore Hutton's central economic argument is joined to his political assertion that 'the semi-modern nature of the British state is a fundamental cause of Britain's economic and social problems' (Hutton, 1995, pp. xi–xii). He contends that Britain possesses a unique structure of values and institutions shaped by her class and political systems which have placed the City of London, Westminster and Whitehall in a symbiotic relationship. The dividend for the City from this relationship has been the maintenance of its role as a centre of international commerce. The dividend for industry in Britain has been the absence of a long-term industrial development bank in either the public or the private sector and one of the highest costs of capital in the world.

INDUSTRIALIZATION AND FINANCE: THE
DISADVANTAGES OF AN 'EARLY START'

Hutton's emphasis on the importance of understanding the contribution made by Britain's political and social history to the failure of its financial institutions to supply domestic industry with adequate long-term investment capital is a theme that has been developed by proponents of what Collins has termed the 'Early Start Thesis' (Collins, 1991, pp. 13–16). This thesis has asserted that Britain's industrial development was impaired by its relatively early start. Britain, in becoming the first industrial nation, developed a unique pattern of market-driven institutions and practices which reflected its pre-industrial economic development and domination of early industrial markets. However, once that domination was challenged, Britain's institutions and practices failed to innovate to meet the competitive threat posed by newly industrializing economies. In the specific case of Britain's financial institutions, one of the most influential theses about the damaging effect of Britain's early start has been the thesis of 'relative economic backwardness' developed by Gerschenkron (Gerschenkron, 1966). Although the basis for his work was primarily an analysis of other national economies in Europe, Gerschenkron's thesis has been widely held to be important for an understanding of Britain's particular pattern of industrialization and subsequent economic performance.

Gerschenkron focuses on the timing of the process of industrialization and in particular on the economic conditions which existed at the time that various national economies commenced what he terms their 'great spurt' of industrialization. His contention is that the more delayed the industrial development of an economy, the more explosive would be its 'great spurt, and the more likely it would be that its industrialization would proceed under some organized direction' (Gerschenkron, 1966, p. 44). Under conditions of relative economic backwardness, where market forces alone were insufficient to advance industrialization, Gerschenkron posits a more activist role for the state. He also contends that the more relatively backward an economy, the more likely that 'ideologies of delayed industrialization' would arise to challenge anti-industrial vested interests (Gerschenkron, 1966, pp. 22–6). However, for Gerschenkron it is the role of 'universal' banks, which combined investment and commercial banking, that he holds to be especially important to the development of modern industry in conditions of moderate economic backwardness. In this respect, Gerschenkron identifies a 'complete gulf' between 'the English bank essentially designed to serve as a source of short-term capital' and the 'paragon of the universal bank', the German bank, 'designed to finance the long-run investment needs of the economy' (Gerschenkron, 1966, p. 13).

Britain's 'great spurt' had occurred primarily in the late eighteenth and early nineteenth century when a legacy of capital accumulation from the earlier centuries of earnings from trade, modernized agriculture and latterly industry itself, had 'obviated the pressures for developing any special institutional device for provision of long-term capital to industry' (Gerschenkron, 1966, p. 14). Moreover, as Collins has suggested, the fixed capital requirements of early industries in Britain could be financed from non-bank sources, notably from the profits earned from a dominance of the market for products and processes whose relatively crude technology and relatively slow rate of technical change did not generate constant demands for large investment in plant and machinery (Collins, 1991, p. 14). Collins cites the work of Pollard whose analysis of fixed capital in Britain during the Industrial Revolution (1760–1830) concluded that the early industrialist was more in need of short-term working capital for the purchase of raw materials, payment of wages, rents and so on, than for long-term capital for fixed capital expenditure on plant and machinery. That could be financed from extra-bank sources, notably the enterprise's retained earnings (Pollard, 1964, pp. 299–314). Britain did not therefore develop, nor did its early industrialization necessarily require, a system of industrial banking. It was only later, during the second industrial revolution, when large-scale and long-term investment was required in the new products and processes of mass production that this deficiency would become a constraint upon industrial competitiveness.

The German economy, by contrast, industrialized against a backdrop of British domination of world markets, albeit domination created from a relatively fragmented industrial structure of many small, often family-owned businesses. For the infant German industries to be able to survive and compete, they had to be established on a much larger and more technically sophisticated basis than their British competitors. This very size and relative technical complexity in turn generated a demand for large-scale, long-term lending of fixed capital, far beyond what could be financed from retained earnings. The role of suppliers of long-term industrial capital therefore was fulfilled by the German universal banks, which enjoyed such a close relationship with industrial enterprises that it was said that they would accompany their industrial progeny 'from the cradle to the grave, from establishment to liquidation' (Gerschenkron, 1966, p. 14). Gerschenkron suggests that German banks not only provided long-term credit to finance German industrial development but also extended their influence far beyond financial control to entrepreneurial and managerial decisions, by virtue of their presence on supervisory boards that were to become the most powerful actors within German corporate organizations. The banks' supervisory influence was assisted during the earlier phase of German industrialization by the desperate shortage of capital amongst heavy industries in particular. When the banks themselves underwent a series of mergers during the late nineteenth century, and found themselves in charge of competing businesses, they were able to identify profitable opportunities for cartelization and amalgamation of their industrial charges. This in turn had the beneficial effect of increasing economies of scale in German heavy industry, but because of the different relationships between banks and industry in Britain there was not a parallel development of industrial banking (Gerschenkron, 1966, p. 15).

In addition to those explanations which focus on the problems created for its later industrial performance by Britain's relatively early economic development, Collins has identified a second explanation for the failure of British banks to develop sufficient provision of long-term investment capital. This is what he has termed the 'Institutionalist' explanation, which in many respects is a variant of the early start thesis and whose proponents have emphasized 'the reactionary, constraining influence of the institutions and institutional relations established during the nineteenth century' (Collins, 1991, pp. 16–18). This 'Institutionalist' schema has featured prominently in the work of many historians (Elbaum and Lazonick, 1986), most notably in that of the Marxist historian, Eric Hobsbawm, who has attributed Britain's relative economic decline to the institutional legacy of 'its early and long-sustained start as an industrial power' (Hobsbawm, 1969, p. 14). Hobsbawm's contention is that Britain remained wedded to the archaic technological and business structures of the first industrial revolution when its competitor industrial economies were embracing a second industrial revolution during the latter half of the nineteenth century.

For Hobsbawm the second industrial revolution possessed four important characteristics. Firstly, an enhanced role was played by science and technology in the two major growth industries of this new phase of industrialism, namely the electrical and chemical industries. Secondly, the factory system of production was systematically extended, most importantly to the manufacture of machinery and consumer durables, using the 'systematic organization of mass-production by means of the planned flow of processes and the "scientific management" of labour' (Hobsbawm, 1969, p. 176). Thirdly, it was discovered that the largest potential market was to be found in the rising incomes of the mass of the working classes in economically advanced countries. Fourthly, there was an increase in the scale of economic enterprise, through the concentration of production and ownership (Hobsbawm, 1969, pp. 172–7). Hobsbawm contends that 'in a capitalist economy (at all events in its nineteenth-century versions) businessmen will be dynamic only insofar as this is rational by the criterion of the individual firm, which is to maximize its gains, minimize its losses, or possibly merely to maintain what it regards as a satisfactory long-term rate of profit' (Hobsbawm, 1969, p. 187). British industry did not innovate or undergo rationalization on a par with that in Germany because entrepreneurs could still make adequate profits from their old investments, allied to the fact that finance capital showed a sustained disinterest in domestic investment opportunities. As a consequence, the British economy as a whole became 'a parasitic rather than a competitive economy', retreating from industry into trade and finance 'where our services reinforced our actual and future competitors' because very satisfactory profits could be made in the process (Hobsbawm, 1969, pp. 191–2).

Hobsbawm's work has been depicted by Leys as 'a rather "idealist" position for a Marxist historian' because it is based on the argument that 'habits of mind learned in the early nineteenth century persisted for more than a hundred years after experience should have suggested scrapping them' (Leys, 1983, p. 36). Collins has also criticized 'Institutionalist' explanations such as that provided by Hobsbawm because of the difficulty of identifying the way in which 'institutional rigidity autonomously inhibits industrial development' (Collins, 1991, p. 17). He cannot envisage how the effect of general institutional structures in nineteenth century Britain could be independent of the effect of wider society's cultural conservatism. Furthermore, Collins argues that institutionalists interpret the meaning given to 'institutional structures' so very widely that the rigidity of such structures becomes little more than a catch-all explanatory repository for 'the extensive list of economic, social and political "failings" that has long been current amongst critics of British capitalist development' (Collins, 1991, pp. 17–18). Having analysed Hobsbawm's work, Leys concludes that what is required to explain Britain's relative economic decline is a combination of 'the primarily economic-historic analysis of Hobsbawm with primarily sociological, cultural and political analyses' in order to be able to link up the different aspects of British society (Leys, 1983, p. 37). It is indeed those explanations which have sought to analyse Britain's financial interests within such a wider socio-political context that constitute the third of Collins' explanatory schema (Collins, 1991, pp. 18–21). Collins asserts that a number of these studies have been inspired, either directly or by way of reaction, by Marxist models of capitalist development. Many have had as their common focus the question of the cohesion or otherwise of the capitalist business elites during Britain's modern social development. Most have pointed to the importance to that development of the role that the City of London has played as the centre for international finance and commerce.

CAPITALISM DIVIDED?

To understand the unique contribution that the City of London had made to the development, or as its legion of critics might prefer the underdevelopment, of the British economy, it is important to recognize the sheer longevity of the City's existence and influence as a powerful financial and commercial presence. Not only has it lain domestically at the heart of the capital city in close proximity to the seats of national power but also it has acted internationally as the facilitator of finance and commerce in the world economy. The City was therefore deeply entrenched in British society long before the Industrial Revolution or the age of universal adult suffrage. Indeed, many of the City's most influential institutions trace their origins back to the late seventeenth century, by which time London had already become the largest city in the world and a major centre for merchants, commodity traders and shipping. As important as their longevity, however, is the fact that many of the City's most important institutions were from their very origins preoccupied by and dependent on business that was more closely tied to the development of the international rather than the domestic economy.

The Bank of England, for example, was founded in 1694 by a group of prominent City financiers and merchants who were granted a charter for their company in return for lending money to the Crown to finance military campaigns overseas. After 1708, when Parliament granted it a legal monopoly of joint stock banking that was to last until 1826 when joint stock banks were legalized beyond a 65 mile radius from London, the Bank of England did not open any regional branches and conducted most of its private banking with the City's major international trading companies. It was therefore, in effect, the Bank of London (Mathias, 1974, pp. 116–7). This concentration on London retarded the development of provincial banking throughout the eighteenth century, during which time the Bank became progressively enmeshed in the state's finances as it assumed responsibility for handling the issue of government stock and subscription for Treasury bills (McRae and Cairncross, 1985, p. 5). The management of the national debt had already become a major issue of public policy by the end of the eighteenth century. In the 1790s, interest payments on the national debt consumed some £11.6 million out of total public expenditure of £33.4 million, and by the 1820s payments had risen to £30.4 million out of total state expenditure of £51.8 million (Mathias, 1974, p. 463).

This very high level of state borrowing created a market in government securities which came to dominate the trading of the London Stock Exchange by the early nineteenth century. A highly developed market in stocks and shares had developed in London by as early as the mid 1690s, but the growth of the government securities market ensured that the Stock Exchange's operations, like those of the Bank of England, were heavily biased towards the interests of the state and international commerce long before industrialization created a demand for long-term investment capital for manufacturing industry (Morgan and Thomas, 1962, p. 21). In addition to the establishment of the Bank of England and the Stock Exchange, the late seventeenth century witnessed an important landmark in the development of another institution that has been accorded a prominent role in some of the most influential explorations of the City's influence on British decline. Although the origins of the Treasury have been traced back to the Norman era, when the term 'Exchequer' was derived from the practice of half-yearly audits, it was not until 1668 that an Order of Council affirmed the Treasury's exclusive control over the state's revenues and expenditure, thereby establishing itself as the leading government department in Whitehall (Hennessy, 1989, p. 25).

The triumvirate of the Bank of England, the City and the Treasury has been described by Ingham as 'the core institutional nexus of British society' since the pre-industrial era (Ingham, 1984, p. 9). This triumvirate lies at the heart of Ingham's influential thesis that 'British capitalism has maintained a distinctive dual character — as the first industrial economy and as the world's major commercial entrepot' (Ingham, 1984, p. 6). Ingham's central argument is that 'the key to understanding Britain's economic development lies in the recognition of the essentially commercial (and not simply financial) character of the City' (Ingham, 1984, p. 5). Indeed, so great has been the domination of the British economy by international commercial capitalism that Ingham asserts that it has had 'a determinant impact on its class and institutional structure', not least in giving the dominant class an 'anti-industrial' character and thereby in disengaging the financial system from domestic industry (Ingham, 1984, pp. 9, 128).

Ingham seeks to demonstrate how the City's preoccupation with stabilizing the short-term operations of its commercial role have had the longer-term effect of rendering the City and the banking system structurally incapable of direct and continuous engagement with production. However, his contention is that the Bank of England and the Treasury have not supported policies favourable to the City simply because the latter has enjoyed the status of the dominant segment or fraction of capital, but because such policies have had a favourable impact on their own independent practices and institutional power (Ingham, 1984, p. 37). Ingham's thesis therefore constitutes an important reaction against and critique of the many Marxist analyses which, in seeking to place the role of the City in British economic development within a wider social and political context, have emphasized the divisions amongst British capitalists between the interests and objectives of the City and industry. Ingham's own emphasis on the explanatory importance of the primarily commercial nature of the City diverges markedly from what he sees as the fundamental weakness of the Marxist approach which is its attempts to identify a specific relationship between finance and industry in British economic development that has enabled the dominant financial fraction of capital to capture and control the state (Ingham, 1984, p. 5).

The importance attributed by Ingham to non-industrial and pre-industrial forms of capitalist enterprise for understanding the performance of the British economy is a theme shared by Cain and Hopkins in the development of their concept of 'gentlemanly capitalism'. Rather than marking a transition from tradition to modernity, gentlemanly capitalism is used to represent 'a selective amalgamation of elements inherited from the past with introductions from the continuously evolving present'. Cain and Hopkins' contention is that the growth of the financial and services sector in the British economy 'proved to be compatible with aristocratic power in the eighteenth century, supported a new gentlemanly order in the nineteenth century, and carried both into the twentieth century' (Cain and Hopkins, 1993b, pp. 298–9). In this process, 'The nineteenth-century gentleman was therefore a compromise between the needs of the landed interest whose power was in decline and the aspirations of the expanding service sector' (Cain and Hopkins, 1993a, p. 33). The middle-class urban gentleman was accorded social recognition by his landed aristocratic peers but the price exacted was to be 'co-opted into the struggle against radicalism and its looming consequence, democracy, and assigned a leading role in introducing an alternative programme of improvement. He was also seen as a counterpoise to the claims of provincial manufacturing industry, which threatened to elevate the provinces over the centre by means of money made in unacceptable ways' (Cain and Hopkins, 1993a, p. 33). Thus, the markets of the City, as a branch of gentlemanly capitalism, 'provided capitalism with an acceptable face by generating income streams that were invisible or indirect' and consequently 'exercised a disproportionate influence on British economic life and economic policy' (Cain and Hopkins, 1993a, pp. 26, 33).

Some of the other most important contributions to the debate on the Left about the role of the City in British decline have appeared in the journal, *New Left Review*. The debate ostensibly began in 1964 when Anderson sought to identify 'The Origins of the Present Crisis' and Nairn to define the nature of 'The British Political Elite' (Anderson, 1963; Nairn, 1963). Both Anderson and Nairn asserted that Britain was an exception to the pattern of economic development in most other capitalist economies because it had never developed a true ruling industrial bourgeoisie. Britain's pre-industrial polity had instead survived the turbulence caused by industrialization, ensuring that the new class of manufacturers remained subordinate economically, politically and culturally to the pre-industrial, aristocratic and agrarian ruling class. This thesis was soon the subject of a withering critique from the eminent historian E.P. Thompson in his essay 'The Peculiarities of the English' where he demonstrated that Anderson and Nairn had underestimated the degree to which Britain had indeed become a capitalist society with a proper and powerful industrial bourgeoisie (Thompson, 1965).

Despite the strength of Thompson's initial critique, Anderson has subsequently developed his original thesis about Britain's exceptionalism. In seeking to identify 'The Figures of Descent', Anderson has argued that the reason for Britain's inability to develop a truly hegemonic industrial bourgeoisie was that a proper industrial revolution had never actually taken place. The consequence for British capitalism was that it never departed from its basis in commercial activity to fully embrace industrial capitalism (Anderson, 1987). This argument has brought Anderson much closer to Ingham's thesis of a division in British capitalism between commerce and industry. It also reflects the influence of Ingham's thesis on a number of prominent Marxist writers, not least Leys who has also contended that despite the Industrial Revolution having produced the new power bloc of manufacturing capital, Britain was never under its hegemony because longstanding and entrenched international relationships permitted the survival of a non-industrial, commercial hegemony (Leys, 1985, p. 22). Indeed, Leys has suggested that if Britain's manufacturers were once dominant in world markets, it was not because they competed successfully against other capitalist manufacturers but because they were able to overwhelm the pre-capitalist production of rival and later developing economies (Leys, 1983, p. 38).

One notable dissenting voice on the Left has been that of the economic historian Barratt Brown who has sought to defend what he terms 'a fairly traditional Marxist view' of the relationship between capital and labour which places central importance on the Industrial Revolution and the role of the industrial bourgeoisie in Britain's economic development (Barratt

Brown, 1988, p. 24). Barratt Brown's principal target has been Ingham's thesis of capitalism divided, although he has also criticized Anderson and Leys because of the way their recent analyses have drawn upon Ingham's ideas. He advances a critique to undermine what he refers to as 'This whole nonsense about a commercial empire' (Barratt Brown, 1988, p. 31). To begin with, Barratt Brown challenges Ingham's claim, accepted by Anderson, that the City's commercial and financial revenues alone in the period 1856 to 1874 grew at a steadily faster rate than Britain's export of manufactures, even though this was an era when the index of Britain's industrial output doubled and when the export of British goods more than doubled. Barratt Brown counters with statistics for British national income in 1871 which show that 38 per cent of national income was derived from manufacturing and mining, but only 22 per cent from trade and transport. Thus, he argues, the large profits gleaned by the City were the preserve of the few, and that the income from merchanting was never as important as that derived from the export of goods or the direct export of capital (Barratt Brown, 1988, pp. 26, 31).

Having taken issue with what he describes as Ingham's 'peculiarly ambiguous definition of commercial activity, in which he asserts that brewing, shipping and on occasions all forms of overseas investment has been incorporated', Barratt Brown turns his attention towards the question of Britain's overseas investment (Barratt Brown, 1988, p. 29). He notes that whilst such investment did indeed boom in the 1870s and between 1905 and 1914, domestic investment at between 5 and 8 per cent of GNP exceeded overseas investment running at between 2 and 3 per cent of GNP in the years 1895 to 1904 (Barratt Brown, 1988, p. 30). Therefore the argument that domestic investment was severely damaged by the volume of overseas investment is at least questionable. Furthermore, Barratt Brown notes that overseas investment by Britain was not limited to the financing of foreign governments but was rather overwhelmingly invested in productive enterprises, for example, mines, railways, plantations and docks because the Empire was an economic business, involving production as much as commerce. The wealth of the great City families was consequently based purely on production from British owned and managed estates in the colonies rather than from commercial activity. Such investment was never exclusive of domestic investment because British capital saw the whole world including Britain as its field of operation. Barratt Brown contends that it still does (Barratt Brown, 1988, p. 36).

Ingham has responded to this critique of his work by asserting that Barratt Brown has failed to grasp his fundamental point which is that the City never realized the major part of its profits from investment in production but gathered it instead from the financial and commercial intermediation that enabled global trading and production to occur (Ingham, 1988, p. 48). To demonstrate the fundamental weakness of Britain's productive economy, Ingham cites statistics which show that from 1815 to 1913 the combined receipts from commerce and banking/finance were virtually identical to those from exports of British products (Ingham, 1988, p. 50). Ingham also cites Barratt Brown's failure to present any new data to support his contention that the City was involved in the financing of production. For Ingham, such an exercise would, in any case, be impossible because 'The chronically low level of investment is an established fact and a unique feature of British development' (Ingham, 1988, p. 59). It is evident from Barratt Brown's reply to Ingham that his claim about Ingham having included brewing in his definition of commercial activities is based on nothing more than a single quotation where the Conservative generosity to 'bankers, ship owners, merchants and brewers' is mentioned (Ingham, 1984, p. 138). Not so easily dismissed is Barratt Brown's challenge to Ingham's assertion of the essentially commercial nature of British overseas investment when he points to a Chatham House study of overseas investment in 1913 that showed that 64 per cent of that investment was in productive industry (Barratt Brown, 1989, p. 126). Barratt Brown further contends that most of Ingham's other criticisms are based on the assumption that he (Barratt Brown) believes that the City is not 'primarily the centre of commercial capital' (Ingham, 1988, p. 46), whereas in fact Barratt Brown's argument is that British capitalism is not, and never was, primarily involved in commercial activity. Barratt Brown concedes that Ingham makes an extremely important point when he distinguishes the City's merchanting function from its financial function, but suggests that by exaggerating the place of commercial capital in the overseas trade balance, Ingham has encouraged Anderson to in turn exaggerate the continuous decline of British industry (Barratt Brown, 1989, p. 126). Barratt Brown himself merely seeks to emphasize the many discontinuities in the development of the British economy, and thereby to challenge Ingham's thesis, built upon by Anderson and Leys, of the continuity of the hegemony of the core institutional nexus, because for him 'the reality is one of a deeply divided ruling class' in Britain (Barratt Brown, 1989, p. 127).

FINANCE AND INDUSTRY 1870–1914

Regardless of how they view the relationship between the elites of finance and industry during the Industrial Revolution, economic historians appear to be largely agreed that British industry did not suffer the supply-side constraint of a shortage of sources of finance for long-term investment.

However, when attention is focused on the relationship between industry and finance in the mid-nineteenth century, Collins, in his summary of the literature analysing developments during this period, asserts that the general picture of British banks concentrating on the provision of short term credit alters little (Collins, 1991, p. 26). After the removal of the Bank of England's monopoly on joint stock banking by legislation in 1826 and 1833, British banks continued to conduct their lending on a predominantly local and small scale whilst the City's lending institutions maintained their distance from the provision of finance to domestic industry. Domestic industry in turn continued to rely on its retained earnings and access to personal private wealth to finance its longer-term investment. However, the debate amongst historians about the impact of financial institutions and practices on industry assumes a much greater intensity when analysing the period from 1870 to 1914 which Pollard has depicted as that of 'Britain's Prime and Britain's Decline' (Pollard, 1989).

From 1870 to 1914, capital was invested overseas from Britain to the extent that on the eve of the First World War, Britain had become the world's most important creditor nation with 41 per cent of gross international investment (Cottrell, 1975, p. 9). About 5 per cent of Britain's GDP was allocated to foreign investment during this period, a sum which amounted to more than one quarter of the total annual value of British exports. Although Britain's rate of saving remained similar to that of Germany and the United States, her two principal industrial rivals during this period, at around 11 to 15 per cent of GNP, the proportion invested domestically averaged only 5 to 7 per cent of GNP during the years 1870 to 1913 compared to around 12 per cent in the two principal rival economies (Pollard, 1989, p. 58). Since Britain's share of world manufactured products fell from 41.4 per cent in 1880 to 32.5 per cent in 1899, reflecting the fact that her rate of industrial production was increasing at only half the rate of her major competitors (Warwick, 1985, p. 100), critics of British financial institutions have argued that the long-term performance of the domestic industrial economy was adversely, perhaps irrevocably, affected by the overseas investment priorities of institutions that were in any case predisposed against the lending of long-term capital to domestic industry. Those better disposed towards British financial institutions have justified the emphasis on overseas investment in terms of the relative maturity of the domestic economy with its fewer clearcut opportunities for high return investment. Furthermore, exports of capital assisted the development of future markets for British manufactures, generated a supply of cheap raw materials and boosted the City's earnings by virtue of its intermediation of the trade generated. It is, in any case, impossible to establish categorically by how much more the domestic economy might have grown had at least some of the exported capital been invested in domestic industry. Nor can it be certain that if overseas investment opportunities had been denied to British investors, they would necessarily have switched their capital into domestic investment. They might have chosen not to invest or indeed save in the first place. As Pollard notes, booms in capital exports during the 1870 to 1914 period at least had the virtue of expanding total investment by up to 3 per cent of GNP (Pollard, 1989, p. 111).

Ingham seeks to explain the flow of investment from Britain in terms of the City's transformation during the nineteenth century into the 'natural' commercial and financial centre of the world economy. He argues that the City's performance was never merely a reflection of Britain's manufacturing superiority and share of world trade, but reflected the benefits not only of an unprecedented one hundred years of peace between the European powers after the end of the Napoleonic wars (his reference to the Pax Britannica appears to discount conflict between powers other than Britain, for example, the Franco Prussian war), but also from Britain's commitment to the domestic gold standard and economic liberalism, especially free trade (Ingham, 1984, p. 96). The gold standard was a product of Britain's political and economic dominance, a reflection of the widespread use of sterling to finance international trade and investment, and the preparedness of successive British governments, acting through the Bank of England, to guarantee sterling's value and convertibility. The commitment to free trade in the markets for money, finance capital and commodities was critical to the maintenance of the City's status as the centre for global commerce (Ingham, 1984, p. 101).

It is Ingham's further contention that the City's development was underwritten by the Treasury's commitment to laissez faire and parsimony in respect of state expenditure. Ironically, it was the Treasury's desire at the end of the Napoleonic wars to detach itself from its reliance on the City for the funding of the state's finances which eventually led to a clear coincidence of interest between the City and the Treasury. As the Treasury sought to control and reduce the state's indebtedness, and alternative sources of funding were established, for example the foundation of the Post Office Savings Bank in 1866, the City sought to overcome the contraction of its lending to the state by expanding its overseas transactions. This export of capital was founded on the basis of free trade and the international confidence in the Bank of England's capacity to manage the gold standard inspired by the state's commitment to non-inflationary fiscal prudence. Thus, Ingham asserts that the Treasury, whose reformers had sought to distance itself from the City, came to support the City's expansion not because it was subservient to the City's interests but because its strict control of state expenditure, like the Bank of England's management of the gold standard, was an independent source of power for it in its own particular institutional sphere (Ingham, 1984, pp. 130–3).

This consolidation of the power of the core institutional nexus in British society enabled non-productive, commercial interests to maintain the hegemony of a non-industrial dominant class (Ingham, 1984, p. 134). Ingham's analysis here draws upon Rubinstein's analysis of the distribution of wealth in early nineteenth-century Britain (Rubinstein, 1977, 1981). Rubinstein concludes that, despite Britain's having been the first industrial economy and the dominant industrial power, the wealthy had remained disproportionately drawn from commerce and finance rather than manufacturing. He argues that this distribution of wealth constitutes one of the keys to understanding 'not merely the wealth, but the anatomy of British elites and through them, the social structure of modern British society since the eighteenth century' (Rubinstein, 1981, p. 61). The less affluent, non-conformist, provincial manufacturing elites had been unable to usurp the political power of the established and more socially cohesive City elites, whose members had often been recruited from the ranks of a public school and Oxbridge educated Establishment. Moreover, because the City's performance had been intimately tied to the financing of international trade and commerce rather than domestic manufacturing, its overseas orientation had been a 'major factor in the chronic under-investment of British industry' (Rubinstein, 1977, p. 116).

Rubinstein's conclusion has been endorsed by Ingham who has suggested that it is not 'too sweeping a judgement to say that ... the City stood in complete indifference (and, in all probability, ignorance) of domestic industry' (Ingham, 1984, p. 150). Pollard too is categorical that the London capital market was not interested in domestic industry, a trend that was accentuated when many of the provincial country and private banks were taken over by the London-based and London-oriented clearing banks. For example, in the years before the First World War, industry in Britain was raising only 10 per cent of its new capital on the London capital market, a sum that represented merely 3 per cent of the sum invested abroad each year (Pollard, 1989, p. 91). However, Pollard has been quick to cite evidence to suggest that industry itself was not interested in the City, and notes that on the eve of the First World War Britain remained the most successful European economy (Pollard, 1989, p. 14). Britain possessed the largest share of the world's manufacturing exports, albeit with a diminishing lead, but only the United States had overtaken Britain in terms of her national income and output levels. Indeed, continental Europe's national product when measured against Britain's had actually declined from 62 per cent of Britain's in 1840 to only 50 per cent in 1910 (Pollard, 1989, p. 6). Such statistics suggest that whatever the debilitating effects on domestic economic growth that may have been caused by the disjuncture in relations and interests between finance and industry during the latter years of the nineteenth century, policy makers could as yet be forgiven if they perceived Britain's economic performance as one of comparative strength rather than relative decline. Nevertheless, Pollard maintains that during this period there was something in British business (he does not specify what it was) that predisposed it towards shortsightedness. The result was that German and American businesses were anticipating and building for the future more successfully than the British (Pollard, 1989, p. 113).

MODERNIZATION FRUSTRATED?

For many historians of British decline, the history of twentieth-century Britain is essentially that of the defeat, or as Newton and Porter portray it, the frustration of a series of modernization movements and state-led strategies that have arisen as a response to Britain's weakening industrial performance. Newton and Porter attribute this frustration of modernization to what they depict as the central feature of the political economy of twentieth-century Britain, namely 'the structural primacy of commerce, principally City-based finance, over production' which has meant that the economic aspects of the British state have been shaped by the hegemony of finance (Newton and Porter, 1988, pp. xii-xiv). Moreover, in the face of the equation of the City's interests with those of the national interest, modernization movements have failed politically to create a united front of producer interests. Thus, from the turn of the century to the eve of the First World War, Newton and Porter contend that the two principal Edwardian modernization movements were riven by the characteristic division of capital in Britain between the commercial and financial interests of the City and the productive interests principally associated with manufacturing industry (Newton and Porter, 1988, p. 2). The Fabian Liberal Imperialist national efficiency movement, though it sought to overhaul certain liberal ideas and institutions, afforded only a partial challenge to the prevailing liberal orthodoxy because of its support of free markets. By contrast, the alternative Liberal Unionist Conservative tariff reform and imperial preference movement associated with Joseph Chamberlain, the Conservative Cabinet minister, former mayor of Birmingham and screw manufacturer, presented a fundamental challenge to the core institutional nexus interests. It demanded a change in the state's priorities such that the interests of production would come first (Newton and Porter, 1988, p. 21). Chamberlain and his allies sought a tariff system which would permit fiscal discrimination in favour of imports from the Empire, in order to create the guaranteed markets that would facilitate domestic industrial efficiency.

Newton and Porter conclude that the tariff reformers failed to alter the relationship between the major fractions of British capital in favour of the interests of production. The reformers were denied the opportunity to apply their corrective modernization strategy because they were excluded from the privileged position of the core institutional nexus, and therefore had to subject their campaign to the vagaries of mainstream electoral politics and the Conservative Party (Newton and Porter, 1988, p. 25). However, during the First World War, the core institutional nexus was denied access to its customary instruments of policy through which it had previously maintained its domestic dominance over economic policy. At the same time, a movement for reconstruction arose on the twin assumptions that the war had destroyed the old social and economic order, and that the institutional reforms forced by total war could be used to construct a new postwar order. Newton and Porter assert that, to its detriment, the reconstruction movement did not generate the same strength of post-war pressure that was generated by the coalition of interests demanding the revival of the prewar liberal economic orthodoxy (Newton and Porter, 1988, pp. 42–3). The domestic inflation crisis in the immediate aftermath of the war led the Coalition government in 1920 to introduce a deflationary budget and to raise the bank rate to 7 per cent to indicate its commitment to the principles of sound finance. The inflation crisis also afforded the City the opportunity to press for an early return to the gold standard to secure the future of sterling as an international currency, and thereby the City's status as the centre of global finance and commerce. The Cunliffe Committee on Currency and Foreign Exchange had in any case recommended the restoration of the gold standard as early as April 1918, several months prior to the Armistice (Longstreth, 1979, p. 165).

Although the core institutional nexus was restored and remained in place during the 1920s, Ingham argues that both the economic base and Britain's ability politically to guarantee the gold standard had been all but destroyed (Ingham, 1984, p. 174). Britain's overseas investments had been heavily depleted during the war and vast debts incurred, with an accompanying loss of invisible earnings to the balance of payments and diminution of the global circulation of sterling. Despite this unfavourable context for its reintroduction, Winston Churchill, the then Chancellor of the Exchequer, was persuaded of the need to return to the gold standard in November 1924 despite the objections of industrialists. Collins suggests that part of the explanation for the eventual restoration of the gold standard in April 1925 lay in the long established political tradition of operating on the gold standard from 1821 to 1914, a practice which had only been interrupted by the extraordinary circumstances created by total war (Collins, 1991, p. 88). Ingham contends that the restoration was believed not only to be in the interests of the City but also regarded as the means by which the Bank of England and the Treasury could restore their former power (Ingham, 1984, p. 173).

The return to the gold standard brought with it a revaluation of sterling which was of particular concern for industrialists given that the key economic problem of the interwar years was the dramatic contraction in British exports. During the 1920s, Britain's share of total world exports declined from 17.9 per cent to 10.8 per cent, and its share of total world exports of manufactured goods from 29.9 per cent to 23.3 per cent (Newton and Porter, 1988, p. 59). In constant price terms, exports in the 1920s averaged only around four-fifths and in the 1930s only two-thirds of their prewar level, and as a percentage of GDP, exports fell from 24 per cent in 1913 to 21 per cent in 1929 and only 15 per cent in 1937 (Collins, 1991, p. 65). The return to the liberal economic orthodoxy was already under challenge, most notably from the leading industrialist, Sir Alfred Mond, and the economist, John Maynard Keynes, when the great depression of 1929 to 1932 reduced British exports by no less than 37.5 per cent and turned a balance of payments surplus of £76 million in 1929 into a deficit of £114 million in 1931 (Newton and Porter, 1988, p. 67). This deterioration in Britain's economic prospects led to an outflow of £200 million from the City in the summer of 1931 that in turn triggered a sterling crisis which brought Britain's maintenance of the gold standard to an end. However, Newton and Porter claim that this latest economic crisis merely displaced rather than undermined the dominance of the core institutional nexus as evinced by the fact that in the face of a depression the incumbent Labour Government pursued a deflationary strategy from 1930 to 1931 (Newton and Porter, 1988, pp. 72–3). This was in marked contrast to the policies pursued in Germany and the United States where deficit financing and counter-cyclical public expenditure was used to revitalize their economies.

There was certainly no shortage of individuals, committees and pressure groups pressing for a change of economic policy in interwar Britain. Best and Humphries cite the 1929 *Final Report of the Balfour Committee on British Industrial Conditions* which pointed to the importance of the 'reconditioning' of industrial organization and equipment if competitiveness in export markets was to be maintained (Best and Humphries, 1986, p. 231). Of even greater importance was the 1931 *Report of the Macmillan Committee on Finance and Industry*, a parliamentary inquiry into the financing of British industry, and the first of three such major inquiries during the twentieth century. The Macmillan Committee identified the existence of an investment gap in the British economy caused by the failure of the City to provide finance for small and medium-sized companies. The Committee's recommendation was that City practice should be changed so that special provision would be made for small share issues but this and other suggestions for the reform of the banking system went largely unheeded (Collins, 1991, p. 85). The Macmillan Committee also recommended the formation of bank industry relationships that would facilitate the negotiation of planned industrial restructuring and the elimination of excessive capacity according to technological and organizational criteria. However, the bankers' own testimonies to the Committee demonstrated their preference for industry-led reorganization. Collins notes the overcautious and very limited initiatives of the City. New institutions were created, such as the Charterhouse Industrial Development Co. Ltd. in 1934, but six years later this particular institution had financed only 17 of more than 7 000 applications for funding (Collins, 1991, p. 86).

The Macmillan Committee managed to prompt the clearing banks into disclosing that around 40 to 55 per cent of their lending was to trade and industry. This, the bankers argued, was illustrative of their commitment to manufacturing industry. However, Collins argues that it is possible to take a much less sanguine view of the pattern of interwar bank loans to industry, in that an analysis of the assets of the London clearing banks reveals that they rarely met even the lower end of their own target of lending 50 to 55 per cent of their desposits in the form of loans and overdrafts (Collins, 1991, pp. 71–2). Indeed, the ratio of the banks advances to deposits declined from 52 per cent in 1928–30 to 41.2 per cent in 1936–38, with the advances to industry as a whole from the ten largest London clearing banks falling by 26 per cent between 1929 and 1936, and advances to heavy industry dropping by 35 per cent, to mining by 40 per cent, and to the textile industry by 51 per cent (Best and Humphries, 1986, p. 230). Since the economy had experienced a major recovery by 1937, Collins contends that economic growth was not being financed by the clearing banks themselves because they had reduced their financial provision to the private sector whilst developing their role as intermediaries between private sector savings and public sector debt. So marked was the transfer of resources from the financing of the private to the public sector that by the late 1930s over half of bank deposits were committed to the public sector (Collins, 1991, p. 73).

Best and Humphries' principal argument about the suppliers of finance in Britain is that from the late nineteenth century to 1939 they 'failed to become involved in the restructuring of industry so as to influence the profitability of enterprise and the demand for long-term industrial capital' (Best and Humphries, 1986, p. 223). The consequence was a lack of integration between finance and industry which adversely affected both the volume and the allocation of British industrial investment, and which in turn damaged the long-term competitiveness of British industry. Furthermore, when the banks did intervene in industry during the depression, it was not through intent but because they had inadvertently become overcommitted to troubled businesses and wished to protect their interests (Best and Humphries, 1986, p. 229). This analysis has been endorsed by Tolliday who describes the banks attempts at industrial intervention as 'clumsy and ill-directed', not least because that intervention was characterized by the application of traditional banking values, maintaining an arms-length approach to industrial restructuring and diminishing their exposure once the economy recovered (Tolliday, 1987, p. 170). Collins concludes that there was greater enthusiasm for industrial reorganization at the Bank of England than at the commercial banks, but that the Bank's involvement was only necessary because of the commercial banks failure to seize the initiative (Collins, 1991, p. 79).

A CONTEMPT FOR PRODUCTION?

Ingham has depicted the period since 1945 as an era of 'mercantile revival and industrial decline' when, as during most of the two previous centuries, the core institutional nexus continued to function (Ingham, 1984, pp. 201–24). As a consequence, despite their having to confront massive economic problems, not least because of the disruption and damage caused to Britain's civil economy by the Second World War, Ingham asserts that successive postwar governments have maintained the political and economic conditions to ensure the City's continuing prosperity as an international financial and commercial centre. These policies of an open economy, a stable, high-value currency, and attractive interest rates for sterling holders are all held by Ingham to have damaged the prospects for postwar industrial modernization. Pollard has been even more scathing in his analysis of Britain's postwar relative industrial decline. He has attributed the poor performance of the economy to the lack of investment in production compared with more rapidly growing economies. Investment in Britain has been so low 'because the whole panoply of government power, as exercised above all by the Treasury, was designed to keep it so' (Pollard, 1982, p. 71). Pollard contends that it has been this 'contempt for production' which has most clearly distinguished the British government from all others in the postwar period. In a similar vein, Lisle-Williams has argued that the Treasury's postwar efforts to minimize fluctuations in economic activity resulted in 'a preoccupation with the balance of payments and the exchange rate that undermined the very basis of economic growth, namely capacity and productivity' (Lisle-Williams, 1986, p. 232).

During the Second World War, even more so than during the First, there had been an overriding concern with, rather than a contempt for, production in Westminster and Whitehall. The interests of the City were sidelined in the face of the demands placed on economic policy by total war. Initially, because of the desire to avoid a postwar legacy of national debt, a policy of higher taxation was adopted to finance the war effort. However, budgetary policy changed after the publication of Keynes 1940 pamphlet, *How to Pay for the War*, which introduced the principle of national income accounting that concentrated on the question of the overall availability of national resources. Under this system, the state was able to dramatically increase its expenditure from its prewar level of £1.933 billion to £5.565 billion in 1945. Abandoning its sporadic interwar efforts to become more involved in the financing of industry, the state became heavily involved in all aspects of the funding and organization of a diversity of modern capital-intensive industries, with the munitions industry alone receiving around £900 million of capital investment from the state (Newton and Porter, 1988, p. 90). So effective was the mobilization of industrial resources that national income grew by 64 per cent between 1939 and 1946 despite the huge disruption caused to Britain's international trade by the war.

To finance the war effort, in addition to grants from the United States of £5.4 billion and the liquidation of £1.1 billion of its overseas investments, Britain had to borrow so massively from abroad that immediately after the end of the war the Attlee Government was confronted with dollar and sterling liabilities of over £3.5 billion and a projected balance of payments deficit of £1.25 billion between 1945 and 1950 (Newton and Porter, 1988, p. 108). Lacking Britain's prewar gold and dollar reserves which had also been liquidated during the war, the Attlee Government sought financial assistance from the United States to assist postwar reconstruction of the domestic economy. But the United States had emerged from the war as the dominant economic power and therefore had as its own priority the restoration of an open international economy to provide a market for its industries. Therefore, the major precondition of its offer to Britain of a $3.75 billion loan in 1946 was the early reintroduction of the convertibility of sterling as a means of resuscitating international trade and commerce. One major implication of its acceptance of this precondition was that the Attlee Government would have to maintain substantial reserves of foreign exchange to settle with sterling holders, at a time when other economies would be able to devote their currency reserves to the financing of imports vital for national reconstruction.

The convertibility of sterling was reintroduced in July 1947 but within five weeks it had been suspended and restrictions introduced on dollar imports as Britain suffered the first of a series of major sterling crises. The global shortage of dollars had led Britain's competitors to increase their exports to Britain from whom they could now secure payment in dollars. This led to such a huge and rapid haemorrhage from Britain's dollar reserves that the very process of reconstruction was called into question. Suspension of convertibility was therefore unavoidable. Dollar imports had to be cut again during the 1949 sterling crisis when the pound was devalued from $4.03 to $2.80. Following the defeat of the Attlee Government in 1951, both Newton and Porter and Longstreth portray the 1950s as a decade of increasing liberalization of financial activity in order for sterling and the City to be restored to their former positions in international commerce (Newton and Porter, 1988, p. 122; Longstreth, 1979, p. 175). However, Longstreth contends that from the reopening of the international market for foreign exchange in 1951 to the attempt in 1957 to reintroduce sterling convertibility, the revival of the City was at the cost to the domestic economy of increased volatility in short-term capital flows, preparing the ground for the eventual divorce of the fortunes of the City from those of sterling (Longstreth, 1979, p. 177).

The conflict of interest between domestic reconstruction and the policies required to maintain the City's international role has been seen by historians as more sharply defined in the mid 1960s when the highwater mark of postwar state-led modernization strategies was reached with the election in 1964 of the first Wilson Government. Ingham asserts that by 1964 there was widespread recognition of the tension between the interests of the City and industrial capital, and that the significance of the election of this particular government 'cannot be overestimated: for the first time in British history, the progressive forces of industrial capital were in accord with a political party in power' (Ingham, 1984, p. 208). However, what Ingham describes as 'industry's bid for hegemony' failed due to the apparent reluctance or inability of the Wilson Government to destroy the core institutional nexus. Whilst that nexus remained in place, major constraints would inevitably be placed upon domestic policy because of the continual threat of the collapse of sterling (Ingham, 1984, pp. 214–5). Thus, the Wilson Government's plans were undermined by the constant threat of an impending sterling crisis which eventually transpired with the November 1967 devaluation of the pound from $2.80 to $2.40, and the announcement of major cuts in public expenditure some two months later.

The Wilson Government did establish the Department of Economic Affairs (DEA), the Ministry of Technology (MinTech) and the Industrial Reorganization Corporation (IRC), ostensibly to ensure that industrial modernization would not be subjected to the Treasury's orthodox monetary control. However, as has been noted in the previous chapter, whilst MinTech and the IRC did succeed in exercising their capacity for industrial intervention, the DEA and the Labour Government's rather anemic National Plan were quickly subordinated to the financial strictures of the Treasury. In his memoirs, George Brown, Wilson's Minister for Economic Affairs, described the story of the DEA as 'the record of a social revolution that failed', a revolution, he claims, that was supposed to replace the orthodox financial accountancy of the Treasury with a novel form of 'social accountancy' (Brown, 1971, p. 87). Brown believed that the DEA would not be subservient but superior to the Treasury in the determination of economic policy. However, he asserts that 'the DEA and the Treasury were running two diametrically opposed policies' (Brown, 1971, p. 104). The central cause of the subordination of social revolution to orthodox financial control was, in Brown's opinion, the failure to clearly establish the nature of the DEA's functions. The DEA threatened 'half a dozen old-established departments' so it had little prospect of threatening the Treasury's primacy in Whitehall, let alone that of the Bank of England and the City (Brown, 1971, pp. 111–2). In a similar vein, as the previous chapters have also demonstrated, the Labour Government's attempts to implement an industrial modernization strategy between 1974 and 1979 were undermined by the primacy of monetary policy as orchestrated by the Treasury internally and the International Monetary Fund externally.

The full implications of Britain's poor postwar economic performance are best understood when relations between the state, finance and industry are placed in a comparative context. The two most comprehensive comparative analyses have been provided by Zysman and Cox, both of which have pointed to the failure of the state in Britain to arm itself with the controls over the financial system that are a prerequisite to an effective industrial policy (Zysman, 1983; Cox, 1986). Thus, Zysman's central argument is that 'discretion in the provision of industrial finance – in the selective allocation of credit – is necessary for the state to enter continuously into the industrial life of private companies and to influence their strategies in the way that a rival or partner would' (Zysman, 1983, p. 76). Although the state in Britain has been forced by economic decline to play a more proactive role in promoting economic growth, Zysman argues that 'the British Government has never controlled the channels of borrowing and lending that would facilitate the selective manipulation of credit allocation by the state' (Zysman, 1983, p. 197). Furthermore, the attempts made by successive postwar British governments to construct 'new institutions that paralleled or challenged the private financial system contributed to a conflict over the distribution of gain from industrial growth', a distributional conflict which in turn 'undermined a common desire for more rapid growth and gave the appearance of pluralistic paralysis' (Zysman, 1983, p. 82).

Zysman's analysis has been criticized by Cox for its 'tendency to underplay the necessity for fundamental conflict and political struggle when it is clear that the domestic financial system is clearly failing to meet the requirements of the domestic economy'. Cox also attacks Zysman's tendency to view 'the financial system as immutable and a constraining invariable', a tendency which Cox regards as a clear oversimplification that underplays the continuous political conflict over the role of the state in the financial system (Cox, 1986, p. 15). Cox's central contention is that there has been a 'fundamental disjuncture in state, finance and industry relationships in Britain', which has been the product of 'continuous political conflict and a failure to develop a national consensus over industrial and financial policy' (Cox, 1986, pp. 46–7). The postwar disjuncture between the state's attitude to financial and industrial policy has 'compounded the consequences of the reliance on a self-regulating financial system'. The state has been unable to implement an active industrial policy because it has not understood the need to control either directly or indirectly the operations of private capital markets which, when left to their own devices, have chosen to ignore the needs of domestic industry and to invest more in overseas industry, property and government debt (Cox, 1986, p. 44).

Cox asserts that 'the trick of successful economic management is to adopt an approach which does not create opportunities for disfunctional ideological, social and political conflicts to overturn the search for industrially and financially rational policies', and that, whilst the Germans and Japanese have not eliminated political conflicts, they have created 'state, finance and industry relationships which minimise the disruptive effects' (Cox, 1986, p. 27). He therefore concludes that the lesson to be gleaned from a comparative analysis of the relationships between the state, finance and industry is that 'those countries which have worked out a national consensus over the need to underwrite the long-term financing of industry, within the logic of capitalist trading relationships, have also been those with the most successful postwar record' (Cox, 1986, p. 57). However, whilst the development of a national consensus is held by Cox to be a prerequisite of a viable state, finance and industry relationship, he also contends that it is not in itself a sufficient condition because the consensus must be directed towards 'both economically rational and domestically sensitive policies and relationships'. Cox suggests that which model is adopted is less important than that 'it works to sustain that consensus within the peculiar, political and social environment operating in individual countries' (Cox, 1986, p. 57).

The principal problem with remedies for Britain's relative economic decline which invoke rationality in politics is that they tend to assume that rationalism in politics is a given with a single, self-evident definition. Rationality, however, is an extremely subjective concept which may be defined according to a multitude of criteria. Britain's postwar economic performance is itself a monument to the constant conflict between what might be considered, from a longer-term perspective and with the benefit of hindsight, administratively and technically rational policies, and what are regarded as politically rational policies according to the all important criterion of short-term electoral expediency. Furthermore, as Cox himself has acknowledged, there has not been agreement in Britain about either the need for a consensus in the first place, or the appropriate forum for creating a consensus and who should participate in it, let alone about what the appropriate state, finance and industry relationship should be. The absence of consensus is well illustrated by Lisle-Williams' discussion of the Wilson Committee's review of the functioning of financial institutions in Britain. The majority view of the Committee was that the supply of industrial finance was not as important a factor in Britain's poor economic performance as those 'aspects of class conflict and culture that shape the context of demand' (Lisle-Williams, 1986, p. 239). There were, however, dissenting opinions both from the Chairman and the trades unionists on the Committee who advocated the creation of an idealized version of the National Enterprise Board, and from the academic economists on the Committee whose preference was for 'semi-autonomous public sector investment'.

FROM BOOM TO BUST: THE CITY AND THE THATCHER GOVERNMENTS

It has been suggested by Coakley and Harris that the Thatcher Governments pursued a 'strategy for finance' during the 1980s, amongst whose objectives was a desire 'to promote the international competitiveness of the City as a global financial centre' primarily through a policy of deregulation of financial markets (Coakley and Harris, 1992, p. 38). They contend that deregulation was advanced by three particular policy measures. Firstly, and shortly after it took office in May 1979, the first Thatcher Government abolished exchange controls over capital movements to and from Britain. In the event, abolition led to a huge net outflow of capital from the recession-bound domestic economy towards more lucrative overseas investment opportunities. Thus, for example, U.K.-based pension funds and insurance companies were able to invest four times as much in overseas equities during the first six months of 1980 as they had been able to during the first half of 1979. From 1979 to 1983 British life insurance companies increased the proportion of their assets held in foreign securities from 2.9 per cent to 9.2 per cent, whilst British pension funds increased their share from 5.5 per cent to 14.7 per cent during the same period (Durham, 1992, p. 46). By 1989, the annual total outflow of capital from Britain had reached a massive £33.1 billion (or £52.8 billion if the contribution from overseas direct investment is included). Britain's net overseas assets, which stood at £32.6 billion in 1981, soared to a peak of £103.6 billion in 1986 as Britain briefly became the world's biggest net creditor. However, the fact that net overseas assets had fallen back dramatically to only £29.6 billion at the end of 1990 is demonstrative of the fact that Britain's surplus on its invisible trade, even at the height of the financial and property boom of the late 1980s, was insufficient to finance its much larger and growing trade deficit in manufactures (Coakley & Harris, 1992, pp. 44–5).

The cumulative outflow of capital from Britain benefited the City not only by generating a stream of profits, dividends and foreign interest, but also by providing City institutions with additional commercial income from fees and commission. However, it was the implementation of the so-called 'Big Bang' in 1986 which provided the second spur to deregulation. It was widely acknowledged both within the Square Mile and beyond that London had long since fallen behind Wall Street and Tokyo in its competitiveness in the global securities markets largely because of its antiquated attitudes and working practices. For example, although British investors had spent around £18 billion on foreign securities in the period 1979 to 1984, the inefficiency of the City had meant that British firms had handled only 5 per cent of this highly lucrative trade (Durham, 1992, p. 46). To surmount this lack of global competitiveness, the Chairman of the London Stock Exchange, Sir Nicholas Goodison, and the Secretary of State, Cecil Parkinson, reached an accord in July 1983 under which the City would implement a number of reforms to its trading practices in return for the dropping of a case brought against the Exchange through the Restrictive Practices Court. The package of reforms implemented through the 'Big Bang' abolished minimum commissions on dealing to promote London's competitiveness, replaced single capacity (that is, the traditional distinction between stockbroker and stockjobber) with dual capacity (that is, the capacity to act as both broker and jobber) to make business more profitable, and extended membership of the Stock Exchange to corporations to generate a larger capital base. It also allowed outsiders to own up to 100 per cent of member firms of the Stock Exchange in order to attract external investment, and replaced face-to-face dealing with computerized transactions to increase efficiency (Durham, 1992, pp. 48–9).

The third principal Thatcherite policy to promote deregulation was the removal of controls over the banking system, including the major distinctions between the banks and building societies. This has enabled the banks to become large-scale lenders in the mortgage market and building societies to expand their range of personal banking services (Coakley and Harris, 1992, pp. 45–6). The irony of this form of deregulation for the Thatcher Governments was that whilst it served the ideological objective of expanding open markets to provide entrepreneurs with the freedom to develop new products, it simultaneously robbed the state of some of its already depleted stock of economic policy instruments for controlling the growth of the money supply in general, and bank credit in particular. Thus, although it is tempting to blame the inflation of the late 1980s on the boost to the money supply given by Nigel Lawson's reforms of the personal and corporate taxation system, greater damage was inflicted by the inflationary consequences of the deregulation of the financial and property markets that occurred in 1986 through the October 'Big Bang', the passage of the Building Societies Act, and the December withdrawal of mortgage lending 'guidance'.

Table 6.1: Bank lending

	percentage of total lending		increase in lending (constant prices)
	1980	1991	1980–91
Manufacturing	27.7	10.8	+49%
Property	3.5	8.3	+801%
Personal	14.3	28.0	+648%
Total	100.0	100.0	+281%

Source: CBI (1992, p. 22)

As Table 6.1 above demonstrates, deregulation led to a rapid and inflationary expansion in lending to the personal and property sectors but this was not accompanied by a similar expansion in lending to manufacturing. In his 1984 Budget, Nigel Lawson had announced the withdrawal of stock relief and 100 per cent first-year investment allowances for manufacturers which only served to accentuate the disparities in the British taxation system between the relative attractiveness of investment in property and investment in manufacturing. Like previous British governments during the twentieth century, the Thatcher Governments had chosen to subordinate the long-term needs and interests of domestic manufacturers to the shorter-term interests of the City of London. On this occasion, however, the Government had unleashed financial forces the strength of whose inflationary implications it neither understood nor possessed the power to control. In his memoirs, Nigel Lawson recalls how 'from 1979–80 to 1987–88 bank and building society lending consistently rose rapidly, at rates fluctuating between 17 and 21 per cent a year' and then surged 'to over 24 per cent in 1988–89'. Furthermore, whilst a '20 per cent growth of bank and building society lending in 1979 represented around £14 billion, equivalent to 7 per cent of total national income', by 1988–89 'the 24 per cent growth of credit represented no less than £82 billion, equivalent to 18 per cent of GDP' (Lawson, 1992, p. 633). In the housing sector, net advances for house purchase increased from £19 billion in 1985–86 to £27 billion in 1986–87, a rise of almost 50 per cent (Lawson, 1992, p. 638). Average house prices rose by 170 per cent between 1982 and 1989 and in real terms by more than 90 per cent. With an apparently guaranteed high return on their initial property investment, and one which was massively subsidized by the state through mortgage income tax relief, whose costs more than doubled during the 1980s to nearly £7 billion in 1989–90, the incentives for investors to enter the property market were many times greater than those to start a new business in manufacturing (Johnson, 1991, p. 149).

The economic boom fuelled by deregulation extended to most areas of the City's financial and commercial dealing. In the foreign banking sector of the City, the number of banks operating in the Square Mile increased to around 521 in early 1989 compared with only 330 in 1975. In the previous year, these banks had accounted for 83 per cent of the international lending conducted by the City (Durham, 1992, pp. 5, 26). In the foreign exchange markets, the Bank of England calculated in 1989 that the City had a daily turnover of $187 billion (up from $90 billion in 1986) compared with $129 billion in New York and $115 billion in Tokyo. Trading in the securities market also expanded rapidly as a consequence of deregulation and the huge boost received from the privatization of British Telecom and British

Gas. The number of shares traded annually by the London Stock Exchange rose from 24 billion in 1981 to 78 billion in 1986. Industry was not entirely excluded from the benefits that accrued from the increase in share dealing. There was a 637 per cent increase in the issue of shares between 1983 and 1987, including a 137 per cent increase between 1986 and 1987. The value of new share issues on the London stock market increased from £1.7 billion in 1983 to £12.7 billion in 1987 (Durham, 1992, pp. 17, 43).

THE DIVIDEND FROM SHORT-TERMISM

The overall benefits to industry's competitiveness of financial deregulation were regularly questioned during the late 1980s especially because of the apparent development of a takeover culture in Britain. The legislative framework for corporate takeovers had been laid down in the 1980 Competition Act which had given the Director-General of Fair Trading the power to refer a proposed merger or any other potentially anti-competitive practice to the Monopolies and Mergers Commission (MMC). The MMC would in turn produce a report which would then be referred to the Secretary of State for Trade and Industry who would ultimately decide whether the MMC's recommendation should be accepted or rejected. Mergers could be referred to the MMC if their result would be to allocate control of at least 25 per cent of a market to a particular company, or if merger created a new company of a particular size (this size increased from £5 million to £15 million in 1980, and then to £30 million in 1984). However, only 3.5 per cent of mergers qualified for referral under these rules, and the vast majority of these were in any case cleared (Johnson, 1991, p. 187).

After the issuing during 1984 of new guidelines governing mergers by Norman Tebbit, the then Secretary of State for Trade and Industry, competition became the principal criterion for evaluating a merger or takeover. The more relaxed regime that the introduction of these guidelines ushered in was a major stimulus to merger and takeover activity. Spending on takeovers increased from £14.9 billion in 1986 to £15.4 billion in 1987, £17.1 billion in 1988 and £26.1 billion in 1989 (Cosh, Hughes and Singh, 1990, p. 36). Advocates of an open market in corporate control had traditionally argued that the possibility of being taken over acted as a major incentive to management to make their business more profitable in order to maintain the confidence of shareholders. However, there was widespread concern in the mid- to late-1980s that British companies were becoming so preoccupied with the short-term threat from and opportunities created by takeover activity, for example, paying out annual dividends to shareholders which were markedly higher than those warranted by actual company performance, that they were neglecting the long term in general and investment in R & D in particular.

When concern about the potentially damaging impact of short-termism on Britain's economic performance were raised at the 1986 CBI Conference, it appointed a 29 man City/Industry Task Force to analyse what the Task Force's eventual report described as the alleged sacrifice of the long-term international competitiveness of manufacturing 'on the altar of short-term financial gain' (CBI, 1987, p. 107). The report's rather surprising conclusion, given that its opening chapter had extensively documented the 'Uncomfortable realities' of Britain's relative economic decline, was that the Task Force could find 'no evidence to link attitudes in the City directly to the long-run decline of the nation's manufacturing sector – nor to its resurgence in recent years' (CBI, 1987, p. 10). The explanation for this conclusion would appear to lie in the timing of the report which was completed at the height of the euphoria surrounding the domestic financial and property boom, and before the October 1987 Stock Market Crash had radically altered business perceptions of the efficiency of volatile securities markets. The conclusion also highlighted the way in which the deregulation of the 1980s had accentuated the divisions of interest within the British economy in general, and the CBI's member companies in particular, between those operating primarily in commercial and financial markets and those competing in manufacturing markets.

More recently, in the aftermath of a recession deeply damaging to the output of the British economy, the House of Commons Trade and Industry Committee has sought to identify the causes and effects of short-termism in the UK economy. In its report, *Competitiveness of UK Manufacturing*, the Committee began by analysing the reasons for the UK's poor investment record. Whilst the Government could point to the fact that the UK's investment in manufacturing as a percentage of value added had been similar to Germany's and indeed higher than in the US for the past 30 years, this overlooked the fact that the UK had experienced a low level of value added. In terms of investment as a percentage of production or investment per manufacturing employee, the UK's record had been poor. Investment in the UK had tended to the cyclical because of the volatility of the national economy. Investment in other more successful economies had tended to be more consistent and therefore allowed companies to acquire and maintain a technological lead over their British competitors. The Committee contended that there are four possible explanations for this disappointing investment record in UK manufacturing. These are the high cost of capital in the UK, a scarcity of investment opportunities offering adequate returns, risk aversion among managers with regard to longer term investments, and a shortage of funds for investment. The Committee suggested that the first three of these explanations can be evaluated by analysing the internal rate of return which UK companies require investment plans to meet (House of Commons, 1994, pp. 52–6).

The Committee reported that in the UK between 1970 and 1990, gilt-edged stocks offering a return to investors of over 10 per cent had meant that returns of around 20 per cent per annum had been required for investment in capital plant in manufacturing. Had the returns on gilt-edged stocks in the City been 6 or 7 per cent, then the required return on industrial investment would have been only 10 to 12 per cent per annum. It was also found that the median required internal rate of return (IRR) in UK manufacturers was 21 to 25 per cent for relatively low risk operational investments and 16 to 20 per cent for strategic investments. At the same time, when the Committee explored the question of payback periods for UK manufacturers, that is, how quickly a company would expect to generate a return on its investment, it found that the median period for operational investments was only 19 to 24 months. In 56 per cent of manufacturing plants, the payback period was less than two years, and less than three years in 89 per cent of plants. The Committee therefore concluded that what differentiated UK companies from their competitors in terms of their investment records, was the internal rates of return required by the companies (House of Commons, 1994, pp. 56–7). These high rates of return were being sought for a number of reasons including the volatility in UK exchange rates and the growth rate of the economy, the generally higher rate of inflation which meant that manufacturers could not necessarily raise prices to compensate, the pressure on companies from their shareholders to deliver high and unvarying dividends, and a higher than average failure rate for investments. The Committee concluded that low investment could be seen as both a cause of problems in UK manufacturing, because it makes it harder for manufacturers to raise their competitiveness and output, and an effect of the problems of UK manufacturing because it reflects the relatively low returns yielded by this particular sector of the British economy (House of Commons, 1994, pp. 59–60).

When the House of Commons Trade and Industry Committee turned its attention to the question of why the UK is relatively weak in its stock of medium-sized firms (employing 100 to 499 people), which accounted for only 15.7 per cent of UK manufacturing employment in 1990 compared to an average of 28.2 per cent in western Europe, it focused on the terms on which funding was available to smaller firms in the UK. The Committee identified the central problem as the fact that the risks and administrative costs of providing funds to smaller firms are greater than in the case of

large firms and therefore greater returns on their investments are expected
by investors. For companies with a turnover exceeding £10 million, the
typical cost of borrowing was 1.5 per cent above base rate, but for
companies whose turnover was between £1 million and £10 million, that
interest rate rose to 2.5 per cent above base rate. Companies with a turnover
of less than £1 million would typically be charged 3 per cent above base
rate by the banks whilst the smallest firms would be charged anything from
3 to 5 per cent above base rate, a figure that would immediately be doubled
if the firms exceeded its overdraft limit. This has put small and medium-
sized businesses in the UK at a particular competitive disadvantage
compared to their continental European rivals because in Germany, for
example, a special bank, the Kreditanstalt fur Wiederaufbau (KfW), exists
to assist smaller firms by re-financing their commercial loans at reduced
interest rates. Similarly, in France, small businesses can obtain soft loans at
2 per cent below base rates (House of Commons, 1994, p. 62). Because of
the absence of a structure of regional banks in the UK, the Committee
concluded that there appeared to be a failure of understanding between the
banks and smaller firms. Moreover, even where investors possessed a
structure of regional offices, such as in the case of 3i Group, they preferred
to act as a 'hands off investor', entrusting management to be able to deliver
the 40 per cent required rate of return which 3i demands on at least some of
its start-up investments (House of Commons, 1994, p. 64).

It is not just smaller firms which have found that short-termism
amongst UK financial institutions has acted as a constraint upon their
performance. The House of Commons Trade and Industry Committee has
also found that large firms have also been the victims of short-termism in
the City of London. In particular, large firms appeared to have suffered
from the decline of private shareholders in the UK (down from 47 per cent
to 21 per cent of shares owned between 1969 and 1992) and the rise of the
pension funds (up from 9 per cent to 35 per cent in the same period) (House
of Commons, 1994, p. 68). Britain is unique in this respect in that its stock
markets are dominated by pension funds and insurance companies whereas
in the US it is private investors who are the dominant shareholders, and in
Germany it is the banks. The Committee reported that the main criticism
that had been made of the City's institutions was that of short-termism.
Profitable long term investments are not being undertaken because City
institutions either require high short-term returns or undervalue long-term
investments.

Concern was also expressed about the relatively high level of dividend
payments from UK companies compared to their Japanese and German
industrial competitors. To account for these high dividend payments, the
Committee identified high yields on competing investments, high interest

rates, the volatility of the UK economy, low expectations of future economic growth, the dominance of the stock market by institutions requiring an income flow, and the maintenance of dividends by managers to show faith in the future of their company and to strengthen their position against hostile takeovers as contributory factors. However, the most important factor contributing to this particular form of short-termism is the UK tax system which encourages shareholders, especially institutional shareholders, to look for income from short-term dividend payments rather than long-term capital gains. Thus, taking account of corporate taxation, whilst pension funds pay a 33 per cent tax on profits retained in the companies whose shares they own, they pay a tax of only 16.25 per cent on their income from dividend payments. The Thatcherite tax reforms of the 1980s accentuated this trend to the extent that 'Between 1982 and 1992, the value to a higher-rate taxpayer of a pre-tax profit of £100, fully distributed as dividend, rose from £17 to £53' (House of Commons, 1994, p. 72). By way of contrast, in the US, Germany and Japan, the taxation system has acted to discourage the distribution of dividends to shareholders and encourages the retention of profits by companies for investment.

The House of Commons' Trade and Industry Committee concluded that 'the problem of short-termism is the result of groups of people responding to a system which requires – indeed insists upon – short-termist behaviour' (House of Commons, 1994, p. 81). For the Committee, the implication of its conclusion that the shortcomings of the UK financial system are systemic was that government action was required. To redress the problem of financing smaller firms and the absence of an effective regional banking structure, it recommended that 'the Government investigate how a loan guarantee scheme could be established which would provide the UK's smaller firms with similar advantages to those obtained in Germany from KfW' (House of Commons, 1994, p. 110). To redress the problem of short-termism amongst the City's financial institutions, with their £900 billion of assets and their ownership of 60 per cent of UK quoted companies, the Committee recommended that the Financial Secretary to the Treasury examine the possibility of changes in the taxation of dividends and capital gains, with the objective of promoting the retention and re-investment of profits, and limited controls on hostile takeovers. It also proposed that in the longer term, the Government should examine alternative means of funding pensions in the UK, and thereby weaken one of the principal propellants of short-termism (House of Commons, 1994, p. 113).

Since the publication of its report, both the Bank of England and the CBI have produced surveys that have borne out the Committee's concerns about short-termism. For example, the CBI's May 1994 investment appraisal survey found that about two-fifths of those using nominal rates of return were seeking a 20 per cent return from their investment, whilst two-fifths of the Bank of England's respondents indicated that they expected investment projects to finance themselves within three years (*Financial Times*, 23 July, 1994; *The Guardian*, 1 August, 1994). Concern about short-termism has also been expressed by the academic community. A study published by the Institute of Fiscal Studies has highlighted the damage to investment levels caused by a shortage of internal company finance arising from excessive dividend payments, whilst a report from the Anglo—German Foundation has recommended greater government intervention, in the form of the establishment of a state-funded small business bank, as a means to counteract the impact of short-termism on small and medium-sized companies (Bond and Meghir, 1994; Mullineux, 1994).

Amongst media commentators, the most prominent and consistent critique of short-termism has been provided by Will Hutton during his tenure as Economics Editor of *The Guardian*. Hutton has asserted that the root cause of Britain's supply side problems remains the fact that British companies must pay one of the highest costs of capital in the industrialized world. Hutton has cited an unpublished analysis produced by the accountants Coopers and Lybrand which demonstrates that the combined cost to British companies of rewarding their shareholders, servicing bank loans and paying taxes is 19.9 per cent (*The Guardian*, 1 August, 1994). It is therefore hardly surprising that so many British companies are looking for returns of more than 20 per cent on their investments because of this very high cost of capital and the context of growing domestic political uncertainty arising from the unpopularity of the Major Government. The danger remains that any domestic economic recovery will be short-lived and undermined by two immediate consequences of short-termism. Firstly, the inflationary pressures arising from domestic manufacturers responding to capacity constraints by raising the prices of their products rather than expanding their capacity to produce because of the costs of capital. This inflationary threat may be accentuated by the steady devaluation of the pound in recent years which has significantly increased the cost of imported raw materials and components. Secondly, the deteriorating balance of payments caused by overseas manufacturers, unencumbered by financial constraints, supplying demand in the British economy for products which domestic businesses are unable to expand to meet because of the prohibitive costs of investing in new plant and equipment. Interest rates may have to rise to levels that further discourage domestic industrial investment merely in order to choke off demand for imports at the risk of an even greater deterioration in the balance of payments at a later date.

To surmount the causes and consequences of short-termism, in *The State We're In*, Hutton has proposed that the British financial system should be 'comprehensively republicanised'. This means that, as part of a wider political settlement, the principles of governance of the financial system in Britain should be articulated and agreed in order to increase their legitimacy. Hutton's broader political agenda includes 'A written constitution; the democratisation of civil society; the republicanisation of finance; the recognition that the market economy has to be managed and regulated, both at home and abroad; the upholding of a welfare state that incorporates social citizenship; the construction of a stable international financial order beyond the nation state' (Hutton, 1995, p. 326). For Hutton, 'What is now required is a national effort to organise a sustained increase in investment' (Hutton, 1995, p. 81). However, because he contends that the economic institutions and   state structures supporting the existing relationship between finance and industry 'are no more ready to respond to such a call than they ever were', Hutton's solution is the creation of an alternative financial culture based on 'stakeholder capitalism', in which the ownership of businesses is broadened so as to generate a greater commitment to long-term investment and an increase in the supply of cheap finance to industry. The responsibility for bringing about this transformation in the operating procedures and priorities of the financial system would lie with a new Central Bank whose structure would reflect the new federal structure of the British state. The Central Bank would itself be supported by a network of regional public banks whose chief executives would in turn be elected by newly-established regional parliaments (Hutton, 1995, p. 298).

Hutton offers a vision of a brave new world for finance and industry in Britain. The Major Government, however, has shown few signs that it is contemplating this scale of systemic reform in order to address the widespread concern amongst manufacturers about short-termism. This was illustrated when the House of Commons' Trade and Industry Committee addressed several of its recommendations directly to the Financial Secretary to the Treasury, Stephen Dorrell, because during the Committee's inquiry, he had publicly expressed concern on several occasions about whether UK financial structures were encouraging entrepreneurial activity. The Treasury had previously launched its own industrial finance initiative to examine the question of the supply of finance to the UK economy, including the issues surrounding capital markets, savings generally, the flow of funds to business, and the implications for taxation and other policies. Unfortunately, when the Major Government published its White Paper, *Competitiveness: Helping Business to Win* (HMSO, 1994), it did not incorporate any of the systemic reforms that the House of Commons Trade and Industry Committee had recommended. Furthermore, the prospects for major changes in policy were not enhanced when a letter to Stephen Dorrell from Lord Hanson, one of Britain's most successful industrialists during the 1980s and a major donor to the Conservative Party, was leaked to the national press. In the letter, Hanson not only accused Dorrell of 'sounding like a socialist' but also stated that the issue of dividend payments was 'nothing to do with the government' (*Financial Times*, 24 November, 1994). It later emerged that Hanson had written to the Prime Minister about the Treasury's review of dividend payments. In the Prime Minister's Cabinet reshuffle, Stephen Dorrell departed the Treasury to become Secretary of State for National Heritage. In the wake of Hanson's attack and Dorrell's departure, it was disclosed that the Treasury had abandoned its review because, according to an unnamed senior civil servant, 'The issue became too much of a hot potato after Hanson attacked the review. No one wanted to pick it up' (*Financial Times*, 24 November, 1994).

THE FUTURE OF THE CITY

Whilst anger amongst UK manufacturers about the City's failure to provide investment capital on a long-term basis at a competitive cost does not appear to have unduly disturbed financial institutions in the Square Mile (it is, after all, hardly a novel phenomenon), the question of the future of London's role as the centre of international commerce has caused some concern. As indicated in the introduction to this chapter, there is a danger when using the shorthand of 'the City' of losing sight of the sheer diversity of markets and financial interests that operate in London. However, even a brief analysis of recent developments surrounding some of the most important markets suggests that the City's competitive advantage is not unassailable. In the specific instance of Lloyd's, for example, the largest single insurance market and one of the City's principal institutions, domestic and international confidence in its future has been severely shaken by the size and implications of the losses that have been experienced by individual investors in Lloyd's in recent years.

In the Lloyd's insurance market, business has traditionally been transacted by insurance brokers, representing those seeking insurance, and underwriters, representing those individual investors (known as Names) who provide the finance for insurance. However, a report from the financial analysts Chatset, who monitor the performance of Lloyd's, has forecast that the Names, whose high risk, high return investments do not enjoy the protection of limited liability, and who already face accumulated losses of

£6.5 billion from four ruinous trading years between 1988 and 1991, will face an additional bill of around £10 billion in the next 20 years (*The Guardian*, 14 December, 1994). This is because insurance syndicates at Lloyd's have not set aside sufficient reserve funds to meet future claims. Chatset estimated that under-reserving had grown from £5 billion at the end of 1991 to £9.7 billion at the end of 1993. Whilst Lloyd's Names had been asked for £1.4 billion for reserves in the past financial year, this had not prevented a further deterioration in the amount of under-reserving. Moreover, Names were unlikely to be able to afford to pay more than another £2 billion in the future, leaving a huge gap between their outstanding financial liabilities and their capacity to pay. Whilst their earlier losses largely relate to recent, one-off disasters such as the pollution caused by the oil tanker, Exxon Valdiz, the explosion on the Piper Alpha oil rig in the North Sea and storm damage in Europe in 1990, future claims on the Names will arise from insurance policies written in the US up to 40 years ago and relating to damage caused by asbestos and other forms of pollution (*Financial Times*, 16 September, 1993). Given the voracity of the US legal system, the size of the eventual losses at Lloyd's are almost impossible to predict.

Lloyd's has taken measures to rebuild investor confidence in its future. In an attempt to prevent its future operations being undermined by prolonged and expensive court action, Lloyd's offered £900 million to its disgruntled Names with the proviso that they drop their litigation against Lloyd's. Given that several thousand Names had been seeking £3.1 billion from Lloyd's, on the grounds that their losses stemmed from negligence and bad advice from market professionals rather than from the inherent high risk of the insurance market they were operating in, it was not surprising when the Names voted down Lloyd's offer. Legal action by a group of 3096 Names, who had invested in four insurance syndicates run by the now defunct Gooda Walker agency, duly proceeded through the High Court which eventually adjudicated that the Names had been victims of negligent underwriting. It was estimated that this judgement could result in an award to the Names of £504 million, although Lloyd's might yet prevent some Names from collecting their compensation payments until full settlement of their losses at Lloyd's (*The Guardian*, 5 October, 21 October, 1994). Subsequently, it has been reported that Lloyd's has been contemplating a new offer of £1.1 billion to the 22 000 Names who have lost money and who have been threatening further litigation (*The Guardian*, 18 November, 1994). However, there is no guarantee that, even if an offer to settle out-of-court is eventually made, that the loss-making Names will accept because, in many cases, the sum on offer in no way matches the extent of their liabilities. The whole matter has been given additional political salience by the fact that at least fifty Conservative MPs and a number of leading theatrical and sporting celebrities are known to be numbered amongst the loss-makers. In any event, irrespective of the eventual settlement that is reached, whether it is within or outwith court, the damage in the interim to the image and reputation of one of the City's major institutions can only be counterproductive.

Another important part of Lloyd's remedial action has been the introduction of a tighter regulatory structure for Lloyd's future transactions accompanied by the decision to admit corporate investors to the insurance markets with a minimum capitalization of £1.5 million in order to restore liquidity and confidence at Lloyd's. The problem with this strategy is that whilst corporate financiers, in the form of 25 investment trusts, have shown themselves to be prepared to commit more than £900 million of new funds to Lloyd's, allowing them to underwrite £1.59 billion of insurance, they are not prepared to finance the past insurance liabilities of Names. Therefore, corporate investment will not flow into Lloyd's without there being prior guarantees that new market entrants will not be liable to bail out debt-stricken Names. In the interim, attempts to meet liabilities from Names consortia that claim to have been bankrupted by their losses are unlikely to meet more than 10 per cent of the money that is owed. In the past five years, the number of agencies operating insurance syndicates at Lloyd's has declined from 388 in 1990 to about 170 at the 1st January 1995. During the same period, the number of Names actively underwriting at Lloyd's has fallen from 28 770 to 14 804 (*Financial Times*, 9 January, 1995). Total underwriting capacity at Lloyd's stood at £10.2 billion in January 1995 compared with £10.9 billion in 1994. Therefore, despite the compensatory increase in corporate investors to offset the declining number of Names, for the foreseeable future, Lloyd's appears to be locked into a vicious spiral of declining market capacity, fewer individual investors, and massive liabilities which the market may not possess sufficient reserves to finance.

The insurance market at Lloyd's is not the only City institution that has faced difficulties in recent years. In the case of London's securities markets, the City's domination of share trading in Europe has been challenged both by the collapse of Taurus, the project to install an electronic share trading system which was intended to give London a virtually unassailable competitive advantage, and by demands for greater transparency in the dealings of 'marketmakers', the securities firms who have been given privileges by the Stock Exchange in return for their legal obligation to purchase and sell large numbers of shares in listed companies, even if market conditions are volatile. Taurus had been designed to replace antiquated paper transactions, which require the possession of a share certificate and a completed stock transfer form, with fully computerized share dealing. It would have saved dealers an estimated minimum of £230 million in share transactions during its first decade of operation. In the event, Taurus failure to become operational cost many domestic and foreign financial institutions many millions of pounds in lost investment, and the Chief Executive of the Stock Exchange his job (*Independent on Sunday*, 14 March, 1993).

The demands for greater transparency in the share dealings of marketmakers in the City has been based on the argument that the current system, under which marketmakers do not have to disclose their dealings in large blocks of shares, means that London derivatives prices (that is, prices in markets such as the London International Financial Futures Exchange which deal in the future price of financial assets) do not necessarily reflect the actual price of shares being bought and sold in the market. Indeed, as Cohen has pointed out, the Stock Exchange has released statistics which show that, because of the failure of the marketmakers to disclose their major transactions, just over half of the previous year's share deals worth more than £1 million were struck at prices better than the best publicly available price (*Financial Times*, 3 August, 1994). This has meant that many investors may have been denied the opportunity to sell their shares at the best available price. The marketmakers have defended their failure to follow the practice in other European markets of immediate disclosure of transactions once completed on the grounds that the existing system guarantees that investors can purchase and sell shares irrespective of the volatility of the market. This, it is claimed, gives London a competitive advantage. Given that the City's principal regulator, the Securities and Investments Board, has produced a report questioning the need for this privileged protection of marketmakers, and that the Office of Fair Trading has launched an investigation to discover whether such practices are anti-competitive, it is clear that the debate about the best route forward for major share dealing in the City will continue for some months. However, the controversy surrounding both the collapse of Taurus and the nature of marketmaking in the City demonstrate the increasing challenge that London faces from other stock markets in the European time zone.

Two of the principal reasons for fears for the future of London's role as the major financial services centre in Europe have been the unification of Germany and the contrasting attitudes of the British and German governments towards further political and economic union in Europe. The unification of Germany has strengthened Germany's position as the most populous and richest single national market in the European Union (EU). The decision announced in October 1993 to locate the EU's potential future central bank in Frankfurt rather than in London was a major commercial and political setback for London. Britain had attempted to block German pressure for Frankfurt to be chosen, but the exercise of the British veto at the Lisbon EC summit in June 1992 was little more than a delaying tactic. London does possess the headquarters of the European Bank for Reconstruction and Development, but this is a political and economic minnow by contrast. Whilst the divisions within the Conservative Party and Government towards further European integration have been all too apparent, attitudes within the City are less clearly discernible. However, an opinion poll of senior managers in the City found that whilst 49 per cent were in favour of full economic and monetary union, 48 per cent were against closer integration. The creation of a single European currency would mean a fall in the number of foreign currencies being traded on London's lucrative foreign exchange markets. Nevertheless, more City executives thought business opportunities would increase rather than decrease as a consequence of European monetary union (*The Guardian*, 9 January, 1995). The fact that Chancellor Kohl, unlike Thatcher or Major, has remained a powerful advocate of further European union may have helped to sway the votes of the other E.U. member states in Germany's favour, especially given the widespread perception on the Continent of Britain's antagonism towards all forms of union. Given the mobility of financial services which, unlike the relatively immobile fixed assets of manufacturing plants, require access only to modern communications, that is, a telephone, computer network and facsimile machine, there remains the possibility that in the longer term larger financial institutions may decide to gravitate away from London and towards Frankfurt or Berlin, the future capital of the unified Germany, in recognition of Germany's status as the most important political and financial actor in the Europe of the twenty-first century.

More immediate threats to the City's prosperity have been posed by a series of financial scandals, terrorist bombing campaigns, and London's overloaded transport infrastructure. Critical questions have been raised about the probity and regulation of transactions within the City following a series of financial scandals, most notably the collapse of the Bank of Credit and Commerce International (BCCI) with unrecoverable debts of $12.4 billion. At the same time as London's reputation for secure trading has been challenged, its longstanding traditition of providing stable political conditions for trading has been interrupted by a series of bomb explosions within the Square Mile. The sheer scale of the property insurance claims which have arisen from the resulting bomb damage raised the spectre of parts of the City becoming uninsurable. Such was the concern that the Lord Mayor of London called for state intervention to underwrite the cost of insuring certain properties in the Square Mile through an indemnity policy similar to that operated by the British Government to cover parts of Belfast.

However, given that France has also suffered from terrorist attacks in the recent past whilst senior German executives in both the public and private sectors have been assassinated in 1989 and 1991, London is not necessarily being put at a major commercial disadvantage by terrorism, especially given the recent ceasefire in Northern Ireland. Of greater potential concern for those who work in the City has been the increasing difficulty of gaining access to the capital because of the failure of public investment in the infrastucture of London's roads, railways and underground system to keep pace with the rapid growth in private sector investment in new property in the City during the 1980s. The delays in the construction of major transport projects, such as the extension to the underground Jubilee Line to Docklands and the East–West Crossrail link between Liverpool Street and Paddington, coupled with the cuts in London Transport's capital investment programme, pose a much larger threat of long-term disruption to commercial activity than the activities of the IRA and international terrorism.

CONCLUSION

It should not be forgotten that the City does enjoy considerable residual strength as a centre of international finance and commerce. Whilst employment in financial services in Britain fell nationally by 10.7 per cent between 1989 and 1992, this decline has to be set against the near doubling of those employed in this sector between 1979 and 1990. Indeed, in 1990, financial services employed 2.8 million people in Britain, around one-eighth of the total workforce (*Financial Times*, 15 June, 1993). London still enjoys a substantial competitive advantage in financial services, not least because of its favourable time zone position which allows dealers to trade for comparatively long periods with both North America and Far Eastern markets. The City also benefits from the widespread use of English in commercial and financial transactions, and the fact that its legal and regulatory framework constitutes the basis for many international contracts. These competitive advantages meant that in 1992 London traded $303 billion daily in its foreign exchange markets compared with $192 billion in New York and $108 billion in Tokyo. Frankfurt was trading only $60 billion daily whilst Paris was trading a relatively paltry $35 billion (*Independent on Sunday*, 18 July, 1993). In trading in overseas securities, London possessed a 93.5 per cent share of the European market in 1992 compared with only 2.3 per cent for Frankfurt and 1 per cent for Paris. During 1994, a record £11.6 billion of new funding for companies was raised on the London Stock Exchange. Indeed, turnover in UK and Irish shares increased in 1994 by 7.7 per cent to £607 billion compared with the previous year. Turnover in overseas equities increased by 24 per cent to £717 billion (*The Guardian*, 31 January, 1994). In the banking sector, the City remained the leading world centre for cross-border lending in 1992, having a 16.5 per cent share of the market, slightly ahead of Japan's 14.2 per cent. As a consequence of its success in global markets, London employs more people in banking and finance (around 800 000) than the entire population of Frankfurt (around 600 000).

Despite the threats posed to it in the shorter term by financial scandals, terrorism and inadequate public transport, and in the longer term by German political, financial and industrial power, the City of London is unlikely to be dethroned from its status as Britain's single most important commercial interest. As Table 6.2 illustrates, London remains a vital source of national income for Britain. In 1992, the net overseas receipts of UK financial institutions increased by 19.8 per cent from £15.7 billion to £18.8 billion. The overall surplus on invisible trade rose to £4.8 billion in 1992 from £2.6 billion in 1991 but herein the dilemma posed by the City remains. These impressive sums were in no sense sufficient to balance Britain's visible trade deficit which rose to £8.6 billion in 1992 from £7.6 billion in 1991, albeit that these figures constituted a welcome improvement on the massive £18.3 billion visible trade deficit in 1990. The general affluence of the City was spread across many markets, with Britain's total income from its portfolio investment increasing by a spectacular 37.7 per cent in 1992 to £10.6 billion. Dealers operating in securities markets increased their net receipts from £791 million to more than £1.4 billion, but this dramatic improvement may have reflected the turmoil in the markets caused by 'Black Wednesday' as much as any improvement in the performance of the British economy.

The dilemma for the incumbent and future British governments remains the same as in the past. Whilst the City's costs to the performance of manufacturing industry are widely acknowledged, the gains in output, productivity and profitability that might accrue to manufacturers from the provision of lower cost capital for long-term investment remain notional, whereas the City's benefits to the balance of payments, whilst they may be smaller in the longer term than those which would accrue from an industrial revival, actually exist and are tangible to those who receive them. In its defence, the City can point to the fact that in 1994 the London Stock Exchange provided a record £11.6 billion of funding for companies as evidence that it is serving the needs of its customers.

Table 6.2: Overseas receipts of UK financial institutions (£ million)

	1982	1984	1986	1988	1990	1992
Banks	2 378	4 353	5 385	4 440	7 231	8 729
Insurance institutions	1 648	2 497	4 898	3 411	2 389	4 340
Fund managers	n/a	n/a	n/a	n/a	202	282
Investment	116	170	189	155	223	293
Unit trusts	63	126	214	254	388	486
Pension funds	326	559	1 032	933	1 390	2 229
Dealers operating in security markets	120	134	583	901	936	1 435
Commodity traders, bullion dealers, and export houses	367	499	440	415	431	454
Baltic Exchange	246	270	221	334	474	401
Lloyd's Register of Shipping	37	27	24	18	29	39
Money market brokers	38	49	58	56	85	92
Finance leasing	68	72	50	40	40	40
Less adjustment	-848	-2 062	-1 658	-630	-64	0
TOTAL	4 559	6 694	11 436	10 327	13 754	18 820

Source: Central Statistical Office.

The City's critics, not least Gordon Brown, Labour's Shadow Chancellor, however, will continue to point to the fact that during the financial year 1993–94, Britain's nine largest banks and building societies generated no less than £13.4 billion in income from non-interest-related charges on their customers, compared with £11.4 billion in 1992 and £7.5 billion in 1988 (*The Sunday Times*, 21 August, 1994). Brown has promised tough new regulations to govern the City under a future Labour Government, including an end to self-regulation of markets to restore public confidence (*Financial Times*, 20 September, 1994). Moreover, a future Labour government is committed to the creation of the Business Development Bank, an industrial development bank modelled on the German KfW which would 'specialise in providing long-term finance for the expansion of small businesses by acting as an intermediary between the short-term demands of financial markets and the longer-term needs of small companies' (Labour Party, 1994, p. 8). On this evidence, there is little to suggest that a future Labour Government is prepared to upset the political structures and institutions upon which the City's financial and commercial power is based, even though, as Hutton has powerfully argued, constitutional reform on an heroic scale may be a prerequisite for remedying Britain's industrial decline.

REFERENCES

Albert, M. (1993), *Capitalism against Capitalism* (London: Whurr).

Anderson, P. (1963), 'Origins of the Present Crisis', *New Left Review*, 23, pp. 26–53.

Anderson, P. (1987), 'The Figures of Descent', *New Left Review*, 161, pp. 20–77.

Barratt Brown, M. (1988), 'Away with all the Great Arches: Anderson's History of British Capitalism', *New Left Review*, 167, pp. 22–52.

Barratt Brown, M. (1989), Commercial and Industrial Capital in England: A Reply to Geoffrey Ingham', *New Left Review*, 178, pp. 124–8.

Best, M. and J. Humphries (1986), 'The City and industrial decline' in Elbaum, B. and W. Lazonick, (eds.), *The Decline of the British Economy* (Oxford: Oxford University Press).

Bond, S. and C. Meghir (1994), *Financial Constraints and Company Investment* (London: Institute of Fiscal Studies).

Brown, G. (1971), *In My Way* (Penguin: Harmondsworth).

Cain, P. and A. Hopkins (1993a), *British Imperialism: Innovation and Expansion 1688–1914* (London: Longman).

Cain P. and A. Hopkins (1993b), *British Imperialism: Crisis and Deconstruction 1914–1990* (London: Longman).

CBI (1987), *Investing for Britain's Future,* Report of the City/Industry Task Force (London: Confederation of British Industry).

CBI (1992), *Making it in Britain: Partnership for World Class Manufacturing,* The Report of the CBI National Manufacturing Council (London: Confederation of British Industry).

Coakley, J. and L. Harris (1992), *The City of Capital: London's Role as a Financial Centre* (Oxford: Blackwell).

Collins, M. (1991), *Banks and Industrial Finance in Britain 1800–1939* (London: Macmillan).

Cosh, A., A. Hughes and A. Singh (1990), *Takeovers and Short-termism in the UK* (London: Institute for Public Policy Research).

Cottrell, P. (1975), *British Overseas Investment in the Nineteenth Century* (London: Macmillan).

Cox, A. (ed.) (1986), *The State, Finance, and Industry: A Comparative Analysis of Postwar Trends in Six Advanced Industrial Economies* (Brighton: Harvester Wheatsheaf).

Durham, K. (1992), *The New City* (London: Macmillan).

Elbaum, B. and W. Lazonick (eds.) (1986), *The Decline of the British Economy* (Oxford: Oxford University Press).

Gerschenkron, A. (1966), *Economic Backwardness in Historical Perspective: A Book of Essays* (Cambridge, Mass.: Belknap Press).

Hennessy, P. (1989), *Whitehall* (London: Fontana Press).

Hobsbawm, E. (1969), *Industry and Empire: From 1750 to the Present Day* (Harmondsworth: Penguin).

House of Commons (1994), *Competitiveness of UK Manufacturing Industry,* Second Report from the House of Commons Trade and Industry Committee, Session 1993–94, HC41-1 (London: HMSO).

Hutton, W. (1995), *The State We're In* (London: Jonathan Cape).

Ingham, G. (1984), *Capitalism Divided? The City and Industry in British Social Development* (London: Macmillan).

Ingham, G. (1988), 'Commercial capital and British development', *New Left Review,* 172, pp. 45–66.

Johnson, C. (1991), *The Economy under Mrs Thatcher 1979–1990* (Penguin: Harmondsworth).

Labour Party (1994), *Winning for Britain: Labour's Strategy for Industrial Success* (London: The Labour Party).

Lawson, N. (1992), *The View from No. 11: Memoirs of a Tory Radical* (London: Bantam).

Leys, C. (1983), *Politics in Britain* (London: Heinemann).

Leys, C. (1985), 'Thatcherism and British manufacturing', *New Left Review,* 151, pp. 5–25.

Lisle-Williams, M. (1986), 'The State, Finance and Industry in Britain', in Cox, A. (ed.), *The State, Finance and Industry: A Comparative Analysis of Postwar Trends in Six Advanced Industrial Economies* (Brighton: Harvester Wheatsheaf).

Longstreth, F. (1979), 'The city, industry and the state', in Crouch, C. (ed.), *State and Economy in Contemporary Capitalism* (London: Croom Helm).

Mathias, P. (1974), *The First Industrial Nation: An Economic History of Britain 1700–1914* (London: Methuen).

McRae, H. and F. Cairncross (1985), *Capital City: London as a Financial Centre* (London: Methuen).

Morgan, E. and W. Thomas (1962), *The Stock Exchange: Its History and Functions* (London: Elek Books).

Mullineux, A. (1994), *Small and Medium-sized Enterprise (SME) Financing in the UK: Lessons from Germany* (London: Anglo–German Foundation).

Nairn, T. (1963), 'The British Political Elite', *New Left Review*, 23, pp. 19–25.

Newton, S. and D. Porter (1988), *Modernization Frustrated: The Politics of Industrial Decline in Britain since 1900* (London: Unwin & Hyman).

Pollard, S. (1964), 'Fixed capital in the Industrial Revolution in Britain', *Journal of Economic History*, 24, pp. 299–314.

Pollard, S. (1982), *The Wasting of the British Economy: British Economic Policy 1845 to the Present* (London: Croom Helm).

Pollard, S. (1989), *Britain's Prime and Britain's Decline: The British Economy 1870–1914* (London: Hodder & Stoughton).

Rubinstein, W.D. (1977), 'Wealth, elites and the class structure of modern Britain', *Past and Present*, 76, pp. 99–126.

Rubinstein, W.D. (1981), *Men of Property* (London: Croom Helm).

Thompson, E.P. (1965), 'The peculiarities of the English', in Thompson, E.P. (ed.), *The Poverty of Theory and Other Essay* (London: Merlin).

Tolliday, S. (1987), *Business, Banking and Politics: The Case of British Steel, 1918–1936* (Harvard: Harvard University Press).

Warwick, P. (1985), 'Did Britain change? An inquiry into the causes of national decline', *Journal of Contemporary History*, 20, pp. 99–133.

Zysman, J. (1983), *Governments, Markets and Growth: Financial Systems and the Politics of Industrial Change* (Oxford: Martin Robertson).

PART C:

Improving Britain's Relative Economic Performance

7. What next for Government and Industry? The Strategic Alignment of National and Corporate Competitiveness

Andrew Cox and Joe Sanderson

INTRODUCTION

Unlike the final chapter of many of the books dealing with the issue of Britain's relative economic decline, this chapter will not put forward an argument in favour of one of the explanations of decline discussed in the previous section. Not only has such a conclusion been written many times before, but it is our belief that it is essentially fruitless to argue that Britain's economic problems can be satisfactorily explained by a single set of variables. Rather, it seems much more realistic to suggest that each explanation, be it the existence of an 'anti-industrial' culture or the political and economic primacy of the City of London, has something to offer. This does not mean, however, that all such explanations are equally valid. The really important point is that none of them represents 'the' answer. In this context, therefore, the main aim of this chapter is not to ask why the British economy has performed relatively poorly since 1939, but rather to consider what lessons for the future might be drawn from the failed efforts of successive governments to deal with this 'problem'. It is our contention that two key lessons can, and urgently should, be learned. On the basis of these lessons, we conclude by outlining what we believe to be one way in which many British firms can acquire and sustain international competitiveness.

LESSON ONE: THE SHORT-TERM POWER OF INITIATION VERSUS THE LONG-TERM POWER OF CONSTRAINT

First, it is clear that the strong and extensive forms of state intervention represented on our continuum of ideal type state market relationships by corporatism, dirigisme and socialism have never been, and are never likely to be, successfully implemented in Britain, because both the electorate and the key socio-economic groups (trade unions, industry and finance) espouse liberal, laissez-faire values. The liberalism of the unions is expressed in their historic commitment to free collective bargaining, while both industrial and financial interests might desire state assistance, but only if it is not accompanied by state interference in investment and output decisions.

The only type of state intervention with any chance of successful implementation, therefore, is the weak and limited form represented on our continuum by Macmillanism. Unfortunately, even this state market relationship is unlikely to be fully worked out in practice, because it relies on the *voluntary* support of business and labour groups for state initiatives. Such support is only likely to be forthcoming so long as the price to be paid in terms of state control remains low. The trade unions may support the idea of state-led industrial modernization, but they are not prepared to accept the resultant burden of manpower planning and incomes policies. Industries with declining international competitiveness may desire state subsidies, but only if they are not conditional on increased state control over managerial decision-making. Similarly, the financial sector is only likely to support state-sponsored modernization if the policies have little or no impact on its freedom to invest in overseas markets. The tension at the heart of Macmillanism is clear. In the short term the state has the power to initiate whatever policies it might desire, but in the long term the implementation of these policies is likely to be modified or to be prevented altogether by the power of constraint residing with key socio-economic groups (Cox, 1984, pp. 3–21).

Evidence for this conclusion can be drawn from the unhappy experience of both major parties in their efforts to use the state as an agent of industrial renewal during the period 1959–70. As the discussion in Chapter one made clear, the state–market relationship created in these years closely resembled what we have dubbed Macmillanism. The defining characteristic of this approach to economic management is that it is based on the voluntary participation and co-operation of the key socio-economic groups.

The decision to take this voluntaristic approach can be directly related to the dominance of liberal values in British society. In other words, the initial choices made by both Labour and Conservative politicians were constrained by their knowledge that any attempt to create a strong and extensive interventionist role for the state would have faced sustained electoral and socio-economic opposition. The problem, however, was that a strategy based on voluntary co-operation with state-sponsored policies was doomed to fail in practice, because it allowed the trade unions and industrial and financial interests to retain their power of constraint.

LESSON TWO: THE CENTRE-RIGHT CONSENSUS IS WRONG

The second key lesson is that the current faith of both major parties in a limited role for the state, creating macroeconomic stability (principally low inflation) and relying on the market to increase investment and stimulate growth, should not be taken as confirmation that these ideas are self-evidently correct. Rather, it is our contention that the new centre-right consensus is deeply flawed. Support for this view is provided by a recent report from Bill Martin, chief economist at the City firm UBS. Martin reviews the Labour Party's economic policy proposals, principally Gordon Brown's so-called 'endogenous growth' policy, and concludes that Labour is mistaken in trying to emulate the macroeconomic stability/low inflation approach to growth currently being pursued by the Conservatives (Martin, 1996). The orthodoxy that low inflation will inevitably lead to a private sector investment boom is simply not supported by the official figures, which show that investment actually fell by 0.7 per cent between 1994 and 1995 and that manufacturing output was down by 0.2 per cent between the third and the fourth quarter of 1995 (*The Observer*, 12 May, 1996, p. 16). While these figures hardly represent a crisis, they are, nevertheless, hard evidence that the new centre-right consensus cannot claim to have solved the problem of Britain's relatively poor economic performance. Indeed, as a recent newspaper article points out: 'Everything is in place for a boom, but companies stubbornly refuse to invest' (*The Guardian*, 20 May, 1996, p. 18).

To understand the emergence of this new centre-right consensus we need to trace developments in the Labour Party since its third successive election defeat in 1987. This defeat allowed the right wing of the party to gain the ascendancy and to launch a radical review of policy. Although the Labour leader Neil Kinnock had begun his career on the left of the party, he was forced to concede that Labour's traditional commitments to nationalization, to state support for industry, and to high taxation and public spending no longer had any resonance with a majority of the electorate. The policy programme of 'laissez-fairism by degrees' carried out by the Conservatives since 1979 had, if anything, become more popular as the 1980s progressed, principally because it chimed with the liberal values which dominate British society. Kinnock, therefore, set about 'modernizing' the Labour Party in order to make it more electable. However, progress was slow in the years until the next election in 1992 and Labour was defeated again. Whatever the reality of policy changes, the electorate simply did not believe that Labour had abandoned its historic commitment to using the state as an agent of social and economic advancement. This defeat precipitated Kinnock's resignation. He was replaced by John Smith, another committed, although somewhat more cautious, modernizer. This should not, however, disguise the fact that before his untimely death Smith achieved perhaps the most fundamental of all the recent reforms, namely the introduction of a 'one member one vote' (OMOV) system to the Labour Party's annual conference. This had the effect of weakening the block votes of the trade unions, which had traditionally been seen as a major source of resistance to new, free-market orientated policy ideas. The value of OMOV for the Labour Party modernizers was demonstrated most graphically by Tony Blair's success in persuading the conference to vote in favour of the abandonment of Clause Four, which contained the Party's historic commitment to public ownership of the means of production.

The significance of this brief history of recent developments in the Labour Party is that these changes have reproduced a situation of consensus as to the proper relationship between the state and the market. In other words, the policy differences between the two major parties are now much more rhetorical than actual. However, the current consensus differs from that prevailing between 1939 and 1979 in that it stresses a limited rather than an activist role for the state. The core belief of this laissez-faire, centre-right orthodoxy is that the only legitimate role for the state is to create macroeconomic conditions under which the market will increase investment and stimulate growth, productivity and employment. The key macroeconomic condition is seen as a low and stable rate of inflation. The other major features of the centre-right consensus have emerged directly from the Conservative strategy of 'laissez-fairism by degrees'. This was discussed in detail in Chapter one, but, briefly stated, it comprises policy initiatives in two key areas: first, deregulation and legal curbs on trade union privileges to create a 'flexible' labour market; and second, the creation of a fundamentally market-based pattern of ownership and control by means of privatization and liberalization.

That the Major government has continued to press forward in both of these areas, and in the battle against inflation, is not particularly surprising; after all, why change a formula that has won four successive elections? The really interesting development since the last general election, and particularly since the election of Tony Blair as Party Leader in 1994, is that Labour has wholeheartedly embraced the state market relationship which has emerged over the last seventeen years. Labour is no longer promising to sweep away the laissez-faire legacy of the Thatcher/Major years, but rather to manage its worst excesses more effectively and to shift the balance of investment away from short-term gains in favour of the long term. The problem with this approach, in our view, is that it does nothing to address the fundamental weaknesses of the British economy. Instead, it merely represents an attempt to render the effects of relative decline slightly more bearable. So what else can be done?

WHAT NEXT FOR GOVERNMENT AND INDUSTRY: QUANTITY OR QUALITY?

In their barest essentials, the two key lessons which we draw from the politico-economic experience of Britain since 1939 are, first, that any government which attempts to use the state as an agent of economic renewal is likely to fail given the power of constraint available to major socio-economic groups, and, second, that the market-based solution currently being pursued has manifestly failed to deliver the investment needed to stimulate growth, productivity and employment. Or, to put this another way, state solutions will never be allowed to work, while free market solutions simply do not work. Furthermore, the historic illegitimacy of strong and extensive state intervention in Britain has been compounded in recent years by the trend towards liberalization and deregulation at both a regional level with the Single Market initiative, and a global level with the recent Uruguay Round agreement. Thus, even if the notion of state-led modernization had widespread support in British society, it seems unlikely that the government would be able to implement such a programme in the face of its regional and global commitments. The British economy would, thus, appear to be between the proverbial rock and a hard place.

We believe that part of the answer to this dilemma lies in a fundamental reassessment of the way in which politicians conceive of their roles and responsibilities. The basic flaw in the thinking of British governments, whether of a right-wing or of a left-wing persuasion, is the view that the only effective choice facing the nation state is between relatively more or relatively less state intervention. This approach is naive in the extreme. The real issue is not the *quantity* of state intervention, but its *quality*. All of the lessons of history teach us that the most successful economies are those in which the state manages to *align* the use of real resources in the economy in such a way that they are *congruent* with the dynamic of international competitiveness. Only by aligning the *real actors and resources* in the economy with this dynamic, can national competitiveness be sustained.

The fundamental failure of politicians in the past has been that they have conceived of the problem of competitiveness as an issue of *ownership and control* rather than as an issue of *facilitation*. Since 1945, the political discourse in this country has revolved around who should own and control the key resources in the economy, rather than focusing on *how much* can be achieved and *by what means*. In short, the history of the postwar era has been a misguided political conflict over the ownership of key assets so that the distribution or redistribution of the fruits of these assets can be controlled. While politicians and their business and labour partners have short-sightedly struggled in a continual 'dog-fight' over ownership issues, they have singularly failed to recognise that the nation's assets are being wasted relative to those of countries in which state and societal relationships are more strategically aligned. It is this focus on a one-sided ownership solution to the problems of economic management that represents the fundamental malaise at the heart of the British body politic.

So how can this malaise be overcome? We believe that part of the answer lies in a fundamental reappraisal by politicians, businessmen and trade unions of the way in which national competitiveness is achieved. The key to this reappraisal is a new way of thinking about business which we call the strategic alignment of national and corporate competitiveness.

WHAT IS THE STRATEGIC ALIGNMENT OF NATIONAL AND CORPORATE COMPETITIVENESS?

Although this is not a difficult concept to grasp, there is little evidence that it has any resonance with the thinking of Britain's political and business elites. *Strategic alignment* involves the simple recognition that 'zero-sum', win–lose conflicts over ownership issues are unlikely to result in national economic competitiveness. This conclusion flows from the fact that when those on the right of the political spectrum win the conflict, the financial sector tends to dominate distribution and investment decisions to the detriment of domestic industry and social redistribution. Conversely, when those on the left win it is the state which controls distribution and investment decisions. The problem is that this state interference causes the financial sector to limit investment, which also has a detrimental effect on domestic industry and social redistribution.

Rather than taking this 'zero-sum' approach to economic management, a *strategic alignment* approach requires politicians to recognise that they cannot effectively manage finance and industry at a microeconomic level, because they do not have the necessary competencies (skills and capabilities). The best they can hope to achieve is to manage macroeconomic aggregates in a way which creates as benign a business environment as possible. The second strand of this approach is an insistence that politicians should stop trying to tell business people what they should or should not become. Politicians do not have any foresight into what the economic successes of the future will or will not be. In essence, most politicians and their economic advisers spend their time exhorting companies and businessmen to copy the successes which other countries and companies have already achieved. This advice is akin to that given by generals who prepare for the next war by learning the lessons of the war they have just fought. This type of thinking is clearly misguided, because technological innovation rapidly changes the circumstances within which armed (and business) conflicts take place. The lesson of history is, therefore, clear: only those who adapt their existing assets (both financial and industrial) and competencies (human skills and capabilities) to the marketplace of the future will succeed.

The *strategic alignment* approach contends, therefore, that national economic success is only possible if those politicians who are the guardians of the state recognise that their role is to *facilitate* a competitive performance by the nation state's key assets, both tangible and intangible. In other words, rather than owning and controlling existing assets, the proper role of the state should be to ensure that these assets perform competitively, as well as to assist in the development of new assets which could become internationally competitive in the future. While the strategic alignment approach does not deny that the state also has a role in bringing about redistribution through taxation in order to mitigate the socially undesirable effects of technological and economic change, this should not be allowed to obscure the state's primary mission.

In our view, this primary mission should be *the development of a segmented and differentiated national policy*, which is sympathetic to the needs of corporate actors who are operating in supply and value chains which are often *mutually exclusive and contradictory*. By mutually exclusive and contradictory supply and value chains, we mean the fact that every corporate actor is embedded in a series of supply and value chains which provide products and services to end consumers in this country or overseas, and from which they seek to obtain corporate value or profitability. Corporations are involved in complex competitive struggles to 'fit' and/or 'stretch' their strategies to the requirements of consumers, in competition with similar-minded corporations which are also seeking to extract value (a margin/profit) from the satisfaction of consumers (Cox, 1996b). In some cases these competitive conflicts over markets are domestic, in others they are regional, and in yet others they are global. This globalization of competition has been stimulated by the policies of deregulation and liberalization pursued by the majority of advanced industrial nations in the 1980s and 1990s. It has created a situation in which there are no longer any hiding places for relatively inefficient and uncompetitive firms.

Since there is little prospect, short of the development of regional trading blocs centred on the EU, the US/NAFTA, and Japan/APEC, of British companies finding a hiding place, it seems inevitable that the only companies which will survive and thrive are those which are 'lean' in production and supply, and which are able to continuously innovate to find new products and services to delight consumers. If the British economy is to be internationally competitive, it will require a national policy approach which recognises this fundamental truth, and which also recognises that *there cannot be one policy approach for the economy as a whole.* Nor can the approach which is adopted be focused on penalising one sector of the economy to the detriment of all of the others. The greatest fallacy of the Thatcher years was the belief that if the hand of the state was taken away from the economy then economic regeneration would occur. The devastating results of a nonsensical policy of wasting oil revenues on an economic boom fuelled by financial and property speculation were predicted at the time, but these views were ignored (Cox, 1984; Cox, 1986). The lesson which must now be learned from this debacle, however, is that *aiding one sector of the economy to the detriment of all of the others cannot be a sustainable national economic policy.*

While this is an obvious point, it does not seem to be well understood by policy-makers and their advisers. The belief that there can be only one legitimate role for the state in economic and financial affairs was partly responsible for the demise of the Heath government in 1974, and was clearly the problem which bedevilled all Labour governments after 1945. The key problem is that policy-makers in the postwar period have not grasped the fact that they must develop a *strategically aligned approach* to economic and financial management. This approach rejects detailed controls and planning in favour of national 'fit' and 'stretch' strategies. By 'fit' strategies we mean those policies which address the major problems that industrial and financial actors must face if they are to compete successfully in the complex supply and value chains within which they are currently embedded. By 'stretch' strategies we mean those policies which address the major problems of innovation that firms must overcome if new supply and value chains are to be created, in order to delight consumers and to give Britain world class innovating companies. The real value of such an approach is that it lays the foundations for the segmented and differentiated approach to national economic policy which, historically, has been singularly lacking in Britain. The way in which this segmented and differentiated national economic policy might be constructed is outlined in Figure 7.1.

As Figure 7.1 shows, the development of a national economic policy must begin with a methodology which allows policy-makers to differentiate between *types of financial and industrial sectors*. This typology must then be matched against *the different types of competitive strategies* which are being employed by the major companies in these particular supply and value chains, that is 'fit' or 'stretch'. Once this is achieved, the key objective of companies and the national government is to work together to develop an understanding of *which are the key assets within these supply and value chains*. This includes both those which exist now and those which may exist in the future. As Figure 7.1 shows further, these key assets can be categorized into those which are technology, human, infrastructure, and process specific. The fundamental purpose of national economic policy should be *to develop a common understanding of the relative importance of these different types of assets for sustaining competitive advantage within specific and discrete supply and value chains*.

It is only by working together to understand the extent to which nationally-based companies possess those assets which are critical for sustainable competitive advantage, that the public and private sectors can arrive at the ground rules for a series of collaborative and differentiated national economic policies. These policies would be both sector and strategy specific. They would either involve *the development of jointly agreed public and private sector initiatives to close competence gaps within existing companies in existing supply and value chains*, or they would provide a basis for *the development of privately or publicly/privately financed (joint equity) companies set up to exploit the*

TYPES OF STRATEGIC CHOICES		ASSETS REQUIRED FOR COMPETITIVENESS								POLICY APPROACH REQUIRED TO FILL GAPS	TIMESCALE FOR FULL COMPETENCE DEVELOPMENT	
		TECHNOLOGY SPECIFIC		HUMAN SPECIFIC		INFRASTRUCTURE SPECIFIC		PROCESS SPECIFIC			PRIVATE ROLE	PUBLIC ROLE
		HAVE	HAVENOT	HAVE	HAVENOT	HAVE	HAVENOT	HAVE	HAVENOT			
STRATEGY AS 'FIT'	FINANCIAL SECTOR SUPPLY AND VALUE CHAINS											
	INDUSTRIAL SECTOR SUPPLY AND VALUE CHAINS											
STRATEGY AS 'STRETCH'	FINANCIAL SECTOR SUPPLY AND VALUE CHAINS											
	INDUSTRIAL SECTOR SUPPLY AND VALUE CHAINS											

© Andrew Cox, CSPM, University of Birmingham, June 1996

Figure 7.1: A methodology for selecting national economic policies for financial and industrial sectors.

potential of newly emerging supply and value chains. The basic approach would, thus, be based on partnership and collaboration between the public and the private sectors. The policies, and the timescales for their implementation, would be jointly agreed. The state's role would rarely focus on control or ownership. Instead, it would primarily be directed towards the facilitation of private sector understanding and towards the development of sector and strategy specific policy frameworks. The overall objective would be singular, namely the development of private companies which are able to compete in global markets, while the means would be sector and strategy specific.

These ideas have many other implications for British government policy. Recent discussions about education and social policy, as well as about economic and industrial policy, betray a complete lack of understanding of the critical importance of supply and value chains for the effective management of relationships and competencies (Cox, 1996a). In order to develop the proper role for government, we must first understand the supply and value chains which exist globally. Unless we understand these supply and value chains, we will be unable to comprehend the capacity of either the private sector or of the public sector to frame policies and strategies which will enable the British economy to compete internationally. Furthermore, unless we first understand the complex ways in which global supply and value chains impact upon existing economic, social and cultural practices in Britain, and how they challenge existing values and processes, we cannot begin to comprehend the changes which are required. And unless we know what is required, we will never be able to fashion appropriate policies for national economic regeneration.

The challenge facing Britain as it approaches the millennium is, thus, only too clear. The question which must urgently be answered is this: *can Britain's policy-makers give up the 'one-eyed' approach to economic management which has historically been adopted by those on both the right and the left of the political spectrum, and focus instead on the development of a public and private sector partnership which recognises that forging a link between corporate and individual competencies and the dynamics of supply and value chains is the way to achieve sustainable international competitiveness?* The key point is that the benefits of this approach to corporate strategic alignment, which we call *strategic procurement management*, are also realisable in national policy-making in both social and economic affairs (Lamming and Cox, 1995; Cox, 1996c).

One of the authors has recently undertaken some work with the Nottingham Health Authority which provides effective support for this assertion. The work demonstrates conclusively that a good deal of health policy in the postwar period has been sub-optimal, because it has failed to recognise the need to strategically align health policy with the effective management of demand and supply within the complex supply and value chains which run through healthcare markets (Nottingham Health Authority, May 1996). The failure of the Conservative government's 'internal market' reforms to achieve their intended effects can be attributed almost wholly to a desire to impose an ideological solution on the healthcare market. Furthermore, this is a solution which completely ignores the question of who owns and controls those assets which are 'critical' within this market. The approach being developed in the Nottingham Health Authority, thus, offers an interesting test case of what might be achieved if a more strategically aligned methodology for managing healthcare supply and value chains was adopted.

Similar thinking could be applied to a range of other policy sectors. In education, for example, the failure of policy in the postwar period has largely been the result of a desire to increase the *quantity* of people passing through the system, without ever addressing the issue of *quality*. In other words, sheer weight of numbers has tended to be seen as more important than the suitability of the *competencies* (skills and capabilities) which the education system is imparting to students. All too often the focus has been on throwing money at the professionals in the hope that they would put it to good use. In practice, of course, educational professionals have only ever been interested in using resources to do more of the same, or what they would prefer to do, in complete ignorance of the national and corporate competencies which are required to sustain national competitiveness.

CONCLUSION

We believe that it is this fundamental misalignment of roles, responsibilities, authority and accountability in health, education and economic policy which lies at the heart of Britain's economic malaise in the postwar period. The tragedy is that by focusing on ownership, control and 'zero-sum' conflicts we have failed to address the key questions which must be answered if international competitiveness is to be sustained. The critical task for the next government must, therefore, be to develop a segmented and differentiated national economic policy, which is based on a sophisticated understanding of the corporate competencies that are necessary to sustain distinct strategies within specific global supply and value chains. Once these corporate competencies have been understood and developed, it becomes possible, within existing resources, to frame social, educational and health policies which will develop the human competencies that sustain corporate, and therefore national, success.

REFERENCES

Cox, A. (1984), *Adversary Politics and Land* (Cambridge: Cambridge University Press).

Cox, A. (ed.) (1986), *The State, Finance and Industry* (Brighton: Harvester Wheatsheaf).

Cox, A. (1996a), 'Relational Competence and Strategic Procurement Management: Towards an Entrepreneurial and Contractual Theory of the Firm', *European Journal of Purchasing and Supply Management*, 2, 1, pp. 57–70.

Cox, A. (1996b), *The Strategic Choices Facing the Firm in the 1990s: Competing on Efficient Operations, Core Competencies, Lean Enterprise or Relational Competence*, Working Paper 2/96 (Birmingham: CSPM, University of Birmingham).

Cox, A. (ed.) (1996c), *Innovations in Procurement Management* (Boston: Earlsgate Press).

Lamming, R. and A. Cox (eds.) (1995), *Strategic Procurement Management in the 1990s: Concepts and Cases* (Boston: Earlsgate Press).

Martin, B (1996), *Labour's Economics: Can Mr Blair do it?* (London: UBS).

Nottingham Health Authority (1996), *Managing Healthcare Strategically in Nottingham* (Nottingham: Nottingham Health Authority).

The Guardian, 'Back to the future, sixties style', 20 May, 1996, p. 18.

The Observer, 'Britain's economy: Clarke takes it on the bounce', 12 May 1996, pp. 16–17.

Index